Autobi‹

Mrs Al

(A girl ca

Made available to the public by the request of June Bell
By

Web   http://www.HealthLifePublications.com

Email   healthlifepublications@outlook.com

1

Preface

After Christmas it was my mother's custom to go home with my brother and sister in law (Alistair and Dee) until after the New Year. When she was at my brothers house In the Christmas holidays of 2003/4 she spent most of the time on the computer writing her autobiography. After her death in 2009 Ali (my brother) presented me with her writings (both religious and autobiographical). I have taken her work and edited it into three separate books and they are available in printed or E form.

Autobiography

Research in Genesis and the names of God

Research into the Beatitudes,
            Sabbath miracles,
            Parables
            Jesus' attitude to women
            Life of Paul (Saul)

At the age of 70+ Alice Bell went to Birmingham University and did undergraduate studies, followed by tutorials with the professors. She learnt to use the computer with the help of my brother (Ali) and spent the last 27 years of her life studying and researching the Bible. She was never still but was reading and working on the computer, doing tapestries, painting pictures, knitting and crocheting, cooking ,but not all at the same time.

She took monthly journals like Current World Archaeology and Biblical Archaeological Review (B.A.R.). From these magazines she was able to see any new books which were being published and she ordered all the books which were in her field of study. It was from this research that she was able to produce her papers and books. One wall of her office was lined with bookcases containing relatively new books which I was able to give to Newbold College (the Adventist University in England) when she was no longer able to study. Any book she read she would mark, indicating the things which interested her. All her life she was an avid reader of history, including historical novels, archaeology and biblical research. She gave talks and preached in the Adventist Church and other churches. Each year she attended Oxford University Summer School biblical conference where she met eminent world scholars. She did not get involved in small talk but loved to tell people about her latest exploits, studies and research.

In the home she was an excellent cook, being able to produce a meal in no time and her cakes were delicious. At church she was a good teacher of the Bible and she was famous for her children's stories. At night she managed on 4 hours sleep. Through the night using her pillow speaker she listened to the BBC world service. She was particularly interested in discovery and invention. I have been helped by my sister Jill with family history, proof reading and partial editing and my brother Alistair in the arranging the writing into book form. Christine McGoldrick, Vinil Roberts, Allan Lanham, Sarah Jarvis and others have helped with proof reading. I am very grateful to everyone who has helped in the production of this book. Ali (my brother) was the main one to teach my mother the computer, but she was also helped by Barnabas Lukapa and others.

June Bell (Daughter of Alice Bell)
2014

(Written for Anne Hyde)

Contents

Bell / Anderson Family Tree

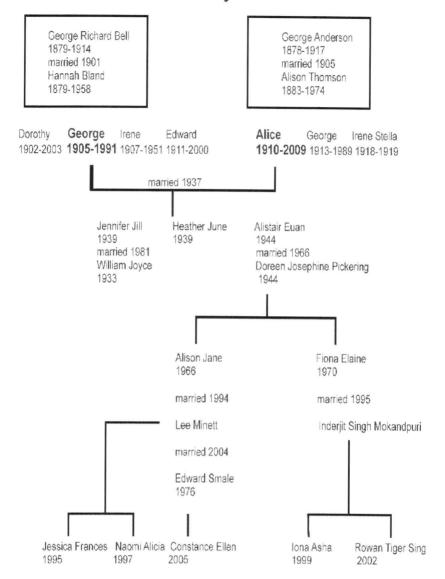

George Richard Bell
1879-1914
married 1901
Hannah Bland
1879-1958

George Anderson
1878-1917
married 1905
Alison Thomson
1883-1974

Dorothy **George** Irene Edward **Alice** George Irene Stella
1902-2003 **1905-1991** 1907-1951 1911-2000 **1910-2009** 1913-1989 1918-1919

married 1937

Jennifer Jill
1939
married 1981
William Joyce
1933

Heather June
1939

Alistair Euan
1944
married 1966
Doreen Josephine Pickering
1944

Alison Jane
1966

married 1994

Lee Minett

married 2004

Edward Smale
1976

Fiona Elaine
1970

married 1995

Inderjit Singh Mokandpuri

Jessica Frances Naomi Alicia Constance Ellen
1995   1997   2005

Iona Asha
1999

Rowan Tiger Sing
2002

5

Introduction

Let's Look at the Bell Family
From time immemorial it has been the custom to recall past ancestors. This is a remembrance towards the end of the life of Alice Bell as she attempts to tell you of her forebears, who they were and how they lived and whose genes have been inherited. Now I am old, and I say to you, my family, 'Remember me when I am gone but do not grieve; just try to understand and have a tender thought'. I tried to do my best to my fellow man. I tried to live according to the best of my ability. As I look back today I recall one of the messages I shared with Dad (George Bell) one Christmas. Being young we shared many happy days together. All the summer days so wonderfully spent and I can recall them. When spring was May and autumn was September, years have come and passed my way. Now I am too old to remember all.

Alice Bell at her desk

Chapter 1

THE EARLY LIFE OF THE GIRL CALLED ALICE

This is my story spanning a period of nine tenths of the 20th century. On reflection today, it seems as if I have lived through a century of miracles. I have seen so many changes since my childhood. Many people living in my childhood days would never have believed possible the miracles I have witnessed in the 20th century. Communication and transport have changed out of all expectation in my lifetime.

I had not been at school very long, at the beginning of the second decade of the 20th century, when one of the children in my class was about to go to India and join his father who was in the British army. I can still recall the wonder and amazement I experienced when I heard my teacher, who must have been very much more knowledgeable than many of his contemporaries, inform his class of very small children that day saying, 'Before we are very much older, we will be able to speak to John in India and he will be able to hear us as we speak'. I can still recall so vividly the wonder of such a prediction. I just could not fully comprehend what was being said. It was startling and vivid to me as a child. The impossibility of what I heard in that classroom has lived with me throughout the long years of my life. Although I listened and I could hear that teacher, at that early age I really could not visualise what I was hearing or even think how far away India was. That information captivated my imagination and it has remained in my memory through the years.

I remember the wonder of seeing aeroplanes flying in the air and eventually being in one myself. I shall never forget the day when my husband George and I had breakfast in Birmingham, had lunch with my son Euan (Alistair) and family in London, on that same day crossing the Atlantic to the mainland of North America, and saying to Dad (George) as we crossed the land "Columbus would never have believed this", then in the evening we had supper in Washington D.C. with Marjory and Bernard Seton, all in one day.

In my lifetime the speed of travel has increased. As a small child I could travel by steam train. Then a journey taking 4-5 hours by steam train can now be done by diesel in 2-3 hours. I also recall my excitement and joy on the first occasion I ever sat in a car belonging to my friend's father. I swelled up with pride at the privilege of just sitting there, just pondering on the thought and knowing that she (not me) would travel 50-60 miles to her holiday destination. It was not only a wonderful experience it was a thrill and joy just being able to sit in this thing called a car. I could hardly contain my wonder.

For years I worked on a little portable typewriter thinking it was a wonderful invention and now I work on a computer. Daily I enjoy the wonder of its capabilities. They are even now beyond my wildest comprehension. That same wonder of childhood never ceases to amaze me.

My Life
A Secret of Life

> The secret of living is learning to pray,
> It's asking Our Father for strength for the day.
> It's walking by faith, every mile that you plod,
> And knowing your prayers, bring you nearer to God.

Paternal Family Background
My father George Anderson was the eldest son of Thomas and Mary Anderson's ten children. Thomas came from a village near Pocklington in Yorkshire. His parents belonged to the first quarter of the 19th century and they lived in the country and they did not travel far. Children had to be registered at the Pocklington parish church, which was some distance away. There was no local transport, and it was difficult to get to there, and so it was not unusual to register the birth of two or three children at the same time. The railways were only just becoming popular. In the 19th century travel in country districts did not differ much from travel during the previous two millenniums. Travel was as quick as a horse could go. My paternal great grandparents were farming people. Farming work was hard in those days with little or no mechanical devices and horses were essential and important for the work on a farm.

My maternal grandmother Mary Elizabeth belonged to Sunderland. As a young girl of seventeen she met my grandfather Thomas Anderson aged twenty, at the Marsden Caves at Roker Park, Sunderland. These caves were a noted and a favourite place for young people to meet on a Saturday night for dancing in the early 19th century. They married when they were still very young and had ten children, George, Jack, James, Frank, Sarah, Elizabeth, Florrie, Louie, and Mary. There were twins both named Rachel. I assume they died at childbirth. At first my grandfather was a contractor in

Sunderland. He had a horse and wagon. Eventually he became a gardener on the estate belonging to the Vaux brewer family in Sunderland.

The 19th century was a time of a social and bloodless revolution. Mechanical inventions were being developed and factories were being built in towns where manufactured goods were being produced in quantity. Young people gravitated from the country to the towns, providing workers for the new factories. This caused a break up of families and changed the structure of the family and civilisation. It reduced the number of farming families in the country and created the need for new housing developments in the towns.

Travel was no longer dependent on a horse. Railways were being developed throughout the land and cars were being made. Transport was gradually changing from horse drawn vehicles, to mechanical vehicles. These mechanical inventions changed the method of production of many goods which had been hand- made and were now being manufactured. Manpower was required in towns where factories were being built for the new industry. It opened up new opportunities for country people to earn a more lucrative living in the town than they had done in the country. With this industrial revolution came new housing developments in the towns. Like other families my grandfather, Thomas Anderson, left his country home in Yorkshire and moved to Sunderland where he spent the rest of his life and eventually died at the age of 80 years.

As quite a young man he had married Mary Elizabeth and his young family grew up in a town environment. This rapidly increasing family of Thomas and Mary Anderson, living in Sunderland, remembered with great anticipation and excitement the arrival of a goose and other goodies from the grandfather's farm near Pocklington as Christmas time drew near, for the Christmas feast. Living was very basic in the 19th and early 20th century. The town people depended on the country people to produce food for the town. Food imports were limited to goods, which did not deteriorate quickly. Foodstuffs from distant parts were very costly. Christmas was one of the few times when the industrial workers in the towns had time and opportunity for feasting and for recreation. Life at that time was still limited to the observance of the four church festivals at Christmas, Easter, Pentecost and Michaelmas. The festivals gave the working people the opportunity for relaxation and the visiting of Fairs and it was the working man's only opportunity for a short break from work and a

9

change of diet. The goose at Christmas time created great excitement in the Anderson family. As a child I can recall my Grandfather Anderson bringing home a large log – the Yule Log. The ancient meaning of Yule is 'good health'. The burning of the Yule log symbolised the burning of the past and the introduction of a new beginning; a time to make New Year resolutions. The church holidays also became the occasion when people paid their rents.

Occasionally, visits were made by some of the young Anderson family to their grandfather's home in Yorkshire. My youngest Aunt Mary, who had been brought up in the town, recalled her regular visits to her Aunt Rachel at the farm near Pocklington. When bedtime came, she was given a candle in a brass candlestick and was told "Take a candle to your chamber dear". Years later she told me how strange she found this country language. Obviously, the Yorkshire village cottage had no gas or electricity; life was very different. My aunt understood the word 'chamber' to refer to the chamber pot for use in the bedroom during the night. To a previous generation the word 'chamber' referred to a room. Implicit in the command was the fact that no modern lighting had yet been installed and outdoor sanitation was still the custom, possibly with a two or three outside dry toilet in the garden. Until her old age my aunt continued to be amused at the language of her ancient relatives. Changing customs bring changes in language.

Eventually Granddad Anderson became head gardener to the Vaux family home at Herrington (a local brewing family). I can recall that home near Herrington, which I visited on a number of occasions in the second decade of the 20th century.
My father was the eldest child and as a young lad of thirteen he felt it incumbent upon him to contribute to the family finances. At an early age he earned money by running errands for local trades' people. As the eldest he felt he had to help his mother financially. His father by this time, like many men of his time, who were earning more money than they had previously earned, had developed a love of beer and the community spirit enjoyed in the pubs. My Aunt Mary later assured me he was never 'dead drunk', but he often spent more than he could afford on alcohol. I can remember, he took to song at that stage of inebriation. At 14 my father started work earning a few shillings, as he helped a little local baker called Hannah Spooner. He learned to love this dear little lady. She treated him as if he were her own son. Visiting her in the early 1920s, when she was quite an old lady, I can still recall the wonderful smell of baking in her home and the love she expressed for my father. She was a little, dumpling of a woman, less than 5 ft in

height. I always saw her with her spotless white apron and a frilly white cap on her head.

It was during my young years I remember hearing the story of my father's obedience, illustrated by the following story. As a young lad and the oldest of the family he felt responsible for his siblings. As a special treat they were allowed to go to a special event in a theatre in Sunderland. He was in charge of his brother Jack. They had been told they had to be home by a certain hour. The play had gone on longer than was expected. Because family discipline was strict, they both left the performance early. Within quarter of an hour of their departure from the theatre, the theatre was burnt down and hundreds of young people died. This became an object lesson in obedience in my family.

At the age of fifteen my father was apprenticed into the merchant navy. On his first voyage to sea he was so seasick he would willingly have broken his contract, but being a proud, determined and responsible young man, he remained at sea to complete his apprenticeship. He made a regular allocation from his salary to his mother, to assist her with the upbringing of his siblings. This continued until he got married in 1905, when he became a financial loss to the family. The whole family remembers the excitement they each experienced when they knew brother George was about to return home. At the end of each voyage he was laden with gifts for all the family. Because he had not completed his education at school, he took time off to study and prepare to take his Captain's ticket. This he achieved at the age of 26. Shipping conditions in those days left a lot to be desired. He was known to say later in life, when describing his first voyage, that: he would not allow a dog of his to go to sea, he was so appalled at the conditions under which the men had to work.

My Grandma Anderson was a frail, gentle, little lady, as I remember her, her back slightly bent. She always seemed to be cooking or cleaning. I can recall three houses in which I visited her, but my picture of her was always being busy with household chores. Cooking odours were reminiscent of her presence. She always seemed to be cooking and creating something with a wonderful smell. I never remember her sitting down to talk to me, except if it was about my father. She would always finish the conversation and sigh, saying, 'George was a good son, the very best'. This statement came up time after time; maybe that is why I remember it. Maybe it was because he was my father or maybe it was because by that time I was a fatherless child. I like to think it was because he was such a good and responsible son to his mother. She missed him as much as we did. Another phrase she would sometimes add: 'He was better than all the others'.

My parents were married in 1905, when my father returned after a long voyage in the Far East. The wedding took place at the Presbyterian Church at Tattem Street, Sunderland. On this occasion he had brought back, among other things, the yardage of beautiful embroidered white silk from Japan for my mother's wedding dress and a silver buckle. I made and embroidered dedication dresses for my twins Jill and June from the skirt material and the silver buckle was divided and given to them for their 21st birthday. The other presents consisted of two tea sets of china and a breakfast set of 'egg shell' china for my mother. One tea set went to his mother, which she brought out on very special occasions. Both families were at the wedding reception. Weddings were simpler in those days. My mother's dress was made with the Japanese silk embroidered material and her going away suit was pale grey. She sailed with my father on his next voyage as far as the Liverpool Canal, where she left the boat. Whenever he came into a British port she travelled to meet him. On one occasion her engagement ring was lost at a hotel. Before my father's last voyage he replaced the lost ring. He bought the best he could buy for his 'darling sweetheart'. It was an outstandingly attractive opal ring, which Jill (my daughter) now owns. Fiona, (my granddaughter) was given the frosted gold bangle which my mother wore on her wedding day.

Before I was born my father was also responsible for raising the money to send his next brother Jack to the South African gold fields. He eventually went to Australia and settled in Brisbane. He also supplied the money to send the third brother James to Canada. When Uncle Jim visited us in Liverpool in the 1950s he told us that when he left Liverpool to sail to New York he only had 6d in his pocket. Such was the financial state of large families with small incomes in the early 20th century, when industrial changes were taking place, which necessitated many young people to migrate to the colonies. In New York Uncle Jim swept streets until he had enough money to go to Canada, where he could make a claim on free land in Saskatchewan (as much land as could be covered in one day's ploughing could be claimed). He claimed land at Meota, which was really only a name on the map. Here he had built a log cabin, and sent for my mother's youngest sister Isabella. Uncle Jim's name is down on the Canadian record of pioneers. They had three children (two girls and a boy), Gladys, James and Cicialia. As his children grew to school age, they moved to Battleford where he had a garage and eventually he became the mayor of the small town. Young Jim, his son, was known to love fishing. One winter his mother made him a coat of rabbit skins to keep him warm, as he sat on the ice over the fishing-hole. He then had to transport his fish to the railway junction, for transit to a town.

My Maternal Family Background

My maternal grandparents came from Knockando, on Speyside near Elgin (Knock means hill). It is a village on a hill, which overlooks a horse-shoe bend on the river Spey near Archiestown. The name Archiestown belongs to local history. Near the beginning of the 19th century a landowner, called Grant, instead of bequeathing his land to the eldest son, divided his land between his three sons. One area became known as Grantown-on-Spey, another area was named Archiestown, and another Williamstown. Many of the Grant Clan migrated to Canada where they were instrumental in the development of the Trans Canadian Railway.

Early in the 19th century, 1817, my great grandfather Donald MacDonald was born. He married Margaret Kerr who was born 1822. Her mother came from Ullapool. When she was widowed, she lived with her daughter and son-in-law, Donald McDonald. It was the custom for the eldest son to be responsible for the care of the extended family (my grandfather took my mother's widowed mother into his family). Margaret Kerr wife of Donald McDonald died 1866 in her early forties, leaving a little family. My grandmother, Elspeth McDonald was her eldest daughter and cared for the family. Donald died l895 at the age of 78 years. The McDonalds lived in the village of Knockando where Donald had a business as a 'flesher' (butcher). In the process of time they bought Boghur (the name means wet peat). The farm was situated on the side of a hill overlooking the horseshoe bend of the Spey.   Eventually it became part of the Wills estate (the tobacco people). The farmhouse was typical of the district. It had a central door with a room on either side of the door and above three dormer windows. The room on the right hand side of the front door, with its flagstone floor, was the room my mother remembers as a child, with its table in front of the window where the brose, bread, scones and oatcakes were made daily. In that room was a box bed, with its closed doors (shutting out the world) and the stairs going up to the dormer bedrooms. It would be in this room that most of the family events took place. As a child my mother visited the farm regularly. To get there her family had to travel by train over the fairly new Tay Bridge. Her grandfather would meet them at the station with a horse and cart to take them up the hill to the farm. Her mother Elspeth

McDonald was on the train the night before the Tay Bridge collapsed as a result of extremely bad weather conditions. Grandma often recalled her visits as a child to Boghur. The occasion when she had scarlatina, and being consoled by one of the old uncles as he sang to her and told her folk tales of the fairies (brownies). The moors, near to the house, were reputed to be inhabited by bogies and brownies. The brownies were said to be able to perform the most unusual and astounding things. Every child was taught to be careful at twilight and dawn. You never knew what they might do. No wonder my mother was fearful.

The farm was 86 acres, with 26 acres arable. According to the census 1861 they employed three servants - a herdsman (the young male who was hired to work on the farm in the Gaelic was called a 'loon'. He slept in the 'chaumer', in the barn. When my husband, George Bell worked at the Murdoch farm in Ayrshire, he slept in a similar cubicle in the barn. In the Gaelic, girls were called 'queens'. The children of Donald and Margaret were Ellen, Donald, Elspeth, Isabella, Margaret, James and Williaine. After her mother died in childbirth, my grandmother Elspeth took over the responsibility of caring for the family. We know she went to Elgin to learn dressmaking, possibly to keep the family clothed. It must have been about this time that the family acquired a sewing machine, which was a fairly new invention. It was used to make clothing for the family. This was more economical. At that time it was customary to hand clothes down from the eldest to the younger members of the family.

Village of Knockando
In the 1950's we as a family went with my mother to see the district where as a child she had visited her grandparents. She vividly recalled travelling on a train from Edinburgh, crossing the Forth Bridge and the Tay Bridge and being met at Archiestown by her grandfather, Donald McDonald with his horse and cart, to be taken up the hill to the farm where her mother had grown up. When she saw the farmhouse again after long years of absence, her joy was evident as she recalled her childhood visits. We stood outside the window, where her grandmother had a long table on which she daily made the scones and oatcakes. We peered in to see where the fire was, where all the cooking was done on the open fire. Here the griddle was used every day to make the scones. The box bed with doors, we could just see in one corner. The stairs went up to the bedrooms. My mother had been a sickly child, and was regularly sent up to Boghur, for the 'good air and good water'. At the time when she needed special comfort,

when sick with scarlatina (scarlet fever), one of the uncles was very good at entertaining her with stories of the 'brownies' (fairies and bogies that haunted the heath). She was able to accept the fairy stories but the poultry and cows terrified her. Apparently she was not a very strong child and went regularly to the country where they hoped she would thrive on the good fresh air and spring water. At the time we visited the farm, Wills, the tobacco family, had acquired the land and were using it as a hunting lodge. Her instant reaction as she looked in the window after all these years was to see the 'ingle neuk' (Danish for fireplace). She remembered sitting on her uncle's knee to hear his stories, as he claimed the attention of the 'sickly child' from the city. She was captivated. He could have been one of the two uncles who came to Leith for the funeral of Donald McDonald, the son of Donald McDonald of Boghur, Knockando, in the 1920s. The memory of her fear returned to her constantly on this visit. The farmhouse was typical of all the farmhouses all over the county, with rooms on either side of the front door, and a dark staircase going up from the living room to the bedrooms upstairs. The three rooms upstairs had dormer windows. Such houses can still be seen today all over 'the North'.

The Kirk was a typical country Congregational Kirk with a yard attached. The day we visited, the wind was blowing from across the heath, almost whistling a dirge among the tombstones, as we stood where our ancestors lay, near to the land where they had spent their working lives. As we viewed the wild ravines of Speyside, the watercourses crossing verdant knolls and the deep entangled dells, reluctantly, almost, we entered the Kirk and were reminded of some of the ancient customs, inherited from Reformation days. There we saw a little old lady, covering all the furniture in the church with white sheeting for the Communion Sunday service. When I spoke to her, I told her of my relationship to the late Donald McDonald of Boghur. She said, "Och, didna I ken wha you are? Didna my mither buy your great grandmother's sewing machine!" This had happened sixty or seventy years before when the farm was sold. Memories are long in these country districts.

Although the old church has now been replaced with a new building, some of the ancient customs are still maintained. The collection is still taken up in what looks like wooden ladles, called by the youngsters of the congregation 'treacle ladles'. The elders of the kirk still process round the kirk on a Sunday with these wooden ladles to collect the offering. The odd little 'bawbees' continue to tinkle as they are thrown into the ladle. On our first visit the old kirk had a small organ, so it must have survived the Reformation controversy about music in the kirk. The Wee Free Church of Scotland for many a long year would not permit an organ in the kirk.   There was a tradition that to have a musical instrument in the kirk was 'to bring the devil into the kirk'. There was a belief that if there was trouble in the kirk it usually started in the choir.   Until quite recently the Wee Free Church only used a tuning fork to give the right note to start the Psalms.   The precentor with his tuning fork directed the singing.   He would sing the first word and the congregation followed his note.

The silent kirk yard at Knockando still tells its own silent story. At the entrance there are three Pictish stones inscribed in Ogham script. An ancient custom was to build a place of worship at the place where previous generations had worshipped. 'The ancients' who farmed this land, who attended this kirk, who brought up their families in the faith of the Word of Gods, built their place of worship on a mound used by the Picts from a previous age.

Each generation builds the present on the past.   So it was with worship. In the place where there had been a pagan temple, when a new group of people arrived with a new type of worship and a new god, the new temple was frequently built on the place of the previous temple or the old 'holy spot' where a god was reputed to have spoken to the ancestors in days gone by or a miracle had taken place. Early Christian churches in Britain were built on the site of pagan temples. When Pope Gregory sent Augustine to Britain he said: "Do not take away everything from the people's worship find a Christian connotation for their customs".   Throughout Britain customs and churches can be traced to our pagan ancestors. St Paul's church in London was built on the site of a pagan temple.   The church at Wednesbury in the West Midlands was built on the site of the temple of Woden.   The parish church at Chester was built on the site of a pagan temple. The Woden Greeks believed that it was essential to strive upwards when a person went to worship. This resulted in pagan temples being built on 'a high place'. Many of the great cathedrals have been built on a mound.

The family Bible in Donald McDonald's farm was written in the Gaelic. Isa, the girl who married William Lorimer at Denny was the girl who inherited the Gaelic Bible. Walking round the ancient burial ground and reading the story of the tombstones, we soon realised that many of the 'rude forefathers ' of the district had lived to a ripe old age. Many of

16

the families in the 19th century at Knockando lived to between 80 and 90 years old. Donald McDonald lived until he was 78 years. They now sleep on the hillside, near the land they worked. This was an ancient custom, which goes back millennia, long before the time of written history. It was also traditional for an extended family to live close to each other, to worship the God of their fathers in life and in death to be buried with their father. Ancient cemeteries witness to this custom.

The Kirk at Knockando is situated on a small hill (Knock meaning hill) and is approached by the Oak Hill Road, a road leading out of Archiestown. The oak tree was the traditional tree where ancient people prayed for fertility and according to the custom of at least 5,000 years ago, the name of the dead person had to be recorded near to the place of burial, to make it possible for them to live throughout eternity. The erasing of the name implied eternity was withheld from the named person. This belief is still implicit in and can be seen by the names on tombstones. On cenotaphs in London we read, "Their name liveth forever," implying the ancient custom.

The age of some of those buried here on this hilltop cemetery testify to a good old age. One tombstone, however, has been questioned. There is reputed to be one tombstone with an age of 120 years, but we did not find it. A local lady communicated an interesting piece of information to us in the census office. She had been speaking to us about the number of distilleries built around the River Spey. Apparently the water in the district is essential for the quality of the whisky produced. It had long been the custom for all workers in the distillery (and there are many) to be allowed two allocations of free whisky weekly. There came the time when the medical doctors were faced with an unusually high number of deaths from cirrhosis of the liver. The National Health authorities appealed to the managers of the distilleries, to reduce the amount of free whisky. In the process of time the number of fatal deaths was reduced. It was later announced that it was the good quality of the water that accounted for some of the long-lived inhabitants of the district.

It was in this delightful area that my maternal grandmother grew up. Although I never remember seeing her, I have heard on frequent occasions the suggestion that she possessed 'the second sight'. This was a popular tradition in the country districts of Scotland. Usually in every district there was at least one woman with 'the second sight'. I think this can be accounted for by the fact that she was an intelligent woman, for her time. She grew up within the bounds of the hills around where the River Spey flows, with its unusual contours of land and its climatic changes of atmosphere. It is not surprising that a tradition of old wives tales developed into fairy tales. No one ever saw a fairy but with a vivid imagination, and the atmospheric conditions, a tradition of folk tales was soon developed. As a child I can recall sitting in the gloaming listening to my mother tell tales she heard as a child and imagining the fairies who were never seen but were always about. Maybe they were the stories she had heard from her uncle at the fireside at Boghur.

Without any medical training, my grandmother was known to frequently help the doctor in the village at the time of difficult births. In later years, when she was living in Sunderland, the local doctor called on her regularly for her services. In those days a child born with a severe affliction was allowed to come to its end naturally. No artificial help was known or could be given.

The old Kirk at Knockando has been knocked down and a new building erected. This was possibly by the new landowners, the Wills tobacco family. The silent kirk-yard is a testimony to the past, telling its own story and making a record of 'the ancients' and their families, often giving a name to a farm or identifying a district by a description of the landscape. Many of these people sleep the sleep of death on the hillside near land they cared for in days gone by.

After the death of her mother, Margaret, my maternal grandmother assumed responsibility and organised her siblings. Donald went to Edinburgh, where he worked for the Prudential Insurance Company, eventually holding an administrative position. One brother went to North London where he became a Salvationist. I never did hear what work he did. Two of his daughters became Mormons and went to Utah. My grandmother arranged for her sister Isa (Isabella) to marry a William Lorimer, a local Knockando boy. She found work for him at the steel works at Denny, Stirlingshire. At this time her husband William Thomson was employed at Dennypace Paper Mill. I can recall my great Aunt Isa very clearly, she was similar to pictures I had of my grandmother, fairly plump and big breasted. I recall two unmarried uncles who came 'down from the north' to Leith in the 1920s at the time of the funeral of my grandmother's brother, Donald. They were reclusive, had long black beards and did not communicate with the other guests. They were just shy country gentlemen, simply not used to urban society.

The Thomson Family

My maternal grandmother, Elspeth McDonald married William Thomson of Lasswade. They had five children, Jack, William, Alison Isabella and an unknown name. Towards the end of the 19th century they lived at Station House, Auchendinny, Lasswade. This village was named after an event concerning a young girl who was fleeing from a life threatening danger. On arriving at a stream, her courage failed her, until she heard a well-known voice shouting Lassie wade, Lassie wade! She entered the water, nearly to thigh level and eventually reached the other side and safety. There is now a sizeable village there named after the ballad and to commemorate her experience.

The house at Lasswade was not much more than a 'butt and ben' (a two roomed house with a bed in the recess in both rooms), set in the middle of a fair sized garden, in which I was told my grandfather grew very good leeks. As a small child my mother recalls all her brothers and sisters being allocated the task of carrying buckets of water from a nearby well, a chore, common in many districts throughout the land. She also remembers a custom her mother had. Every evening she would leave the cottage and take a quiet walk in the nearby beauty spot of Roslin Glen. This custom is rather revealing of her character. She had come down from the beauty and isolation of the Spey Valley to the industrial belt between Edinburgh and Glasgow. It must have been a culture shock to her, after living in the isolation and beauty of Speyside to be confronted with industrialism and her present circumstances. Her reaction was to retreat to the nearby beauty of Roslin Glen, night by night in the mellow evening light, where she could enjoy the greenness of the trees and the reflections of streams in the valley, reminding her of the lovely Speyside she had left behind. It was her one opportunity to renew her resources amidst the fairy-like beauty of Roslin Glen. Walter Scott, who spent the first years of his married life here, wrote of it:

> To Auchendinny's hazel shade
> And haunted wood house lees,
> Who knows not Melville's beechy grove
> And Roslin's rocky glen,
> Dalkeith which all the virtues loved
> And classic Hawthorn den.

Sir Walter Scott in his 'Antiquary' knew what the name of Penicuik meant. He was in the habit of whimsically calling his home 'Mons Cuculi', Latin for 'Hill of the Cuckoo'.

19

In the days of my grandparents, men worked long hours, five and a half days in the week. On Saturday, the grandparents would take the children to Penicuik, to shop. This was the most exciting event of the week. During the time they spent at Auchendinny, until my mother was ten, the children attended the big school on the hill, not to the local school. I never did find out why they went there, unless it offered a better education. My grandfather worked at the Cockenzie Paper Mill, Penicuik, a little over two miles away from 'Station House', Auchendinny where they lived. I do not know if I am imagining it, but I assume he must have been a good workman with ambition, who was not content with his lot. A friend, who knew him, (possibly a man from the village of Penicuik) who was now a manager at the Dennypace Paper Mill, offered him a job that was better paid. After accepting this new job he moved his family to Dennyloanhead. It was here they had much better accommodation. The house had upstairs and downstairs, a nice garden at the back. Home life was possibly very much improved by this move. Not content with his own advancement, he was able to get work for his brother-in-law, William Lorimer at the local steel works. This move brought Elspeth's sister Isa, who was married to William Lorimer, down south to Dennyloanhead. This move must have been at my grandmother's instigation. She was a great organiser of other people. It would please her greatly to have her sister Isa (Isabella) so close to her. They lived almost opposite each other. This was a time when the immigrants from the north were infiltrating south to be near relations in the industrial belt. A new and ever-growing work force was required in this new industrial belt between Edinburgh and Glasgow. The Thomson family now attended a one room school about two miles distant. The teacher had to teach all ages and discipline was very strict. Any misdemeanour was punished with the taws (a leather strap with three strands at the end).

This was a memorable time for my mother and her sister Bella. For the first time they had new green velvet dresses and new hats. It was a big event to have new clothes. Clothes were usually passed down from an elder child to the next one down. I feel sure the new clothes must have indicated a financial advancement. The joy they both experienced was a perpetual memory to my mother. Until this time all clothes had possibly been made by their mother. A new dress for Easter has been a custom for hundreds of years. The girls wore their new hats and accompanied the family to church as proud as peacocks. They sat in the front row of the gallery. To ensure good behaviour in this prominent place, they were handed peppermints

20

from time to time, to keep them quiet during the sermon.

While at Dennypace Paper Mill, my grandfather was approached by a friend in Sunderland offering him a management job at the paper mill at Grangetown, Sunderland. He moved his family from Dennyloanhead to Sunderland only to find out that his new job was occasioned as a result of a local strike at the mill. There had been a series of strikes (this was near the time when workmen were feeling their power to control their working conditions). On arrival at Sunderland, my grandfather was furious. He had always believed in doing a fair day's work for a fair day's pay. Learning that he had been brought down to help to quell a strike made him really annoyed. He had moved the whole family well over a hundred miles and now he felt he just had to make the best of a bad job. My grandmother has been quoted as saying almost in condemnation "Will. what kind 'o country have ye brought us to? We ha'e never lived among fighting folks a'fore". She had never heard of such things as strikes and thought they were very degrading. It was this move, which determined the future of the family. From now on they lived in Sunderland.

I have not been able to obtain the year my grandfather died. It must have been before all the children had reached the age of being able to work. All I know is that he was still quite a young man. At the funeral the Presbyterian minister advised my grandmother to take up nursing in order to maintain her family. She did not feel she could do that and leave the family unsupervised. The local doctor had already used her services with childbirth. This she continued to do for some time. When the eldest boy Jack was old enough to work, he was employed at the paper mill. He married Bella Clifford, at the age of nineteen, which all the family thought was too young. I suspect it was the loss of his money that was the problem. It was the custom when children went out to work; they would bring the pay packet home unopened to mother. They were then allocated a small amount of pocket money. Uncle Jack and Aunt Bella had either three or four children. Then Maggie, the next daughter, was employed at the mill. She married John Good, and I recall visiting them just after the First World War. They gave my brother and me a model steam ship in good working order. It was about 24-25 inches long and had been made by Uncle John Good, who was an engineer. We had it for a long time and sailed it on a lake in the park until one day, in the middle of the lake, there was an explosion and it blew up!

My mother Alison eventually worked at the paper mill when she was old enough. There she earned 10/- (50p) per week, which her mother claimed. My mother received 3d (1.5p) pocket money out of her wages. By this time she had met my father. The story goes that her friend had made a blind date with a sea faring man, who requested she bring a girl friend along with her. At this first meeting, my father took one look at my mother and he was hooked for life. Being sea faring, they met infrequently, so they started writing to each other. Once my father fell in love with my mother, he determined to get married. To raise enough money to take his master's ticket and to get married, he joined a ship owned by Currie's doing long two-year trips to the Far East, (trading up and down the coast). It was during this time he earned sufficient money to take time off work to enable him to take his examination for his 'captain's ticket' and to set up a home for his sweetheart. While trading in the Far East he bought some beautifully embroidered material of fine Japanese silk for a wedding dress for his sweetheart. His cabin must have been stacked with presents. I can account for at least three tea sets (packed so carefully not one piece was broken) one for his mother and two for his sweetheart, as well as a small 'eggshell' breakfast set, kimonos, fans, and ornaments for the family.

During this time (a two year sea voyage) my mother was sent up to Leith for the good of her health, and the 'good Scottish air', to her uncle Donald McDonald who lived at 20, Leith Links Place, (this is directly in front of Leith Links). Uncle Donald encouraged his sister, my grandmother, to move her family to Leith. It was customary for elder brothers to show a caring concern for the family in times of trouble and distress. Donald suggested Elspeth should rent a new flat being built at King's Road, Portobello and then to take in lodgers, as a means of earning money. Apparently this is what she did. The feature of the Portobello house, my mother always recalled, was the lovely bow window of the first floor flat of the red sandstone building. It was here they had two lodgers, to supplement the family income. Will was now of an age when he could work at a local steel foundry. After a short time, Will got married to a girl from Lasswade (I seem to remember there was a family relationship).

My mother was by this time writing regularly to my father, her sailor boy, and my father was corresponding and working with a view to marriage. After two years his ship eventually docked at Leith docks. It was late at night, but with his sweetheart so near, he walked in the dark from Leith docks to Portobello, possibly 4-6 miles. After two years at sea he could not wait for transport till the next day. In this strange town he had to find the girl he planned to marry. Eventually arrangements were made for the family, my mother, her mother and her young sister Bella, to leave the flat at Portobello, and move back to Sunderland to be near my father's family and find accommodation there. My mother's younger sister Bella was at this time in correspondence with my father's brother Jim. The Thomson family, mother, Alison and Bella, moved back to Sunderland, to be near my father's family and some of my mother's family. My father insisted that Elspeth should make her home with them. They had the upstairs flat in the house of a very old lady who lived on the ground floor. It was from here that they were married.

My parents were married at the Presbyterian Church, Tattam Street, Sunderland in 1905. After a short honeymoon my mother accompanied my father on the ship as far as the Manchester Canal. The following year they rented a new house in Vallette Road, Grangetown, Sunderland, on a new housing estate. My mother recalled it was very nicely furnished. It was her pride and joy. A china cabinet was bought to display the china brought from Japan. It came from a house sale, from the local doctor's house. The cabinet was reputed to be 100 years old then. Grandma Thomson continued to live with my mother and Bella. She used to say: "Your daddy would not have had it otherwise". It would have been a disgrace not to have my mother living with us. They stayed at Vallette Road for between 4 and 5 years. It was then decided that as my father was doing shorter trips and calling at Leith more often than at Sunderland, it would be advisable to move to Leith. Until then every Sunday after church, they all walked out from Sunderland to Herrington to have tea with Grandma Anderson. This was a great big weekly family picnic, not only for relations but also for many friends.

George Anderson

My Anderson Family

The origin of my Anderson family began, when as a young man my father caught one glimpse of Alison Thomson. From then my father was hooked for life. Family gossip records their wedding. Every leave he had was like a second honeymoon. My parents were married at the Presbyterian Church, Tattam Street. At the wedding both families were represented. My mother's wedding dress was made with the fine embroidered Japanese silk my father had brought home. After a short honeymoon my mother accompanied my father's ship as far as the Liverpool Ship Canal. Then she met him at his ports of call.

Before I was born in 1910, my parents and my maternal grandmother had moved from Sunderland to Leith, to 4, Hermitage Terrace (in 1968 changed its name to Rosevale Terrace and can be accessed from East Hermitage Place and Somerset Place), to be near the shipping port of Leith where my father's ship docked fairly frequently. He sailed with Curries Shipping Line and eventually with the Ben Line. Now that he had his own home, long trips were out. Short trips could be 4 – 6 weeks. As in Sunderland, they had made their home in a new housing estate, so on this move to Leith they moved to a new house at 4, Hermitage Terrace, Leith. This house was part of 'a new venture in housing', which had been in progress during the last forty or fifty years. It was a development like that of Bourneville in the West Midlands, Rowntree's in York and Fry's in Bristol had developed. These houses offered new facilities, such as inside plumbing, water and sanitation.

Houses were required for the influx of country people to the industrial towns. In Leith a new building scheme had been started in 1865 by David Paterson. He was a partner with William Cochrane & Co., Corn Merchants. They had purchased the Restalrig Park estate, which stretched from Arthur's Seat to Leith Links. They planned to build houses particularly for workers, which were known as low type

24

houses.　This was a contrast to the high-rise flats, popular in Edinburgh that had become rather dilapidated. These houses were to provide front doors and a small front garden. There were flats on the first and second floor level. They contained inside toilet facilities and some of them had a bathroom. They were designed in what was called the Colony type housing and were in rows. Hermitage Terrace, where I was born, was built along the east end of one of these colony's on the site of the old Hermitage House, which had been bought on the site of the corn merchant, William Cochrane's old home. During the building period the company went bankrupt and the Industrial Co-operative Society took over the project in 1878 when the first builders had run out of money. A local builder, A & W Fingies eventually completed the houses. This was a progressive period in house building. With the rapid advance of industrialism, great advances were made in 'modern' house building to accommodate the influx of people from the country.

Hermitage Terrace was a row of blocks of flats, six flats in each block. They were typical of the period, with two small rooms. The terrace was built on a small mound and was reached by about 12 steps. In each block of the complex there were six flats, two on the ground floor, facing a sloping square of grass and two on the middle floor and two on the top floor. They were all rented.

Our flat consisted of two rooms and was lit by gas. Each room had a box bed recess in it, which was usually curtained off during the day. It was quite usual to keep what was called a 'hurly' underneath the bed. A hurly was a mattress on wheels that could be pulled out at night. There was a separate area cut off from the main room where there was a sink, a gas stove and on the wall a cupboard for dishes. In the entrance hall was the toilet (indoor sanitation) and a cubical for keeping coal, but no bathroom. The coal lorry came round weekly (coal fires were the main source of heating). Tradesmen in those days travelled from street to street, calling out their wares. The coal man shouted "Co-al, co-al 1/- a bag, co-al!" Those who wanted coal would indicate from the window, and the 'coalie' would carry a cwt, (hundredweight) of coal on his back up to the appropriate house. Bread vans would call daily in each street. Then there was a group of rather colourful men who came round intermittently calling 'Rag and bo-anes'. In exchange for jam jars they would give the child a big balloon. They were very popular with children because of the balloons. Children always listened for his cry.

Leith was near the fishing port of Granton. The fisher wives from this village would call regularly, calling:

"Caller herring straight frae the Firth.
Wh'll buy my herring?"

They were dressed in navy blue flannel petticoats, a red and white striped coloured blouse, and a tartan scarf on the head. On the head would be a leather strap, holding the creel of fish (the creel was made of cane). It was an oval shaped basket made of wicker work, containing the fish that rested on the back of the fishwife and was supported by a leather strap over the head of the fishwife. The fishwives were a colourful group of people. I recall their hands always looked very red and cold. They came from a very close-knit fishing community at Granton, and spoke in their own peculiar dialect. They were locally famous for their choir. In the summer months they performed in the bandstand in Princess Street Gardens and drew big crowds, especially visitors who loved their colourful costumes. In the winter they gave concerts indoors. The front room of this flat was usually used as a sitting room or a bedroom according to the family requirements.

It was in 1910 at 4, Hermitage Terrace (now Rosevale), Leith, that a, 8 1/2 lbs baby was born called Alice Anderson. My maternal grandmother assisted at my birth. She introduced me to the world by saying: "She's a bonnie wee lass". My Grandma had been assisting at the birth of babies for many years and in many places, whether she lived 'up north' or in Sunderland. Wherever she had lived, the local doctor sought her assistance at childbirth. She had no midwifery training but had a great deal of natural and inherent knowledge. From a young girl, after the death of her mother, she had been caring for the needs of the family and was possibly old and wise before her time. In those days when a child was born, badly handicapped at birth, the doctor or the nurse who had little or no medical means of maintaining life did the only thing they knew, they let nature take its course. Child mortality was very high. It was survival of the fittest.

My sea-fairing father did not set eyes on me until I was nearly three months old. I'm told it was a very joyful time when he came home to see his first child. He had been caring and supporting his brothers and sisters for years. Now he claimed his very own. His own first child was a replica of his beloved sweetheart. I was called Alice and not Alison, as my mother had been named. In her home she had been known in the abbreviated form, 'Allie'. Outside the home she was

'Alice'. I think the name Alison was unusual in England. Because my father had fallen in love with Alice, as my mother was known, I was called Alice. Of my father I have a few but very vivid and memorable memories, which I have retained and treasured throughout life. Possibly because of being brought up most of the time in a 'one parent home' the few memories I have are important.

Living in flats at the beginning of the 20th century was like living in a village. Much of the world had gone through the silent bloodless revolution of industrialism. It had brought the country people to the town in search of work. In the urban areas, neighbours were seldom the local residents. They were incomers and incomers were inclined to make close friends with other incomers. By the time I was able to crawl, I found my way up the stairs to a friendly family of newcomers from Inverness. They immediately adopted me as one of their own. They were a family who had migrated from 'the north' (Inverness-shire) for work. In the 19th century there had been 'the Clearings' in Scotland. As a toddler I was willingly adopted into the 'Sinclair' family. I called our near neighbour 'Granny Sinclair, and her husband was 'Daddy Sinclair'. I have a vivid memory of a very small old lady; to me she seemed to be constantly bending, maybe to my height. She wore a little white nab cap and a white apron. Daddy Sinclair was an old white-haired man, with a white grisly beard, sitting at the fireside, reading his Bible. He had become interested in the 'International Bible Students movement'. The adult brother and sister were Auntie Bessie and Uncle Roddie. This adoption lasted until they died. Auntie Bessie worked in the Civil Service. After the death of my father, she visited us every Sunday for lunch, and gave George and me a 6d (old money) to put in a little metal saving tube, which held 40 sixpences. Auntie Bessie took us to our first theatre. I should think it was a pantomime. She eventually married Jim McKenzie. June, my daughter, has a vase she left my mother, just before she died.

Large landowners had taken over much of the land for hunting, shooting, fishing and sheep rearing. The local people gradually lost their crofts and their means of a livelihood and many of them migrated to the industrial belt between Edinburgh and Glasgow. During the second half of the 19th century and the beginning of the 20th century many migrated from 'up north' to the newly developing towns in the industrial belt. It was here the new industries were offering plenty of work for those willing to work. At the same time in England, manufacturing industries were replacing the old country crafts. The migration from the country villages to the industrial towns was constant. This caused the break-up of many families and introduced a new social order to the 20th century. It had been a bloodless revolution and it was responsible for a great social change in society. These early migrants were not always received well by the local residents. It is difficult for townspeople to understand the ways of country people. Under the circumstances the country people had to adapt to the townspeople. This was very difficult for them to understand each other's ways. Such integration can take a generation or two. As I can recall, most of our friends were immigrants from 'the north'.

While living in Hermitage Place (now Rosevale terrace) I became sick with scarlet fever, and was taken to Colinton Fever Isolation Hospital for six weeks isolation. While there my father returned home. He was indignant that I had been taken to hospital, and hastened out that night to see me. My long golden fair hair had been cropped, (it grew again). I recall standing up in a cot, being very excited to see him. Being taken to hospital can be a very frightening experience for a small child.

When I was about 4 years old we moved to 3, Blackie Road, to one of the new style flats which were being built at that time. Going there was something new and exciting. We were to have a bathroom. The flats were offered 'To Let' with this new facility of a bathroom and were very desirable.

My brother George was born when I was 2 years and 4 months. By this time my maternal grandmother had died and was buried at Seafield cemetery. My father paid for the funeral; he was very fond of his mother-in-law, especially her hearty laugh. This was before I was three years old. A new phase of our new life began at 3, Blackie Road, Leith, which was at right angles to Restalrig Road. For the use of this flat we paid a quarterly rent to the Corn Merchant who had been instrumental in this new housing development. He owned a wood yard near Leith Academy, where I eventually went to school. The Industrial Co-operative Society had been started in Lancashire in 1844. It was a group of people who were interested in justice and the distribution of wealth. It soon spread all over the country. The Co-op sold things like bakery, butchery, grocery goods, but not milk and clothes. Most working people became shoppers at the Co-op. Money paid for goods was placed in a small circular container, which was transferred on a pulley to the treasury office. If change was required, it came on this connecting wire to the counter. Money, in the form of 'Dividend' was paid by the Co-op to all shoppers and was calculated on the amount of money spent in a quarter. The dividend varied from about a shilling (12d old money) 5p, either way, for every pound spent in their shops. All the monies were recorded in a black account book. Accounts were made up every quarter and out of this dividend money we were able to pay our rent.

Number 3, Blackie Road, Leith (Edinburgh)

Alison Anderson with daughter Alice

Here in our new home our main living room looked out onto Restalrig Road, named after the Restalrig Park (part of the land bought for this new housing development, fifty or more years before). The flat was lit by gas. All streets at that time were lit by gas. Every evening before sunset, 'leerie' the lamp lighter would come along, (some walked, others had a bicycle). 'Leerie' had a light attached to a long stick, which he pushed up through a hole in the glass covering the street light, this turned on the street lamp. This must have been the first satisfactory attempt at street lighting. 'Leerie' then returned again after sunrise the next morning to extinguish the light. Robert Louis Stevenson, who visited his grandmother's flat, situated opposite the Botanic Gardens, wrote a poem about 'Leerie' who waved to the little sick child every evening when he was lighting the lamp outside grandmother's house. Robert looked out of his grandmother's front window every night, when he was able.

The room we lived in was lit by gas. It had the usual recess in it, to hold a bed and a hurlie. Next to that recess was a coal house (all house heating was done with coal). The fireplace in the kitchen was made of black metal, which had to be black-leaded frequently to retain its clean shining appearance. The fire was contained in a metal cube fronted by bars, to retain the coal fire. At the side of the fire was an oven. At tea time toast was frequently made in front of the bars of the fire. The toasting fork always hung by the side of the fireplace and one of the children usually had to be responsible for the making of the toast. This skill was acquired and burnt toast was not at all popular. There was a round moveable top on the fire and this was used to support a pan for cooking. This fire provided the heat for cooking and room heat.

Diet in Scotland at the beginning of the 20th Century
Porridge, made from ground oatmeal was the regular breakfast in Scotland. Oats had been part of man's diet for millennia. In my day it was bought in bags containing 3 ½ lbs, in coarse, medium and fine textures. Medium was usually used for the morning porridge. Porridge was made with oatmeal, water and salt to taste. It took a long time to cook so it was usually started the previous evening. At night, the last task before going to bed was to prepare the porridge. It was left on the hob to simmer over the dying embers of the fire. By morning only a short time was required to complete the cooking. It was served in soup plates the next morning, with milk (occasionally golden syrup). It was known to have a soothing and healing effect. If a member of the family was sick a thin gruel was made with oatmeal and milk and this was believed to cure anything. When we were sickly, the gruel was made with the oatmeal and milk. This was sieved through muslin and was reputed to heal most complaints.

As I was growing up in Scotland, it became popular to have freshly baked morning rolls at breakfast time. The baker's shop would be open about 7 a.m. then the youngest mobile child in the family was usually appointed to go to the baker's shop to buy the fresh morning rolls. There they also sold a freshly cooked triangular scone called a bran scone. In previous centuries oatmeal had been part of the staple diet in Scotland. Oatmeal was cheap and nutritious. It was often grown on the croft. Today we are told it contains all we need for a healthy diet except Vitamin A and B7. In the country districts it would be milled locally.

As I was growing up I can recall students arriving from 'the north' during and after the First World War with a sack of oatmeal, which was to become part of their staple diet while studying at University. Wordsworth, of the Lake District, said of students: 'It is good to have plain living for high thinking". Fish at that time could be bought very cheaply at a 1d or 2d for a haddock. We had a friend who had a large house near the University, where she let rooms out to university students during term time. Morning and evening, they would make their oatmeal porridge (brose was a different way of cooking it). Many students rented a room, sometimes even sharing a room. With this inexpensive way of living they managed to live while they obtained a university education. Financial help could be earned by winning a bursary toward university fees. A few bursaries were offered only to excellent students.

It became a custom, in the Highlands, to send the eldest son in this way to university for his education. When he graduated and commenced work he, would be expected to contribute to the next son's education, and so on until all the family had the opportunity of an education. I can recall back in the 1960s, when travelling on the Isle of Lewis, meeting a lady on a bus. She lived in a 'butt and ben' and had six children. All of them were now in the professions of medicine, law, dentistry and one girl was a matron in a large Liverpool hospital, all having been educated by this system.

Oatmeal was also used for making little flat cakes (oatcakes) as a substitute for bread in country districts where shop bread was only baked once or twice a week. Oatcakes and scones would be made daily on a girddle (flat iron), which was heated on top of the fire. They were served as cake at the end of the meal.

Not long before George, my husband; died we were on the Isle of Skye in front of a broch, (a fairly large round building reminiscent of the Bronze or Iron age). It gradually became smaller as it increased in height until at the top it could be covered with a large stone. I was explaining to George how and why they were built - they can be traced right across Mediterranean countries, up the coast of Spain and France, up the west coast of Britain as far as Norway. Nearby us there was an American couple attempting to listen to what I was saying. I eventually went over and asked if they had seen such a building before, and did they know when and how they were used. Obviously they didn't, so I explained that they were built as a defence against raiders. The cattle occupied the ground floor at night. There was an internal circular staircase right up to the top. The first floor was the living space where the parents slept. The next floor was for the families sleeping quarters. A small upper room was for the servants. It was an easy building to defend. They were used two to three thousand years ago. My explanation to them was a description of how simply people in this country lived in days gone by. The lady said: "Isn't that strange, I have been to a number of doctors in America for years and no one could advise me how to get rid of my problem. Then recently one doctor told me to eat any foods made with oats and eat only white fish, and the diet cured me".

Most of our cooking was done on the top of the fire, which is possibly why we had a lot of vegetable broth at lunchtime. I remember my first attempt at cookery. It was making ginger biscuits, which were cooked in the oven at the side of the fire. In the process of time we had a gas stove at the side of the fireplace. I must have been about eight years old before it was installed. This was a fairly new invention. It also was black like the fireplace. It must have been a great advantage when we could have instant heat and a given temperature for cooking. The stove had three or four jets on top giving instant heat for cooking and an oven with a constant heat for baking. This would have been invaluable, especially in the summer. It was a wonderful modern addition to any house. Being able to turn the heat on and off by the twist of a knob was revolutionary. It would reduce the workload and shorten the time for cooking.

In front of the kitchen window was a sink and at its side a tub where 'the laundry washing' could be done. Clothes were washed with the help of a rubbing board. This was a wooden board covered with a corrugated surface. I cannot recall washing powder, only soap. The process was to lay the garment on the board and cover it with soap, and then rub it on the board to get rid of the dirty marks. In those days clothes became really dirty. I can recall the dirty marks on the collars of clothes. This had to be scrubbed clean. Baths were usually taken on a Friday night. Clothes lasted much longer than they do today. Usually we had winter clothes and summer clothes. One set of clothes for in the week and one set for church. Clothes were changed only once a week after the Friday night bath. On washing day, white clothes were boiled after washing to retain their whiteness. After boiling, they had to be rinsed. They were then put through a small wringer, attached to the washing tub to extract as much water as possible, before being hung on a pulley, hanging from the ceiling. This could have been because of the inclement weather. This must have created a very damp atmosphere in the house. There was a drying green outside the back of the flats, but not much drying took place there due to the inclement weather. Inside the house the atmosphere was smoky due to the open coal fires and outside of the house chimneys were belching out sooty dust most of the year. Chimneys had to be swept regularly by a chimney sweep. He could be seen any day of the week. His face and clothes were very black. His instruments for the cleaning of the chimneys were brushes on long extendible sticks.

Every Monday was washday. Tuesday was ironing day, Wednesday mending day. In the afternoon's mending would be done. Stockings were usually home knitted on four knitting needles. It was quite an accomplishment to be able to turn a good heel when knitting a stocking. The mother of the family usually had a sock on her knitting needles all the time. Stockings were made with fine wool. They lasted until the wool became too thin to hold another darn. Socks usually lasted for a season. Darning was accomplished on a wooden holder shaped like a mushroom. There were white cotton socks for the summer. I think they were possibly bought. Button boots were the stylish footwear but very expensive. Included in a dressing table set, there was usually a silver button hook that made the buttoning boots easier. I remember while buttoning my boots, catching the hook on the lower part of my eye (another cause of one of my fears). I was fortunate having boots, many children at that period of history ran about bare footed summer and winter. Poverty was very real affecting both clothes and food.

Central in the kitchen was a big square deal table surrounded by four dining room chairs covered with black leather and two bigger easy leather chairs. Behind the table was a big mahogany chest of drawers, which had come down with my grandmother from 'the north'. The family clothing was kept in it. There was one deep central drawer where towels were kept. I can still recall how that mahogany shone. The floor was covered with red linoleum, which was kept well polished. Every Friday night was floor-polishing night. My brother George and I had great fun sitting on polishing rags and sliding on the floor to bring it to a high state of polish. There was a rug (made from rags) in every house in those days. Old clothes were not thrown out. They were cut into small pieces and with a rug hook were worked onto a canvas backing to make rugs (little or nothing was wasted).
 One of our treasured possessions was a gramophone, with a big horn. On the horn was the picture of the dog listening to 'His Master's Voice'. I can vaguely remember the excitement of the gramophone being bought. Being out on a shopping expedition with my father always created great excitement. We never knew what we were going to buy. The buying of a gramophone was a wonderful and memorable event. The records I particularly remember were 'I Love a Lassie' and

'When the Fields are White with Daisies I'll return'. I should think they were my father's own special choice. Did they indicate his wishful thinking? He spent so little time at home with his family. Every year when I see the daisies on the lawn at the beginning of summer I remember that favourite record: when the fields are white with daisies I'll return. 'Will you stop your Tickling Jock:' and 'Roaming in the Gloaming with a Lassie by my Side'. They were current pop songs at that time. Some of them were sung by Harry Lauder, a singer comedian from Hamilton. At that time there was no radio and all these tunes were popularised at the theatre and recorded on gramophone records, which had to be wound up, for every song.

The bedroom was not very big. The window looked out onto Blackie Road. On dull days I frequently played in the bedroom. I could look out of the window and wave to my friend in her bedroom window on the other side of the road. Hanging on the wall was a large picture of ten or twelve cloud formations. This early picture has helped me to identify clouds and watch the changing skies. I am still fascinated with clouds (when travelling by air it is the clouds that still fascinate me).

When my father was not at home, I slept at the foot of the kitchen bed and my brother was alongside my mother at the top of the bed. This was not unusual at that time. In large families very often the girls were in one bed and all the boys in another. As I grew bigger, a bed was made up for me on a couch next to the kitchen bed, which was turned round to prevent me falling out. When my father was in residence I slept in the bedroom in a big brass bed. Sleeping there I examined all the cloud formations. On the other side of the bedroom wall was the kitchen of our neighbours 'the Smiths'. They were a large family of eight children. They had either very black or ginger curly hair that was very attractive, but got infested with nits. Mother Smith made attempts to rid the infestation, but I think they got re-infested in bed from the pillows at night. I used to be able to hear their chatter while in bed at night. In this room also was the camphor wood chest, brought home from China by my father and was used as a blanket box. To be allowed to see what was inside it was always an exciting event. On a shelf, which has now disappeared, there were quite a number of pieces of my late grandmother's jet jewellery and other trinkets which any little girl would delight in, especially if she could put them on. This chest had come from the Far East, but it held a few treasures; it was known as the 'blanket box'. After my father's death, I can recall the visit of my Uncle Frank, the youngest of my father's brothers and the only one in England (the others were in Canada, Australia, and South Africa). After my father's death, my mother had requested him:

"Please take away that revolver". She was afraid even to touch it. I imagine that as captain or first officer on board a ship my father had to be capable of using firearms.

In the sitting room we had the piano, a very nice mahogany china cabinet, a set of easy chairs and settee in green embossed velvet and a small cabinet (in the Chippendale style), which I now have. It was nearly a hundred years old when my mother bought it in Sunderland at a sale at the house of a local doctor. The cabinet held a set of Harmsworth's Encyclopaedia's, some bound copies of 'Sunday at Home' and copies of 'The Quiver'. The only other book I remember was a copy of one of Marie Corelli's. She was a popular writer at that time. There was the usual aspidistra, which was regularly washed and cared for. No wonder Gracie Fields sang a popular song about it. They were found in nearly every parlour. It stood on a slim elegant mahogany stand. The fireplace had a brass curb in front of which was a black fur rug. It was usual to use this room on a Sunday and as children we loved to lie down on the fur rug while reading. On the mantelpiece there were Japanese vases, fans and lacquered wood ornaments. The walls held two oil paintings of a ship my father had sailed on. The paintings portrayed the ship in the calm and in the storm. In this room was a cupboard in which jam was stored. We had an Aunt Lizzie who visited us every summer and arrived with 14 lbs of black currants. Her arrival meant we all had to engage in topping and tailing the black currants before the jam could be made. It also was the secret place for presents, which had to be kept under lock and key.

This room holds some of my earliest memories. It was covered with a green carpet. This was unusual. Carpets had not become popular in small homes. Linoleum was the popular floor covering. It was easy to keep clean. This was before the days of a vacuum cleaner. There was a common conception that it was almost impossible to keep carpets clean. They had to be regularly brushed with a small stiff brush and then they were taken down to the green regularly to have the dust beaten out. This room enjoyed a corner window from which Blackie Road and Restalrig Road could be viewed. When not at church, it was the practice on a Sunday morning to sit at the window once the church bells started to chime and watch the procession of people as they came out of their houses to go to church. Nearly every family went to church, either morning or afternoon. Children went to Sunday school in the afternoon. As the bells chimed, they seemed to say:-

O Come to church and don't be late
And put your pennies in the plate.

Or was it:-

Lord in this hour
Be thou my guide.
That by thy power.
No foot may slide.

At the peel of the bells whole families emerged from the front doors, clothed in their Sunday best. It was the nearest thing to a mannequin parade we ever had and it became one of the big events of the week, never to be missed. I never hear the chimes of church bells but it takes me back to that corner window in Blackie Road as the church bells called the faithful of Leith to worship. We paid a 'rental' to St James Parish Church for a seat in the church. The custom had become popular in the 19th century. From that window we could also see our neighbours going about their daily duties. We saw the shops they visited, the people with whom they spoke and generally kept an eye to the comings and goings of the neighbourhood and of course it was there we looked for our Daddy when he came home.

The window seat was our view on the world around us where we often looked out onto the street below. There was no radio in those days. People made their own entertainment and visited each other in the evening. This particular window was our viewpoint on the outside world and was the central focus of my early life. Just on the opposite corner from the window was the fish shop (a fresh fish shop). It was a busy place from early morning till evening. Next door was the green grocer. In those days, before refrigeration, we bought our vegetables daily for the soup. I often had to visit the shop before school for 1d worth of carrots, turnips and leeks for the soup. Our family economy did not allow for extravagance. At the bottom corner of the road was the chemist. His shop was still there in the millennium year 2,000. Next to him was the baker, where the bread and scones were sold. On the opposite side of the shop was the most important place for a small child. It was a sweet shop. There were bottles of boiled sweets of every kind, which could be bought on the way to school if we had any money, at a 1d a time. That was all we ever had to spend. It was a good place to spend the Saturday 1d. Sometimes we only spent ½d. at a time. Money was very scarce and precious.

Under the sitting room window was an ironmonger where paraffin was sold. Many families still had paraffin lamps. As I was growing up, I sometimes helped out in that shop for a while, when and if the owner had to slip away. I can't account for this privilege, but I recall being left in charge of the shop for a short time. I also did this at the paper shop, which was underneath our kitchen window. The lady at the paper shop was a Miss Drummond, who was an expert at doing oil painting of flowers on black velvet ribbon. Ladies at that time often wore a black velvet band of ribbon around the head to hold up the hair or sometimes round the neck. I also remember serving at night at the dairy next to the ironmonger's. They remained open until 8:30 p.m. every evening Milk was served from gill and pint containers from a large churn (milk bottles had not arrived as a popular container).

It was at this window seat on one memorable occasion, when my mother and my brother George and I were all at the window excitedly waiting for my father's arrival home from the sea. He had been away at sea longer than I could remember. It could have been six or eight weeks. It was not unusual for the ship to be diverted to another port and the homecoming was delayed. We used to go to the Shipping Office with my mother. It may have been to collect her salary allowance or to find out the approximate time of the arrival of my father's ship. Very few people had telephones in those days. My mother kept in touch with the Shipping Office at Leith Docks . We would all be sitting at our window, in great excitement. We knew it was the day of Daddy's arrival. On this occasion I was about three years old. We were so excited, jumping up and down. Daddy was coming back home. That meant surprises. It was exciting. It could mean presents. We had been at the window quite a long time just looking. Then imagine the excitement, my mother sighted him. "There's your Daddy". By this time we were jumping with joy. Anxious to meet him, I don't think anything could have held me back. I was off like the wind, as fast as my little legs could carry me, down the stairs, down Restalrig Road and straight into the arms of the wrong man. My father must have been near enough to see what had happened and he rescued me. I was teased about that event so many times. Such was the experience of a small child growing up without her Daddy. Often I have wondered what made me remember this mistake. Was it the excitement beforehand? Or was it the horror of the wrong man? Or was it the teasing? It may have been a sense of shame at making such a mistake. I never lived that mistake down. It lives with me now.

The remembrances I have of my father would not be complete without the oft-told tale of him coming back from the Baltic. He must have been sailing as first officer. The captain of his ship was given to enjoying too much strong drink. On this occasion he was 'dead drunk' when the ship was due to sail from Oslo. It has been reported that my father locked the captain in his cabin and brought the ship safely back to Newcastle. He had to account to the Shipping Office for this offence. They secretly thanked him for saving the ship and cargo. The captain was duly reprimanded. My father was moved to another vessel. From the stories I have heard recounted he was very quick in everything he did. Men used to say "It's difficult keeping up with Anderson". He did not have a great deal of patience with people who were slow (maybe I have inherited this). Another memory, which I think took place at Leith. We must have been visiting him on the ship at Leith docks. I do not recall getting onto the ship, but I do remember getting off. I was carried down an outside ladder backwards by him. I must have been safe enough in his arms but I was very fearful. I can still see the ladder, see the drop and feel fear, as I was carried down backwards.

Another memory of about the same period was at the home of my paternal grandparents at Herrington, near Sunderland. My grandfather was head gardener to the Vaux, brewery family. The gardener's house was near a crossroad in Herrington. The two gardeners had two reasonably large houses in the grounds of the estate. Granddad's house was on the right hand side. The second similar house was further back off the road on the left of the garden. I went back to see the house about forty years later and it was just as I remembered it.

All the family were there for Christmas. My father was home to enjoy the festivities with us. I can't recall how many bedrooms there were, but I do know we had to go through one bedroom to the one we as a family were occupying. It was Christmas morning 1914, so I would be four years old and I was hoping for a doll's pram and maybe a doll. Into the bedroom on Christmas morning came my excited father wheeling a big doll's pram. He made straight away for my brother with the pram. I was devastated. The one thing I was hoping for and longing for was going to my brother. This was soon rectified and I had a lovely big doll's pram and a doll. The pram was nearly as big as me, as is often the case with small children. The doll could open and close its eyes. It had curly hair. It was nearly as big as a small baby.

It may have been on this same holiday, I remember there was a green parrot in the living room. Quite possibly my father had brought it home from abroad. It had quite a vocabulary, not always of decent repeatable language. My father was always known to have sweets in his pocket to share all round. He gave this green parrot a chocolate ginger (my mother's favourite sweets), which caused the green bird to scream a host of swear words. Grandma Anderson ordered the bird out of the house when she heard its language. The moral never give a parrot a chocolate ginger in front of children. I do not know if that bird had a natural death, but I never remember seeing it again.

Another vivid memory from the past was at this same house which was situated at a crossroads in the village. At the diagonally opposite corner of the crossing was the village blacksmith. It was here I faced one of my most memorable fears (fear can be indelibly retained in the memory). On this occasion there was a fire of some proportion at the blacksmith's shop on the other side of the road. I do not recall the appearance of a fire engine but only the smoke, the smell of burning hair and the screams of men getting horses out down a slipway. This horror is still with me. Before long all the people in the immediate vicinity seemed to be there. Whether it was the smell, the noise, the smoke or the fear, it certainly left an indelible impression on a very small girl.

My grandparent's house was a typical country house backed by tall trees. The front garden served both gardeners houses. It had a low wall around the front garden where neighbours met to chat in the evening. The living room and kitchen seemed to occupy the ground floor. In my memory it was always full of people (that is impossible it must be an aberration). I do know all the family and their friends from Sunderland would arrive at Herrington every Sunday afternoon on a tramcar for tea at Grandma Anderson's, so I must only remember Sundays. This I think is what still lives in my memory, the people and the noisy friendly conversation. My grandmother was noted for being a wonderful cook. She was also very hospitable. I hope I have inherited some of that quality. I do not ever remember her ever having a gas stove on which to cook. Everything was done in an oven at the side of the fire. Sundays were wonderful days. Sometimes the tables would be taken out to the garden and there would be lots of people laughing and talking to me.

In this garden I also have a vivid evening memory of my Aunt Mary. She would possibly be a teenager at the time and I recall her out in the garden in the cool of the day, near sunset. She was moving around in an almost slow dance rhythm as she sang: 'If you were the only girl in the world and I was the only boy'. It must have been the current pop song at the time. I think she possibly was enjoying one of her early love affairs. Why I have this vivid memory I do not know, maybe I had been allowed to stay up later than usual with older people. When I hear that song today my memory goes back to that summer evening at Herrington. To get to Herrington from Edinburgh, we travelled by train. My grandfather would meet us with a horse and cart at the Sunderland station to take us back to Herrington just as my mother's grandfather met her at Knockando to take her to Boghur. It all sounds so very primitive but at that time it was a normal means of transport in the country.

By the time I was between six and seven years old, the First World War was in progress. My father was sailing between Britain and Canada. The Atlantic was a danger zone. German torpedoes were destroying British merchant ships. For the first three years of the war my father sailed between Montreal in Canada and Britain without an incident. During this time of war, when food was at a premium, my father triumphantly came home with a whole cheese. His ship had returned from Montreal, Canada. Cheese must have been part of the cargo. The custom men gave him the whole cheese, as it could not be sold because of the test hole through it. It was something we were able to share with friends at a time of very restricted foodstuffs. Another memory I still recollect at that time was of seeing the sweeping searchlights across the night sky, and the noise of gunfire, which was very frightening. These events had obviously been discussed around the evening supper table when I was a child. My grandmother's family all realised how imminent was destruction by bombers. How dreadful I did not know. When living in Leith we had been advised that at the sound of an air raid warning, we had to go to the safest place in the building for shelter. In our block of flats this was the square well at the foot of our communal stairs. On the occasion of the first and only air raid, I remember I was bundled out of bed, dressed in the fur coat my father had brought home from Vladivostok for 'his little girl'. In it I had to meet my inevitable first air raid. During the raid all the inhabitants of our flats sat there huddled together in the stair well. The effect on me, well, I was fearful and I was sick, all down my precious new treasured possession, my fur coat. It may have been caused by fright from the unusual noise of the air raid sirens, or the noise of the bombs. It could well have been the fear of the unknown, or it could have been the anticipation of all the horrors I had heard discussed and imagined, but we survived. The following day we travelled up to Edinburgh to see the damage. The bombs had fallen near the University, demolishing a number of flats. The conversation was heard: "Look at the destruction by these dreadful Germans".

In 1917 we travelled to Sunderland. German submarines had had a devastating effect on the merchant ships. The country depended on their safety to bring the essential food into the country. The Government decreed that the loss of merchant ships was so great that they had to be equipped with guns to defend themselves. My father, as First Officer, had to be trained in the use of the gunnery. It was now the law of the land that all merchant ships should carry guns. This was our last time together as a complete family and our last visit to Sunderland before my father was drowned. He had to report for six weeks training in gunfire. He was sailing between Britain and Quebec, Canada. During this visit I have been told my mother woke up crying during the night. Daddy asked "Whatever was wrong?" She had a dream and in her dream she saw my father's ship being hit with a torpedo. She saw him on the deck giving orders. The small boats were lowered and she was shouting "Jump George Jump!" He was on the bridge and did not jump. As the boat tipped over in its 'last curtsy' she saw his boat go down, with him on the bridge. Did she have 'second sight' like her mother before her? As she wakened, she was told not to be silly, that was only a dream. Hadn't he crossed the Atlantic time after time and had dodged the U-boats. Sad to relate, this is just what actually happened to the Fremona. According to law, the ship had to sail in convoy. This was the first and only time he had crossed the Atlantic in convoy. They had left Quebec and were heading for the Port of Saint Nazaire in France. They were only a few miles away from that destination, when they were attacked by U - boats. My father's ship had a direct hit. Eleven men took to the lifeboats and were saved, including the chief engineer, whom my mother met later. He lived in Edinburgh and described the attack exactly as she had seen it in her dream. My father was on the bridge when the boat disappeared under the waves.

The war office had presumed my father was dead; but my mother hoped that he had been picked up and would eventually be returned as a prisoner of war, but it was not to be. She did not give up hope until she had spoken to the chief engineer. This event changed the pattern of our family life. Now when my mother went out, it was not as the happy wife of a successful man but as a young widow, dressed in black (widow's weeds). Her broad brimmed black hat supported a black veil. This was the style of mourning every widow was expected to wear in 1918. The mourning was worn for a period of a year. Life was never again to be the same for our family.

Months later, my mother met the chief engineer, who lived in Edinburgh. He had been picked up and had been a prisoner of war. He told my mother: "I saw the ship go down and Anderson was on the bridge. He went down with the ship as it went under".

School days
School days started at Leith Academy when I was five years old. This necessitated a walk of more than a mile. Down Restalrig Road, the crossing of a main road on which there was a tramcar line, into the Leith Links, which was a large area of common land. Through the Links was a road, the continuation of Restalrig Road which led to Leith Docks.

The Links
The Links was the site of two ancient mounds, possibly going back to the Bronze Age. They were locally called 'Giant's Graves' and were reminiscent of many other burial mounds of the Bronze and Iron Age.

I do not remember anything about my first days at school, but my first year's education is memorable for two things. I vividly remember the song we had to sing to all the parents at the end of the first term, when we were dressed as Dutch children wearing clogs:

I'm a little Dutch girl, I live in Holland,
Holland is a land of dykes and seas.
When I look around I see many windmills,
Willy willy, willy in the breeze.

The one and only lesson I recall was on weather. We created a weather chart for the month of February. A large oblong piece of brown paper, divided into 28 squares, to represent the days of February, was given to each child. Each day we had to record the weather on our chart. There were many sunny days in February 1915. Every February I recall this early lesson.

My father George Anderson born 1879-1917
Born in Sunderland. He was a UK Mercantile Marine and first Mate on the Fremona when he was drowned on July 31 1917, aged 38.

The Fremona was a cargo ship of 2,922 gross tons, built in 1887 by Gourlay Bros. Dundee for E Thomson + sons. In 1907 it was sold to Cairn Line, Dundee (Cairns. Noble +Co, Newcastle). It was carrying grain flour and lumber which were vital supplies for the UK.

At the outbreak of war my father ship was seconded to the navy for the war effort.
He made many crossing of the Atlantic bringing vital food supplies from North America to the UK. Just before his last voyage he had been to Chatham Navel Dock Yard to have his ship the **Fremona** fitted with a gun and have training in its use. This was the first time the ships were travelling with guns and in a convoy. He was 10 miles of Ile de Bas, just off the coast of France on route for St Nazaire and Leith when his ship was torpedoed by a UC 47 German submarine. He and some of the crew went down with the ship (the chief engineer and 10 of the crew survived). After the war the chief engineer told my mother how the ship went down. His name is 1 of 35,767 on the Tower Hill Memorial, in London (near the Tower of London). He was the 1st mate and died together with 10 other sailors.
His last letter was to his sister in law and posted from Montreal and dated 4th July 1917.

My father's death
The year of my father's death was followed by a year of readjustment. We left Leith and went to Sunderland. My mother was expecting her third child. We did not have any near relatives in Scotland so we returned to my maternal grandmother's home for the birth of a girl called Irene Stella. The War Office had just presumed my father to be dead. We did not know if he was dead or alive. It was thought better to be at his mother's home in the meantime. There was a vague possibility that he may be a prisoner of war, and this hope remained with my mother for at least two or three years. At the end of the war she visited the arrival of ships at Leith Docks with 'returned prisoners of war' in the hope that my father might be among the prisoners. There were usually large numbers of widows and mothers of missing men, anxiously gazing at these haggard, deplorable, dejected, piteous men, as they trudged off the prison ships, usually in pathetic groups, from the various prison camps. Many were badly mutilated, some were blind, there were those who had lost their memories and did not appreciate they were nearly back home to their loved ones. Time after time for many of these grieving relatives, it was a hope deferred. Hundreds of people during these years continued to live in a kind of limbo.

Sunderland

During the last year of the war we stayed at Sunderland and it was during that time I had a big surprise. I vividly recall being taken by my maternal grandmother's hand into my mother's bedroom on the ground floor of the cottage as she said to me: "See what we have here". There, nestled in my mother's arms, was a new born baby, Irene Stella. We stayed at Sunderland at this small cottage for the next six months, during which time I attended the village school at Herrington just over a mile away. It was on the main tram line to Sunderland, so every day I went to school on the tram. The school was a building with two rooms. In the middle of the main room was a big black stove to heat the building. In the winter the children's wet clothes were dried around the stove. We did not have any writing books, we wrote with pencils on a slate. It took me some time to catch up with my education when I returned to Leith.

During the time we were in Sunderland we were invited to visit Aunt Louie's home for tea at a mining village called Shinney Row in County Durham. She was my mother's sister-in-law. She, like my mother, had been widowed. She had two children (boys Hugh and Ernie). It was shortly before the end of hostilities and wartime rations still prevailed. Many merchant ships were sunk right until the end of the war and the basic necessities of life had been destroyed. Bread was in short supply. This visit could have been late 1917 or early in 1918. This visit to my aunt is a day I shall never forget as the bread we had that day had a frightfully sour taste, and even now I can recall it. Most North of England people baked their own bread. The flour Aunt Louie had used could have been very old stock, (possibly brought out at a time of great shortage) however the taste was terrible. The flour she used must have been in store for a time. It has remained a taste of war time. Apart from the catastrophe of sour bread, life with all its deprivations, both physical and mental, had to continue. My cousins and I played with child-like abandon, just like children of any age. We had all lived through nearly four years of a war with all its restrictions and we had both lost our fathers. We were living in what was a war zone, yet the memory was of a cheerful song. We all sang together a hopeful, cheerful song, which must have been a hopeful family ditty. Their paternal grandfather was in the building trade and as family they looked forward to better times to come and sang in the hope that things would soon be better. Their grandparents, for four years had only done repair work. No house building was possible. The boys led in this family jingle in which I joined and have never forgotten, although

I did not appreciate or understand its significance until much later in life. We sang in anticipation of a return to a time of normality for the family. No lights had been visible during at night, no house building had been done for years. We sang as we hoped for:

> One fine night, when the moon shines bright
> And my father builds another street of houses

This ditty had developed in the Ritchie family towards the end of the war in the hope that no longer would they be disturbed by bombers by night, when people could only go out by the light of the moon. I should think it was a family ditty, in the hope that soon the day would come when the war would be over, and life would return to normal in grandfather's business and building would resume in the village. It was a wistful hope, and possibly the topic of family conversation. A family request expressed as a street song. The war had been very frightening for everyone, especially children. County Durham had been badly damaged with the bombs dropped by the zeppelins.

About this time, I remember, one night I had a frightful nightmare and woke the others in the bedroom (the cottage bedroom was the width of the roof and had three beds in it). In my nightmare I saw all the local people of the village hanging up on trees and heard their screams. They seemed to be in the last throes of death. That frightful fear has recurred time and time again to me. During the Second World War (and even now, after all these years) that same fear has recurred in my dreams. It could have been related to the few occasions on which I had managed to stop up beyond my bedtime and listened to the adult conversations at the supper table, where I heard the horror stories of what 'these wicked Germans' were doing to prisoners of war. This, I think, I had confronted in my dreams. I imagine that my brother and I were the only children in my grandmother's house at that time. I had possibly secreted myself in my own little hiding place and heard the family talk about 'these wicked Germans' and what they were reputed to do, particularly to women and small children. (In the living room in that cottage I had my own little hiding place, in the centre of a big dresser). There I could be unobserved for a long time. It was a very big dresser. The lower part of the dresser consisted of two stacks of drawers and in between each stack was a horseshoe shaped space into which I used to creep, and where I was able to listen to the adults without being seen. It was just big enough to be an escape hatch. When I was there, the grown-ups could forget I was not in bed. Conversation must have been very noisy and at supper time when all the family were home and round the table. It would be especially vivid if there had been recent bombing activity. However, I woke that night screaming. I had seen in my dream something that was possibly a visual extension of the conversation to which I had listened (I will never know). The picture, the horror and the fear of that dream still returns to haunt me.

Six months in Herrington

During this period, while we lived in the long straggling village of Herrington, I went to the village school, situated in the next village. Our house was on one of the corners of the crossroads. On the opposite corner of the crossroads was a pub, and opposite the pub was a blacksmith's shop. It was here the tramcar stopped to pick up passengers going into Sunderland. Every morning, with my Aunt Mary, I travelled to school in the next village on the tramcar. The school was a building with only two rooms. Children of all ages attended. On one snowy morning the tramcar developed a fire and everybody had to get out quickly in the snow. Such was my fright, I was taking no chances, I ran all the way home and had a wonderful day making a slide when I should have been in school. The fire was soon put out and the tramcar progressed on its journey without me. The school room was heated by a big black stove and I was lucky enough to sit near it. In the winter the farm children would arrive wet from walking through the fields. Their wet clothes would be dried round the stove. There were very few books and we wrote in pencil on slates. My village education made it very difficult for me to catch up when I returned to Leith Academy. On my return to Leith I was talking like a Geordie. This became an attraction to my friends who spoke in a Scottish dialect. They often had me repeat what I had said in my Geordie accent, much to their amusement.

Return to Leith

School life resumed at Leith shortly before the Armistice which was in on the 11th day of the 11th month of 1918. After the national despair of 1917 when German torpedoes nearly brought the war to a halt in favour of Germany, things gradually begun to look a little brighter. As 1918 progressed, there was a glimmer of hope that the war situation favoured the Allies. One unusual event towards the end of the war took place in the trenches at Mons in Belgium. At a very critical time in the war an apparition was seen in the night sky. It appeared like an angel hovering over men who were in great danger in the trenches. They took it as an omen and their despair was changed to hope.

Newspapers and the Armistice

Newspapers propagated the story and it became a national inspiration. This was before the advent of the radio. The newspaper was our only way of receiving national and local information. Our paper was the Edinburgh Evening News. It was delivered to the news agent between 5-6 pm. I am sure that at that time there were more avid readers of the newspaper than there is now. Before the advent of newspapers, people had depended on travellers arriving at the village cross to retell important news items. For a few weeks before the Armistice, newspapers were avidly anticipating the end of the war. However, the end was deferred until the 11th November. Then suddenly the church bells rang out. People had been waiting anxiously to hear the final announcement of peace. When the sound of the bells rang out the message, (this was an ancient and primitive method of conveying information) there was a rush from the houses to the streets in the excitement of the moment. The bells pealed out: Peace is declared. Lessons stopped at school and we were joyfully made aware of the significance of the event. It was a day to remember, 'the 11th hour, of the 11th day, in the 11th month, 1918. During the succeeding days the shops decorated their windows with national emblems. The war was over was the topic of conversation. The most memorable shop decoration was in an old established florist shop in Princess Street, Edinburgh. They had one big window decorated with an angel hovering over frightened soldiers in their dugouts giving them protection and hope. This florist's shop window was an instant memorial to the miracle story of 'The Angel of Mons'. All who passed by could visualise the apparition as it had appeared hovering over the despairing soldiers, at a very critical time in the history of the hostilities and had been witnessed by hundreds of frightened men who were in immanent danger and this gave them confidence. Tradition accounts for this miracle as being a determining factor in victory.

The return of the soldiers

The close of hostilities brought with it the return of soldiers, many of them badly mutilated from the effects of warfare. Men who had been badly shell shocked would never work again. Some were blind. The working population of the country was never going to be the same again. Women, who had worked to help in the war effort, were almost compelled to continue to fill the places men had once filled. After the first euphoria following the Armistice, came a period of disillusionment and then widespread unemployment such as had never before been witnessed.

The war and social conditions
The war was responsible for the re-structuring of social conditions throughout the land. Many homes were bereft of a father and sons. There were few homes where there was no loss of a loved one. Children were growing up in homes with only one parent and widows were left with children who had no father to support them. Many parents had lost their sons. Many young women had lost their sweethearts and never married and had children. Many parents in the Highlands had lost three or four of their sons. A whole generation was deprived of its youth.

After the war
The gradual renewal prevailing after the Armistice was expressed not only in a reaction to the horrors of warfare, but it also expressed a rebellion to the restrictions of the previous age. This period of joy, elation, and almost gay abandon, broke into a time of gradual rebellion. The work structure of the nation went through a difficult period of change affecting the position of male and female in society. Before the war, ladies' dresses were ankle length. Immediately after the war, the skirt hemline gradually crept up almost to above the knee. The raising of the skirt above the ankle was a very daring venture. Until this time, no man expected to catch a glimpse of a lady's ankle, except when viewed on the stage of the theatre, when singers like the Cockney Florrie Forde, had exposed her ankle, during the singing of one of her very suggestive songs. She raised her skirt level an inch or two, a movement that sent her audience, especially the men, into gales of laughter as she sang, "just a little bit, just a little bit".

The new social freedom after the wartime years was now expressed in the clothes ladies wore. The skirt line which had trailed at ground level, became higher and higher, until many skirts eventually above the knee. Until the post-war years unmarried ladies wore their hair long, which was an indication of virginity. A woman 'put her hair up' when she got married, then it was pinned up into various styles. The hairstyles had become shorter and shorter. One hair cut was called a shingle (hair was cut to ear level and graded at the back of the head). A more adventurous style was the Eton crop; this was just like a young boy's hairstyle. What had once been taboo now became acceptable. Reference to skirt lines became the topic of songs in the variety theatres. What had been shameful in the 19th century was permissible in the 20th century. The 19th century had seen an industrial revolution and the 20th century saw a social revolution.

For over three millennia long hair of the female had been an indication of virginity. The absence of men in industry during the First World War necessitated the presence of women in an industrial situation. A woman who had long hair would have introduced an element of danger. With the end of the war, the position of women in industry began and a silent social change. This was demonstrated nationally by the gradual disappearance of the ancient social customs.

In the second and third decades of the 20th century, as well as hair, the skirts became shorter and shorter. These changes in the early stages of their development were current with the early feminist and sexual equality movements. What had once been taboo and shameful in the 19th century was permissible in the 20th century. During the war women had participated in men's work, wearing men's working overalls. They hid their hair, so were almost indistinguishable from men on the factory floor. Reference to skirt lines became the topic of songs in the variety theatre songs and dance rhythms. They reflected the spirit of the age.

Return to Leith Academy
I had returned to the discipline of Leith Academy and living in a Scottish flat. This was not unlike living in a village for friendliness. We knew all the neighbours on our stair. At least three of the mothers there were widows. On rainy days it was customary for the children who lived in the flats to assemble on the upper stair level and play games. We played mothers and fathers. We not only used our own dolls if we had them but we made dolls clothes. Some dolls were basically a clothes peg. This was an on-going game. We improvised shops and stocked them with simple herbs, flower petals seeds, and dock leaves etc. It was a time of wonderful 'make believe'. The person serving in the shop made pokes out of newspaper, just like the real shopkeeper did at that time. We gossiped as we sold our wares. We had story telling times. Who could tell the best story? We read stories. We did not feel deprived, we used what we had and 'made believe'. This system of play filled the lives of children in the early part of the 20th century. We had little or no alternative. We had no Council playground, but we did not miss one. None of us had many toys. We did not miss what we never had. Lack of toys was not a problem. Many of our toys were invented or home-made.

Street games in summer
In the summer there were street games. We played in streets where

there was little or no traffic. Games did not cost money. An empty can was all that was required - 'kick the can'. The chosen child was called 'It'. He had to close his eyes and count loudly and slowly up to ten. This gave the group time to run and hide. Then on summer evenings we would play at singing games in the street. One person would be elected to be 'It' or the farmer. The group made a circle and the farmer stood in the middle of the circle. Those in the circle danced around the farmer, singing:

> The farmer's in his den.
> The farmer's in his den.
> Haigh-ho my Daddy O
> The farmer wants a wife.

The farmer then had to choose a wife to join him in the circle. The singing circle recommenced singing:

> The wife wants a child.
> The wife wants a child.
> Haigh O my Daddy O
> The wife wants a child.

Someone was chosen to be the child and joined the inner circle. Then we sang:

> The child wants a nurse.
> The child wants a nurse.
> Haigh-O my Daddy O
> The child wants a nurse.

Last of all came the nurse to the inner circle. Then the game began all over again. The nurse became the farmer.

Another circle game was played at the Links. We were required to sit on the grass in a circle. Someone was chosen to walk around the outside of the circle with a handkerchief secreted behind the back. Then we all sang:

> I sent a letter to my love,
> And on the way I dropped it.
> D D dropped it
> D D dropped it
> And on the way I dropped it.

The one who had the handkerchief dropped it secretly behind one of those in the circle. Then they had to get around the circle to the place where the handkerchief had been dropped without the person with the handkerchief noticing. The person who had not noticed the drop restarted the game. The person became 'It' and the game recommenced. This required a little dexterity.

A skipping game was played when two children turned the rope, as the rest of the group sang:

> Each peach pear plum in comes my chum.

The child in the skipping rope would call another child into the rope singing:

> Each, peach, pear, plum, in comes my chum.

One by one, as the rope was turned, this continued until there was no more room for another child.

Poverty

One memory that I have retained from these long gone days was the depth of poverty that was evident, even to me as a child. There were a few fashionable districts in the city, with houses that were well designed. There were also a large number of slum dwellings. Often they had been part of the fashionable area of the town in a by-gone age. They were now dilapidated and had been divided into very small living quarters where people lived in abject poverty. It was not unusual for many of the children from these slum-like dwellings to be sent to school bare-footed in the winter. Their clothes were not always adequate in cold weather. Their school was arrogantly referred to as 'the ragged school'. Such a school near Leith Academy was called 'Links Place School'. There the children were known as 'Links Place Keillies'. Their poverty was not entirely the result of low wages. It frequently resulted from the large quantities of alcohol being consumed by the father of the household. Many men were paid on a Friday night at the pub just outside the gates of the factory where they worked. Here the wage packet was opened, and so much liquid refreshment consumed, it was not unknown for the worker to arrive home, having spent a large proportion of his wages on alcohol. This left very little money to pay rent and feed the children, let alone to clothe them. This became a habitual way of life for many working men during this Industrial Revolution. The outcome of such conditions gave a rise to at least two groups of people who devised a means of dealing with this situation.

The Church of England Temperance Society
The Church of England founded the Temperance Society in New York in 1808. Its influence soon spread to the Mother Country where it was just as essential. The Junior Division of the Temperance Society was targeted at children.

The Water Rats and Captain John Hope
About the same time in Edinburgh, a boy's group started to function called 'the Water Rats', who, under Captain John Hope, an Edinburgh lawyer, formed a 'League of Juvenile Abstainers'. He was a man whose thinking was well ahead of his time. He attracted a group of young boys who lived in appalling conditions. They came to him in tattered clothing. He dressed them in uniform. They came bare-footed. He offered them boots if they attended for twelve months, and signed a pledge to abstain from alcohol. Full attendance brought 60 marks and two pairs of boots made by a local boot maker, who used leather of the best quality. He hired Army sergeants from Edinburgh Castle to drill the boys, and encouraged a local minister from a church at Stockbridge to provide a hall for the use of their activities. In the process of time, he had boys who had been hopeless and helpless playing the flute and other brass instruments in the band. Many boys flocked to become part of the 'Water Rats'. What John Hope had begun eventually became 'The Boy's Brigade'.

John Hope was a fitness fanatic and did not smoke or touch alcohol or even drink tea. As a boy he raced the stagecoach from Portobello to Pinkie near Musselburgh, to save the fare. He was a life-long bachelor and his passion was to protect youngsters from the evils besetting the working classes. His movement started 1859.

John Hope enrolled only abstainers to the age limit of 17 years.

The cadets were issued with a shirt that was called a Garibaldi. It was red and named after the great Italian patriot, blue serge knickerbockers and brown canvas leggings.

Boots were particularly important as the boys who came from poor homes usually had wafer-thin footwear or none at all.

He ran the scheme at his own expense by which each young lad could earn a new pair of boots every year for regular attendance at drill nights (taken from George Robinson in 'The Scots Magazine' July 1996. p. 42-43.

The Salvation Army and other churches

The Salvation Army and other churches conducted similar entertainments on a Friday night for the juvenile section of the Temperance Society in Leith. In many districts a free programme was organised on a Friday night: to entertain, to influence and to teach children of the evils and abuse of alcohol. The operators of these programmes taught children the damage done by an overuse of alcohol and encouraged them to sign a pledge, promising to abstain from alcohol and tobacco. This was done in the atmosphere of a concert, where there was singing, story-telling and other forms of entertainment, usually with the use of what had recently been invented, magic lantern. It functioned with the use of glass coloured slides projected through an illuminated magnifying glass. In the early days of its use a little oil lamp was used. Later, when the electric bulb became available, it produced the necessary illumination. This became a fascinating draw for children. It was almost like a magnet, drawing children into the Temperance entertainment. Slides to instruct and to tell a story were used. This magic lantern was one of the exciting inventions of the 19th century, before the advent of the cinema. Whole stories were told with the use of these coloured pictures, such as 'Uncle Tom's Cabin' etc. Churches used this new device to illustrate Biblical stories. It became a very popular addition to the children's night out at the 'Band of Hope'. Its use attracted large attendances. Knowing the deprivation children experienced at home, they must have looked forward to the entertainment offered on a Friday night by the Temperance Society. It had been the worst night of the week when, not only the mother, but the children had to confront the 'evils of drink' evident in their homes. Children were encouraged to sign a pledge, 'to abstain from drinking alcohol, smoking tobacco and taking opium'. This was influential in changing what had been a blot on the social life of the nation. (My research paper on wine puts this topic into perspective. It gives the proper use and historical background. Many readers of the paper have found it illuminating and it can be found in my book on the New Testament).

Poverty and Drunkenness

The problem of poverty and drunkenness was felt throughout the land. As a child I frequently had to face the results of this national problem on the doorstep of our home. We had constant visits from people who were hungry, begging at the door of our flat, not for money, but for food. They were people who were very thankful to be offered a good sandwich. Some beggars remain in my memory. There were the gypsies. They were not real beggars. Their dress identified who they were. They appeared at the door, offering clothes pegs for sale that they had made themselves. The pegs had cost nothing to make. They usually carried a few pegs, but this was not usually the purpose of the visit. Even if you did not buy the clothes pegs, they would prolong the visit by saying: "You have a lucky face". Really, the gypsies wanted to tell the owner's fortune and thereby hope to earn some money. They had a very acute perception of people. They were astute observers of features and body language seen through the open door, and would pick up information innocently conveyed in conversations. Then they would tell a fortune without an iota of truth, based on something they had observed. Many people believed they had a method of identifying the doors where people were vulnerable to their fortune telling, which usually brought additional money.

The Old fiddler
Then there was the 'old fiddler' who made a regular round to the flats. He knew the flats where he could find shelter for the night and where a resident would give him sandwiches and tea. He would sleep in the 'stair well' at different blocks of flats on a regular rotation. It was customary to hear different residents to say "I haven't seen the old fiddler for some time". His calls were fairly regular. At one time he had been a famous professional violinist in the concert halls. Now he was infamous. In his younger days he had enjoyed the glitter in the concert hall and had a career marked with success, until be became too fond of alcohol. Then, instead of his talent giving him 'a good life', now he had to depend on his violin to earn him a few coppers and to provide him with his crust of bread. This reduced him to his state of poverty due to over indulgence on whisky. On the nights he came to our flats he was really not welcomed by some of the tenants. Most people did not mind his occasional visits. Some householders, recalling his past, would take pity on him, give him some sandwiches, fill his tea kettle and give him a few coppers. Some were heard to say, "There, but for the grace of God go I". He was a sad specimen of humanity, a good subject for the Band of Hope speakers. I can recall seeing him, huddled up in a corner on a cold winter's night and remember and recall the smell of tobacco, or it may have been his lack of hygiene.

The Beggar and the Blind Man
When we were out shopping in Leith Walk there was another old man.

He had a long patriarchal beard and a shuffling gait, no doubt due to the condition of his footwear. He seemed to be clothed in layer upon layer of rags. He also had seen better days, so we were told. His hat was always worn at a jaunty angle and it looked as though every garment he had acquired was put on top of the previous one. His undesirable condition became a parable and a moral to teach us the horrors of what descends on a person who drinks too much alcohol. The old blind man had his regular pitch where he stood near the foot of Leith Walk. Here he read from his Braille Bible daily. He had possibly grown up in a Christian home where the reading of the Bible was a daily occurrence. He was always equipped with his enamel cup, which he would rattle for the collection of coins when he heard footsteps approaching. As children when we passed him, we were allowed to put a coin in his cup. In those early days there was little or no public assistance. People in desperation went to the Work House, which was a terrible disgrace. It meant they had got to the end of their tether, they could no longer beg. The Old Age Pension that had recently been instituted by Lloyd George, was 10/- per week and was available for people with a permanent residence, but this did not help the vagrants.

Our tea set

Opposite his pitch was the shop where as a child our violet tea set was bought for 7/- (35p). I retained a few oddments of the set until my nineties, when Jill my daughter, found an almost complete replica for £15. It has been so nice to use similar dishes to those belonging to my childhood.

Advertising, breakfast cereal and jam

One of my exciting and vivid recollections during these early years was my introduction to the subtlety and devious power of advertising. This happened in a grocer's shop in Restalrig Road. A prepared breakfast food came onto the market just after the end of the First World War. This was possibly the beginning of one of the early prepared foods in Britain such as we buy today. It may have been 'Force' (I am not sure).

Prepared breakfast food was developed in America in the last quarter of the 19th century. Dr Kellogg (an Adventist) became acquainted with the first efforts at making a 'ready-to-eat' breakfast cereal. A new health movement was sweeping across America in which Dr Kellogg became involved. He further developed what had been done by a small local group of health fanatics at Battle Creek. He developed further what they had devised, until he had made a presentable, saleable biscuit made entirely with wheat and ready for use at the breakfast table without any cooking. Advertising was just developing as a new industry in The States. Dr Kellogg recognised the wisdom of this new selling device that was in its infancy, and was prepared to use it. His biscuits were advertised in the newspapers as 'every flake a grain of wheat'. At the same time the good doctor had a nurse travelling around the States during the summer months giving health lectures and propagating his breakfast cereal. It had an instant appeal as a health giving, labour saving device. Dr. Kellogg soon had his instant breakfast food advertised in Europe. Other manufacturers soon got on to the bandwagon with him, making an instant breakfast food popular. A similar type of breakfast cereal was advertised by one of the shops in Restalrig Road. It captivated a junior audience. So much of this market eventually depended upon children's support. It almost ousted the use of oatmeal porridge from the traditional breakfast food in Scotland. The logo was aimed particularly at the children of the nation. This American idea soon became an international eating habit. The new movement for healthy eating which had begun in North America soon came to Europe and the new modern practice of advertising developed like wildfire. Its appeal was instant when it came to Restalrig Road.

For years the people of Scotland had prepared their own breakfast cereal. It had been a time-consuming task, starting the previous evening, as it simmered on the smouldering fire during the night, and was just heated up in the morning. With the introduction of this new breakfast cereal that only required the addition of milk, the use of oatmeal porridge went into decline. It was an attraction to most housewives. It was an exciting innovation for children. In the carton, holding the biscuits, was another subtle technique used to attract the multitude of children who would eat the prepared cereal. Enclosed within each packet was the segment of a circle, on which was displayed part of a picture. The circle had been divided into six or eight sections. Each packet contained one section of the picture. Anyone who could collect a complete picture was offered a prize. The problem arose when it was realised that the picture could be completed except for one section. There may have been a few of the missing segments but no one I knew ever found the missing segment and I never heard of anyone who got a prize, I was always short of one section and so were my friends. This was a wonderful exciting event for many children but also a big disappointment. I kept looking for that missing section. We had to buy the cereal time and time again. Porridge was off the breakfast menu. We kept buying the cartons of the new breakfast food. I was known not to enjoy oatmeal porridge, so this was a great attraction to me.

About the same time I can recall a similar device in a small grocer's shop in Restalrig Road. The grocer had two windows attached to his shop. One was taken over by the jam firm called 'Robertson's' who became notable for 'Golden Shred' Marmalade. They soon became involved in one of these early advertising schemes, which were gaining popularity throughout the land. The little grocer in Restalrig Road was chosen for this local advertising experiment.

Robertson's had developed this marmalade where the peel was cut into pieces the shape of a fish (like a goldfish). Jars of marmalade filled the window. Behind the jars was one of these new electric lights illuminating the new type of marmalade, making the window look like a big goldfish bowl. Electricity was just beginning to become popular (we did not yet have electricity in our home). The light illuminating the marmalade was electric. This attracted a constant flow of observers. It was possibly my early introduction to the power of electricity and to advertising. (Our flat was lit by gas). This electrical display was a great attraction in the neighbourhood. Most passers-by stopped to look.

The Buttercup Dairy
The Buttercup Dairy had an advertising device. 'The Buttercup Dairy' sold only butter, cheese and eggs. Their shop was in Duke Street just behind Leith Academy. At this time of early advertising they introduced an interesting device, which was wanted by all children in the neighbourhood and only obtainable when a certain amount of money was spent at the Buttercup Dairy. It cost little to make. It was made from a square of cardboard. Then a piece of brown paper, half the size of the square, was attached to two sides of the square, making a loose triangular attachment on the cardboard. It was then folded in two. The advertising gimmick printed on the cardboard. "We crack as we go to the Buttercup". When folded diagonally and held firmly in the hand, and then strongly flicked, the paper came out with a crackling sound. It was a toy that cost nothing. All the children in the district wanted one. They were obtainable only when buying from 'The Buttercup Dairy'. Every child cracking the device was furthering the custom of the Buttercup Dairy as they said: 'We crack as we go to the Buttercup'.

The Green (an area at the rear of the flats for drying clothes)

During the war appeals had been constantly made for money for the care of the wounded soldiers. Attached to most flats in our district there was a drying green (garden) where clothes could be hung up to dry. Carpets were also taken down there regularly to be beaten, to get rid of the dust. This was usually done with a cane carpet beater. These greens became a place towards the end of the War, where local concerts, as a result of the communal efforts of the community were held. The proceeds from the concerts were used to help the wounded soldiers. Generally the concerts consisted of poetry, songs and little plays. The actors were our near neighbours who tried to dress up in an unrecognisable outfit. They must have looked frightful, but everybody appeared to enjoy the fun and entertainment. Some of these concerts were performed in the back green attached to the flat. The audience was local. People paid a few pence for entry. Before the concert finished we usually had to join in singing. The response I remember to the poems and songs was a loud appreciation. Not being used to sophisticated entertainment the concert in the back green was accepted as a wonderful entertainment, well worth a penny or two. The actors were very inventive, and all enjoyed fun. I recall three sisters of a friend dressed up as birds singing:

Three craws sat upon a wa' sat upon a wa', sat upon a wa'.
Three craws sat upon a wa' on a cold and frosty morning.
The first craw couldna' craw at a' couldna craw at a'
Couldna craw at a'. The 'first craw couldna craw at a'
On a cold and frosty morning.

Second craw cried for its Ma, cried for its Ma, cried for its Ma,
Second craw cried for its Ma on a cold and frosty morning.
Third craw crawed and crawed and crawed, crawed
And craweded and crawed and Crawed on a cold and frosty
morning.

The last verse has slipped my memory, but the concerts were great fun and very popular.

As a youngster I was a Brownie. I expect I went weekly with some friends to the Brownies. We had an identifying brown uniform and we were expected to learn deportment, obedience and discipline. To be a good Brownie we were required to pass a number of memory tests, including the motto:

On my honour I will try to do my duty to God and the King and help other people at all times, to obey the Brownie Law and be of service to mankind'.

While at the Brownies, we gave concerts to different groups of people. One very vivid concert was given at a church in the Edinburgh High Street. My Brownie Pack had to become farmyard animals for that concert. Our song I still remember.

> Moo, Moo, Moo, we give milk and butter and cheese.
> Buzz buzz, buzz, buzz, buzz, Honey is better than these.
> Cluck cluck,cluck, cluck, cluck, we lay brown eggs for you.
> We wake you up at the break of day with a Cock a doodle Doo!

My special friends

My special friend at that time was Barbara Sinclair. She lived on the other side of Restalrig Road. Her father, like mine, was seafaring, in the merchant navy. He was seldom at home. Her sister Kathleen, a very pretty girl, was much older than we were. She was the first person I knew to study to become a teacher at Moray House in Edinburgh (the educational college which is still there). When the Titanic sailed, her aunt was on it. She was a very elegant lady with light golden hair. Unfortunately she was drowned. Barbara's granny lived with them. She was less than 5 ft. in height, a very tiny woman, who was always dressed in black, with the addition of a big white lace collar. She always wore a white 'mutch', rather like Queen Victoria. Her dress indicated she was a widow. She was a very good storyteller. I recall her telling us about the beach at Wick. It sounded really magical. We were told a tale about a girl digging for gold. Granny said: "If you dig deeply enough you will find gold", when the two families (the Sinclair's and the Anderson's), went to Port Seton (east along the Firth of Forth from Edinburgh) for a picnic. Barbara and I dug very deep for gold but we never did find any. I recalled this when we travelled with Fiona, my granddaughter, to the beach at Wick (we did not do any digging.) We always treated Granny with great respect. When we went on a picnic to Port Seton, the first thing we had to do was to pick winkles off the rocks. They were then boiled on the camp-fire and when cooked we had them for lunch, picking the winkles out of the shell with a pin. In the Sinclair house there was a large attic, with a few large toys like a rocking horse and a doll's house. I spent many happy hours there.

I had friends near Blackie Road called 'the Anderson twins'; we were not related. They were called Lily and Daisy. Their father was a local school master. They were not identical, one had fair hair and one had dark hair. Their mother had died at childbirth and their sister 'Netta' brought them up. On reflection, I think the father never got over his wife's sudden death. He was a very unapproachable man. We had to be quiet when he was about. When he was around, games in the house were very subdued. When he wasn't there, we had lots of fun. They lived in a villa type house.

The other friend I had was called Peggy Davidson. She was a lovely girl, with fair curly hair that was always pleated. Her father was an estate agent. They had a car and I shall never forget the pride and wonder I felt, as I sat in a car for the first time. It seemed miraculous. The front windscreen could open at the bottom end. It seemed magical making it work. They had foot muffs to help keep them warm in the winter. One member of the family was very delicate and she was wrapped up in a very expensive looking travelling rug. There was an L shaped handle that went into a hole in the front of the car to start the engine. There must have been leather seats because I can still recall the smell of leather. The lamps for use at night were on either side of the front of the car. They were not electric. I may be wrong but I think they had to be lit manually. They were called acetylene lamps. I felt so thrilled, I felt myself swelling up with pride at being able to sit in a car. I could never imagine ever having one.

This was a very difficult time in British history and there had been such devastation during the war ('at the front'). A whole young generation of men had been practically wiped out (disappeared). They were 'the lost generation'.

60

Chapter 2

How the family joined the Adventist Church in Edinburgh

I was introduced to the Adventist Church possibly in 1920 when I was of 10 years of age. My father Captain George Anderson had been drowned in 1917 off the coast of St. Nazaire, France. A torpedo hit the boat, some of the sailors escaped from the ship, but my father was seen on the bridge as the ship went down. From that time onwards we were a one-parent family.

Almost every family in the land was affected by the loss of a family member in the 1914-'18 war. All were asking the same question. Where are the dead? What happens to us after death?

Where are the Dead? Lectures given at the Adventist Church in Edinburgh

We lived in Leith, (Edinburgh) Scotland, in a three room tenement flat. My mother had seen in the leaflet and the advert in the Edinburgh Evening News for a lecture to be held on Sunday in the local cinema entitled "Where are the Dead?" This was the question, she and hundreds of war widows were asking. The lecturer was a gentleman called Lionel Barras. He was not dressed like a minister, but in a morning suit. I cannot recall the lecture, but I do know the audience were requested to leave their name and address, as a request for a copy of the lecture. This was eventually delivered by a small thin little lady dressed in navy blue, wearing a very old fashioned suit. On her feet were well polished button boots. She had a small black bag which contained a Bible and a copy of the lecture. Lionel Barras went to London from Edinburgh and by the time I went to College 1925, he had left the ministry.

On my arrival home from school I saw this stranger, sitting at our kitchen table with an open Bible. I can recall being told her name and the purpose of her visit. Her name was Annie Clarke. She hailed from Lancaster. I later learned that her family was among the early Adventists in that city. She had been to the Church College in Holloway London to train as a Bible Worker. She was dressed in an austere manner of a bygone age and with button boots (no longer in fashion). It was fascinating to listen to her as she gave her Bible study. In those days most people went to church and children attended Sunday school so they had knowledge of the Bible, but Annie Clark gave us a new understanding and changed the direction of our lives. We met new friends with the same curiosity for Bible studies as ourselves. We met in a hired hall in Picardy Place (not a church) and this became our spiritual home.

We met visitors from different parts of the world many of whom were medical students. Many were from British colonies and came to Edinburgh up- date their qualifications. (see p.53 Dr Cave Dr Rouble)

Jane Archibald

Jane Archibald was a most unusual lady for the era in which she lived. I regret that so little is remembered of her today. She, like Annie Clark, always wore a navy blue tailored suit, and a little round hat, perched on her silver grey hair. I think she also wore the button boots. She often reminisced on the American pioneers, who had come to Britain and their influence. I think she had attended the college in Holloway (I have forgotten its name). Jane Archibald was an outstanding character apart from her knowledge of scripture which seemed to me to be prodigious. Her thinking was in advance of her day and age. She was an early feminist. I can recall older members at church frequently saying: "she preaches a better sermon than the ministers," and she possibly did. She had a very keen logical mind which she used to good effect. I assume those early workers, both men and women all had similar tuition, but she had developed her teaching in greater depth than some of the men. She took a constant interest in me and possibly the other young people, but I do think she must have anticipated sending me to College which was now at Stanborough Park, Watford. She took an interest in my schooling. She indoctrinated me in the fact that my mind was as good as any man's.

For many years many years many years Jane Archibald took the responsibility of the churches in Scotland when they were short of a minister. The members used to say: "She's as good as a minister". I have realized for some time that Jane Archibald had a strong influence on me. Within recent years when reminiscing with the few of my college friends (1925-1929) and those of my day and generation, I have been informed that they regarded me as a more intellectual than any of my group and I don't think that says a lot but my intellectual aims were possibly a little higher. I should have graduated a year earlier than I did but the faculty added to the Bible worker's curriculum because of my young age. I did a ministerial course, except for Hebrew. I started as a young Bible worker at the age of 18. I was mentally and intellectually judging myself against the men with whom I worked (was that Jane Archibald's influence?). Then in the 50s when the feminist movement was developing, it made an instant appeal to me. My husband and I had 6 months in the States in the early 70s and I grasped what was developing over there. On my return home I made a detailed study of 'Women in the Bible' and eventually preaching in many of the local Midland churches on the topic, as well as Glasgow, Edinburgh, Liverpool, Hull, Plymouth, Exeter, Gloucester and Newbold College (Adventist University). I have since met at least three ministers who recall my talk, at the College. I inquired from them: do you remember what I spoke on? The answer was 'yes'. This topic did not go down very well with the Caribbean men, or with some of the white men. Some still hold it against me, as though it was the only thing I could preach on.

Jane Archibald was one of the most effective of Scotland's workers, not only her influence on me, but the responsibility which she accepted and exerted, with her constant biblical influence in the development of the church in Scotland. Many men came and did good work but then left, leaving Jane Archibald to continue their work. She worked tirelessly until the day of her death.
 At the age of 15 years I went to Stanborough College in Watford (the Adventist College).

There was another lady a Miss Robertson and her family came from the Borders. Her sister ran a Health Institution; I think this was at Moffat. She was assisted at the services by Ethel Robertson, who for many years was a Bible Worker in Scotland, who later married Frank Bollam from Newcastle. He was a colportuer (a seller of religious literature who called at peoples doors). His mother wrote a children's story book, similar to Uncle Arthur's Bedtime Stories which he sold for many years. They attended the Glasgow church well into the 1930s. It was at this time Alfred Bacon was superintendent of Scotland, supported by Jane Archibald, a Bible Worker. The two Elders of the Glasgow church were Andrew Barr senior and Bro Bleasly (a dentist); they worked well together. Andrew Barr's son went to Egypt in the 20s having previously attended the new college at Stanborough Park.

Mother did some paid work
About this time my mother went out to work for a short period. Before her marriage, like her father, she had worked at the Paper Mill in Sunderland. Seeing an advert in the Edinburgh Evening News for a person qualified in this type of work, to work on their own, she applied. Apparently there had been a fire at a paper mill and a local man had bought the remaining stock from the fire. It had to be prepared for re-

sale. I expect my mother applied for this work because bringing up two children on a pension was not easy. She was accepted for the work. During that time, we had lunch at the home of a church member. She was a **Mrs Annie Dunlop**, who had two boys**, Eddie and Bertie**, both younger than we were. I do not remember what we had for lunch but there was always soup. Mrs Dunlop came from Nairn, and had been brought up on a regular diet of soup and possibly oatmeal. She with her sister had left the country town of Nairn for the capital. There she found employment as a waitress in a Princess Street café where she met her husband, who was killed 'at the front' before her second child was born. I remember him (Bertie) as a baby, sitting on his mother's knee being fed with a Nestles milk mixture. She was listening to the Bible study. This looked very strange to me. I do not think I had ever seen a baby being fed like this before.

Other families
The other family with whom we became friendly were the **Gullands**. Mrs Gulland was also a widow. She had been left with four children, two boys and two girls. She had belonged to a farming family at Haddington and migrated to Edinburgh after her marriage. The youngest girl was named 'Alice'. We soon became good friends, although she was a year older than me. The Gulland girls were away at school during the week. My vivid memory was when I went to their home one Friday afternoon and Mrs Gulland was baking plain soda and treacle scones (great piles of them) - they were delicious! On one occasion we had a country holiday with them in a cottage near Haddington - it was great fun. We climbed Trappin Law, a small hill just less than 1,000 feet high, a Roman site. In the early 1920s the archaeologists found some early Christian communion vessels. They were exhibited in the Queen Street Museum, Edinburgh, but I believe they have now been moved to the new museum.

Miss Coloquin and the Gypsies
When visiting the Gullands we passed Miss Coloquin's home (another church member). She was a maiden lady from Perthshire. She with her sister belonged to an affluent family who had been brought up with the idea of sharing her wealth with others who were not so well off. She occupied a basement flat. In the autumn she followed a gypsy family with numerous children and made friends with them. Then she persuaded them to let her have three of the children for the winter, so that she could begin to give them an education. They were real gypsies, not 'tinks'. Tinks were reputed to have come from Ireland. Before she took them to her basement flat she took them to the

hospital to be de-loused. She clothed them and during the winter she educated them. At that time there was no provision made by the Education authority for the education of gypsy children. They then became part of the young people of our church.

Growing up amongst missionary minded people I became enthusiastic and anxious to raise money to support missionary projects. With the help of my Mrs Cave, I helped to organise a concert at which £3 was raised. I only recall the gypsy contribution. It was very memorable. The eldest gypsy had a recitation to say. She recited in her low voice with very elongated vowels:

> There was a man named Samson,
> Who was very good and strong.
> For the Lord had greatly blessed him,
> And his hair grew thick and long.
> He married a bad woman
> Who he thought was very fair.
> She teased him till he told her,
> That his strength lay in his hair.

This slowly enunciated verse, spoken in a very low Highland dialect, captivated the audience. Many, who heard it, can remember how it sounded. We still try to repeat it in the dialect in which it was given. The other children were dressed up as snowflakes (in white paper dresses). They were wearing house slippers (their foot- wear was usually much more substantial). They had to come in skipping and saying:

> "Here we come, little white flakes of the drifting snow".

When they came on to the platform, one of the children clumsily stepped on her sister's white paper dress. Instead of ignoring it, she turned round accusingly saying: "She's toored ma frock, she's toored ma frock"! We could not continue, until the problem of the 'toored frock' was discussed and solved. In the audience there was a titter of laughter all round. These children were really the stars of the evening. I can still repeat a line from one of the poems my little gypsy friends learned all those years ago. Her poem was called springtime. It described what happened at springtime. As I see the first dandelions on the lawn, I say either silently or audibly:

> "The dandelions are popping up, in every field you pass".

This is a truism; it is exactly what happens from year to year and when I see the dandelions popping up it reminds me of the children and I think I hear that slow, low Highland dialect. Their contribution has been a lasting addition to my vocabulary. The family was only with us for a short time but it was effective. One of the other songs at that concert, which I think very few would forget was:

Little water wagtail had a little nest,
Down where the rushes grew.
If they stood on stone or rail,
They were taught to wag their tail,
For little water wagtail knew.

Years later we heard news concerning these little girls. One of the girls became a music teacher, another worked in an office. Miss Coloquin's sacrifice brought forth real fruit!

Chapter 3

SCHOOL DAYS

According to my father's wishes, his children had to receive the best education available. Where we lived there were several council schools in the district. I was sent to Leith Academy, a school built of red sandstone towards the end of the 19th century. It was situated at the west end of Leith Links. Its position was next to St Andrew's Church of Scotland. Opposite was a Brewery and not far off was the Kirkgate, which in previous days had been one of the main thoroughfares of Leith, leading from the town down to the docks.

Leith Academy was originally built on an ancient foundation of the 16th century. Until the Reformation, education had been under the control of the church. About this same time, the Law School attached to Oxford University moved to the Middle Temple, London and became independent from the church. It was the first department to move away from the control of the church. In Scotland education also became subject to a similar change. In 1560, at Leith, a school was established under a Board under the control of the Town.

By 1896 Leith School Board decided that the High School at St Andrew's Place was no longer satisfying the demands of education in Leith and voted to replace it with a building more suited to the purpose. The old school was demolished and in its place a handsome red sandstone Victorian building, incorporating the cupola and clock tower of its predecessor, was built.

This new Leith Academy became, and still is, an impressive and readily identifiable Leith landmark. It was officially opened October 22 1898. It functioned as Leith Academy, providing Primary and Secondary education until the l930s when the senior department moved to new accommodation, leaving the building to the primary school'.

Memories of 20th Century Education in Leith
Time spent at school occupies a large and determining place in the life of a child. I can say my school helped to mould me into the person I have become. As a kindergarten child my fees were 5/- per quarter (today that does not seem to be much, but I suppose it was quite a lot in the second decade of the 20th century). There were three quarters in the school year. I had to wear the school uniform. It consisted of a

navy blue gym-slip with white blouse, black stockings and a royal blue blazer with the badge of the school, showing a sailing ship capped by the motto 'Persevere'. This distinguished us from all other schools in Leith.

I started school in 1915 when the Rector was a Mr O.M. Tait, a benign gentleman, I should think between 50-60 years old. All the students held him in reverence and awe. His hair was greying and he was slightly bald. In my memory he always seemed to be dressed in a light grey suit, which added to his dignity. His office was central to the building and students who were sent to the Rector because of bad behaviour, sat outside his office, usually looking dejected and frightened. There was a Headmistress for the junior school. I cannot recall her name but she was a very distinguished looking lady, in her black silk blouse which had a high neck line, trimmed with lace and small beads. She always seemed to wear a string of black beads around her neck. She was possibly in mourning. As she strode around her black skirt seemed to sweep to the floor.

There came a time when the school was outgrowing its capacity and additional buildings were built for the Secondary Department. The new buildings included a new gymnasium and a number of classrooms. These were built behind the main school building.

I had to walk the best part of a mile, down Restalrig Road, across a main road on which the tramcars ran, then through the Links to the school. 'The Links' was an area of open grassland. On the south side of the Links was 'Links Place' and on the north, the buildings were approaching the docks. A road divided 'The Links' which was a continuation of Restalrig Road, reaching right down to the docks. Daily, as I went to school, I saw two ancient features called by the locals **'The Giant's Graves'**. It is very possible that they were ancient tombs belonging to the Iron Age, when it was a custom to bury important people in mounds. These mounds are found throughout Europe in groups and sometimes in isolation. **Arthur Seat** in Edinburgh is an area where there are remains of a very early civilisation (an ancient ruin still remains standing in a strategic position on the hillside). It is therefore not surprising that mounds are to be found in the district. According to tradition, the men under the mounds in Leith Links were giants. It is very possible that there could have been an ancient king or warrior buried in the district. When I was growing up 'The Links' became a play centre where swings were a great attraction.

It has been recorded that in 1459, when James II ruled, that **the game (golf)** was to be forbidden in Scotland, as it was interfering with archery practice.

Archery practice was the recreation practised everywhere by the male youth, to make them proficient at a time of warfare. Obviously the king did not wish this essential practice to be limited.

James IV however favoured the game of golf when time permitted. Council accounts note that he acquired clubs and golf balls ' for the playing of golf at Leith' in those days. Golf balls were expensive items and at Banff Burgh Court there is even a record of a boy who had stolen a golf ball and 'he was then ordered to be taken to Gallows Hill to be hanged on the gallows'.

In 1898 a small firm, J.P. Cochrane & Co. in Albert Street (the first street over the Leith border) with a staff of six produced the Rex and Paragon gutta ball. In the 1900s they moved to Morano Place with 180 employees and were turning out 3,000 balls per week. There is a shop in the High Street, Edinburgh where they claim to have sold the first golf balls.

Not having Council playgrounds in those days, the Links became our playground during the holidays. At holiday times, after the keeper had cut the grass, it became a place where children congregated to make grass houses. They consisted of rows of grass, three to four inches high, made in lines in the outline of the rooms of a house or a shop. A group of children created an imaginary grass village and we played there in the long summer days (I do not remember wet ones, they may have been when we played indoors). The eastern Links had at one time been the place where Dutch sailors had played a ball game, centuries ago, with a stick, which in the process of time developed into golf.

The first song I remember learning at school:

> I'm a little Dutch girl I live in Holland,
> Holland is a land of dykes and seas,
> When I look around I see many windmills,
> Willey in the breeze.

We had not only to learn the song but we dressed up as Dutch girls (including the clogs) to perform in front of the parents. This was my first public appearance.   My other vivid memory during my kindergarten days was the production of a weather chart for the month of February. We each had a brown square of paper, divided into 28 small squares. The weather was observed and discussed each day. It was then indicated on our chart. At the end of the month we had many more sunny days than dull days in February. Every February that early weather chart comes to mind and I am yearly reminded of the returning sun. I never fail to remind others of that weather wisdom.

School began with the ringing of a school bell when all the children assembled in the playground in designated lines, according to their particular class. Our teacher would collect us at the cloakroom and march us to a large dark room on the ground floor, where Assembly would be conducted.

The playground was important. It was where we could skip and play before lessons and play at playtime. We had a variety of games we played, with skipping ropes. There were communal ones when two girls twisted the rope and each child had an opportunity to jump into the rope as it was being turned. We joined in singing:

> In the garden stands a lady
> Who she is I do not know,
> All she wants isn't gold or silver
> All she wants is a nice young man
> So call in (the name of the next girl) my fair lady.

Skipping ropes were popular with the girls in the winter when it was cold.   At another season we played 'peavers'.   This was another playground game. To play this game 'peavers' we required a small piece of polished marble, about two and a half inches in diameter (these peavers could be bought for a penny from the yard where tombstones were carved). If it was impossible to buy a peaver, an empty tin box would do. A piece of ground would be marked out in six blocks of squares, numbered 1-6. The peaver had to be moved with the side of the foot from square 1-6. If it landed on a line, the player was 'out'. Then they had to wait for another turn. To be able to get round all the squares gave you a game. The number of games won was important. A hide and seek game was also played which was rather difficult in the playground. The prohibited area for this game was the toilets block (I remember the area with horror because the toilets were low and smelly!)

The classes in school were between 50-60 pupils (boys and girls). My teacher was called Miss Taylor in the junior school. My recollection of her was always seeing her dressed in a long dark skirt nearly reaching to the floor and a white blouse. She had complete command of the class. For much of her teaching she used the blackboard. Her countenance was severe. Her dark hair was parted in the middle and from the parting a roll of hair encircled her head, which was covered by a hairnet. She taught her class from her desk, as she sat on a fairly high chair in the right hand corner of the classroom, from where she could observe all the children. The only time she moved from the desk was to write on the blackboard. We, the pupils, were expected to sit quietly unless her voice of authority determined otherwise. From her seat of authority at her desk, she instructed us in our use of English, which had to be pronounced clearly and articulated precisely. To develop our knowledge of Maths, we began our first lesson in the morning with mental arithmetic. During the term we had frequent visits from student teachers and specialist teachers as we were instructed in our Scottish local and national history. Our Geography lesson opened up the world around to us. Miss Taylor conducted the singing class once or twice a week from her so-fa chart. We learned to read music. As a special treat we made a short journey over to the new gymnasium for physical education, which included country dancing. Any disobedience, such as whispering to the person next to you or eating a sweet, merited the use of the strap. A strap, (locally called 'the taws') consisted of a strip of leather divided at the end into three tongues, (tradition declared this increased the pain). There was a general conception that it was kept soaked in whisky to make it more painful. I never recall getting the strap. For extreme disobedience the child was sent to the Head master for punishment. That was a terrible disgrace. Any child awaiting punishment from the Rector sat outside the Rector's study door until called in. This punishment was very degrading and was dreaded by most pupils

The school day began with a worship service, introduced by one of the staff. It was concluded with the saying of the Lord's Prayer. This Assembly was held in a ground floor hall. After the Assembly we went to our respective classrooms, then lessons commenced, beginning with rote practise of tables and spellings.

Pupil teachers paid us a visit occasionally. This brought a welcome interest into the day's lesson. Often they read a poem and discussed it with the class and we possibly had to memorise part of it. I looked

71

forward to these visits and really enjoyed them. Usually a poem was chosen with a story. It was possibly the story and the rhythm that captivated me. As the years went by we learned quite a few of them by rote, a custom for which I have forever been thankful. In adult life a long lost verse has meaningfully come back to me. Years later, George (my husband) and I had a few hours on our own together in London, one warm sunny Sunday evening, at the end of a long busy day. We were in the centre of London having just listened to the starlings on their return from their countryside-feeding place. Just before twilight they returned to nest on London's plane trees on the embankment. We wended our way to London Bridge; standing there in the sunset glow I was reminded of:

> Dull would be the soul who could pass by
> A sight so touching in its majesty,
> This city doth like a garment wear.
>
> The beauty of the morning, silent bare
> Ships, towers, domes, theatres and temples lie
> All bright and glittering in the smokeless air.
>
> The river glideth at its own sweet will:
> Dear God! The very houses seem asleep;
> And all that mighty heart is lying still.

As I recalled and repeated the beauty of the poem, we stood together sharing part of that nightly beauty; it was an uplifting, revealing experience, long remembered. Although the poem was directed to the morning beauty, on that night, in the evening golden glow it still held a mystery and beauty seldom seen. We felt privileged to see and partake in that evening hour the opportunity of seeing such a magical sight.

Not far from Westminster Bridge is Lambeth church where there is a memorable small window, depicting a travelling salesman, with a pack on his back. When he died, he left £2.10.0 (£2.50p) to be given to the Lambeth church. With that money a small piece of land was bought. Shortly after the Second World War the land was sold for 2 1/2 million pounds. Two poems from that period that made quite an impression on me were 'Enoch Aden' and 'The Laird O Cockpen'. I still try to quote from them from time to time. The class was always admonished to be on very good behaviour when a pupil teacher came to visit us. It must have been a welcome relaxation when we were able to enjoy poetry. Miss Taylor conducted our music lessons. She used a chart with 'tonic so-fa.' The one song I remember from that period, although there must have been many others, was:

O for the wings of a dove.
Far away, far away would I fly.

(This may have been wishful thinking.)

I passed my exam for the Leith Academy, which had recently been extended to include the gymnasium and new classrooms. This was a great event. Instead of being under the supervision of one teacher, we had a different teacher for each class. This added movement to the school day. Instead of being taken out to play games in the playground, we went to the newly constructed gymnasium.

All this was happening at the end of the First World War. School attendance had increased. Additional classrooms were required urgently, so temporary buildings were erected in the boy's playground. They were similar to Nissen huts used after World War II. In the playground, they built four classrooms on either side of a corridor. The history class I attended faced the road (not inwards towards the playground). The Secondary department covered a 'six year' period. Boys and girls classes were separate. Boys were identified 'B' 'D' 'F' 'E' and girls were 'A' 'C' and 'G'. I was group 'C'. This section of the school was called 'The Higher Grade'. In this division of education our minds were beginning to be stretched. We looked at new topics. All teachers in the Secondary school had to have a degree. This was not so in the Council schools. I look back on this period of my education with pleasure. I was particularly fascinated as I was introduced to Maths. The teacher was a dapper little ginger headed man who made Maths fascinating. I can recall on more than one occasion getting 100% for algebra.

History was my most exciting lesson. The history teacher stimulated my interest. He opened my mind to the story of past ages. What had happened in bygone times just where and how man lived was a revelation. Mr MacKay was an unusual man. He is mentioned in the 100th Anniversary book. He walked the length and breadth of Scotland looking at the stone relics left behind by previous generations. He was able to communicate the excitement of ancient civilisations. He has had a lasting influence on my life. His history lessons captivated me. They were conducted in the temporary

73

buildings in the boy's playground. As a teacher he was not a disciplinarian. He did not usually need to exert discipline. He made history the most exciting event in school. Like many other students, I used to be fascinated in his class, but not all the class shared my enthusiasm or were as receptive. On one occasion, he was really involved in the topic he was teaching, when one of the boys who had heard the ice cream man outside the window quietly climbed out of the lowly placed window and bought an ice cream for himself. Cockie MacKay, (our affectionate name for him) obliviously did not notice what had happened. He continued with the topic. Suddenly he saw this apparition climbing back through the window: 'Where have you been?" ask the teacher. "Just to buy an ice cream," the boy replied. This all goes to show, that what absorbs one student, leaves another unimpressed.

The influence of my teaching at Leith Academy has lasted throughout my life. I spent from the age of five to fifteen at Leith Academy. The next era of my life was about to begin. It was at Leith Academy where I learned to love books, which became like shells, waiting to be opened with a pearl of wisdom inside. My love of books continued until the end of my long life.

I left Leith academy at the age of 15 and continued my education at Stanborough college in Watford (the Adventist College).

Chapter 4

People I knew in my early life

Sunderland
Early recollections were of being in the midst of chattering adults, around the supper table, usually at the end of the day when my grandparent's large family had all returned home to enjoy the cooking of my maternal grandmother (she was a wonderful cook and my taste recollection is of the taste of different herbs, possibly from the garden). I ought to have been in bed, but I must have made myself invisible by and scrambling into the recess (cubbyhole) between the two sides of the big dresser where I could hear adult conversation, and be forgotten in the tumult of the family chatter.

Leith – Edinburgh
I was about 10-12 years of age when we had joined the church. During this period my home and school life was fairly quiet and uneventful. I met people at the church who had arrived in Edinburgh from distant lands, like the United States of America, South America, the West Indies, and South Africa. They had come to Edinburgh to gain the British qualification that would permit them to practise medicine within the British Empire. This was a time of great missionary expansion throughout the world. In my naivety, the meeting of these strangers from the far flung parts of the world was a very impressive influence on me. They spoke English in a different dialect to our Scottish dialect. Sometimes their dress was unusual. I was being introduced to the great wide world outside the confines of my beloved Scotland. Every week I was being introduced to something different. This opened my eyes to the necessity of school work in order to learn about the great beyond. I was asking questions that had never occurred to me before. I longed to know what was beyond Leith and Edinburgh and the world had suddenly become a big place. School geography became more interesting, and was a way for the exciting acquisition of knowledge which suddenly became important. I became much more inquisitive and enjoyed the idea of reading and learning.

Leith Academy
I attended Leith Academy, a school with an ancient foundation, and there I had a remarkable history teacher, lovingly called **Cockie McKay**, who inspired me with his interest in the past and although the knowledge of ancient history is much more developed today, his

captivating method of teaching has rubbed off on me. I am still currently a devout student of archaeological history which has influenced my personal ability to interestingly convey my knowledge to groups. There is a connection between much of what we do today with what happened millennia ago. At 93 years of age I still give talks to groups. Many of my talks are based on archaeological findings. This year (2003) I have only given 12 talks, but a few years ago I was giving between 50–60 talks between September and March.

Cockie McKay, my History Teacher

June took me back to Leith in the early '90s, when we were invited to visit the muniment room in my old school, Leith Academy and my dear 'Cockie McKay' was honoured by having his picture on the wall in the muniment room. It had been placed there during the 100th anniversary celebrations as being one of the outstanding teachers of the century. He was the one teacher mentioned in the Anniversary booklet and it was well deserved. He was not a strict disciplinarian but he knew how to retain our attention. The classrooms at the end of the war (1918) were in Nissan huts. One boy in the class had climbed out of the window to buy an ice cream from the Italian Johnny on the pavement outside. On his return he was noticed by Cockie McKay who questioned him "And where have you been?" The lad defiantly answered "O just to buy an ice cream". He was suitably punished, but the class had retained interest and attention throughout the incident. He was a man living before his time. Before hiking had become a popular pastime he was walking Hadrian's Wall and other interesting historical sites. We had one site just outside of the school playground. It was an early burial mound colloquially called the giant's grave.

The Dunlops

During my last two years at school I had lunch at the house of Annie Dunlop and her two children. They, like our family, had been left fatherless as a result of the War. The flat where they lived was really in the slums, but it was all they could afford. Both boys became eminent doctors. They had been influenced by the number of missionary doctors constantly passing through the Edinburgh Adventist church. Eddie got a State honour while he was in Boston and Bert contributed to the Adventist hospital work in South America, Trinidad, West Indies and Hong Kong.

Miss Coloquohn and the Gypsies

While attending the church I met an unusual lady. She belonged to a wealthy family from Perthshire. She was not married and like some of the other members of her family she felt a strong social responsibility for the underprivileged. She had left her comfortable home in Perthshire and hired a basement flat in Edinburgh. She then toured in the Highlands of Scotland where she saw gypsy children who never had the opportunity of education. She realized that these children would never be able to enter the world as it was then developing. This realization drove her to make friends with a few gypsy families, and then in the autumn of the year she persuaded their parents to let her educate three of their children. The gypsy families were living as generations of their forebears before them had lived with their horse driven caravan. They lived on what grew in the hedges and on what other people threw away. The only money they had was earned in the harvest fields and by the sale of the clothes and pegs they made. The materials cost them nothing and they were sold in the villages and towns. The year was possibly 1922 or 1923 when Miss Coloquohn collected three gypsy children from their parents one autumn and brought them down to Edinburgh. They were taken to a centre, to be deloused and bathed and then they were transferred to her residence in a basement flat off Broughton Street, Edinburgh. This must have been a staggering culture shock for them. It must have been like jumping through the time zone of centuries in a few hours. In one day they moved from the simplicity and the freedom of living in the wide open spaces of the Highlands where they moved the caravan and travelled at the rate of the pulling power of a horse. In Edinburgh, modern transport whisked them into noisy, smelly urbanity, where vehicular transport was noisy and speedy. Their arrival at the basement flat must have been magical where they just had to touch a little spot on the wall and suddenly there was produced dazzling light, many times brighter than a candle or oil lamp. They had never been in a house before, never seen electric light, and never been in a bedroom. They had usually eaten outside the caravan. In the evening it would be around a camp fire and by candle light. Within one day they made this change which it had taken the world centuries. They had crossed that time gap in a few hours. Their lives were being changed forever from the simplicity of an ancient style of living to the modern world. They had leapt through a time gap of centuries in a few hours.

During the winter Miss Coloquohn taught them to read and to write and they had to learn music. Not the simple whistle made out of a reed which the father had played, but they were introduced to the piano and learned to read music. What can their mental reactions have been? It could have been a frightening experience for them.

Three lonely little children confined within the walls of a house with a maiden lady intent on introducing them to the triumphs of modernity. She brought them to church on Sabbath and that was another unusual experience for them, being with a group of people none of whom they had seen before who were all singing together. Then there were the classes they had to attend where they heard stories that were not at all familiar. Eventually they regularly repeated Bible verses and learned the Bible stories and when there was a special program once every quarter they contributed to it. On one occasion one of them in her very strong Highland accent publicly told the story of Samson.

> There wos a maan named Samson,
> Who waas very good and strong
> For the Loord haad geatlly blest him
> And his hair grew thick and loong.
> He married a baad wooman whom he thought waas very fair
> She teased him till he told her
> That his strength lay in his hair.

Years later, a number of the members who had heard this gypsy's elocution still remembered the little girls.

Then I remember one concert they took part in. One of them was a snow flake and she had her white paper dress and when her sister stepped on her dress she forgot what she had to say, she turned indignantly to her sister saying in the middle of her part and very audibly in her broad Highland dialect accusing her sister saying:

> "You've toored my frock!"

This caused much laughter in the audience. The girls wore slippers that night. They were used to wearing very strong footwear so I think the slippers could have been the cause of the problem. They visited Miss Coloquohn for three consecutive winters and were returned home for the summer. She emphasized to them that she was only their teacher guardian and they should not forget their mother or father and of course she returned them home every summer. The last I heard of them was that one worked as a secretary, one was engaged in dressmaking and one taught music.

Dr Rouble

In 1921 we had Dr Rouble, his wife and their adopted niece Martha Jane arrive from the States. He eventually became the resident doctor at the Stanboroughs in 1924. Just before leaving the States, they had adopted Martha Jane whose parents had recently died. On their arrival in Edinburgh, she was just becoming acquainted with her new parents. She had never been out of the States before and she was going to be taught at home. She would not meet any children in Edinburgh, which must have made her feel isolated and be rather difficult for the little girl. I was invited to visit on a weekly basis, so I suppose I played an important part in her adjustment with her new parents. On my arrival at the flat, I was given delicious hot chocolate which I thought was wonderful, never having tasted drinking chocolate before. To get to their home I had to travel on two tram cars, the first one from Leith to Pilrig on the Leith tram car, then from Pilrig to the Meadows on the Edinburgh cable tram car. Pilrig was the boundary between Leith and Edinburgh and each city had its own public transport. To make it possible for this cable car to turn round to make its return journey back to Edinburgh, the conductor had to get out of the tram car and with a long rope he turned the long cable connection on the roof of the tram car around, and so it was possible for the tram car to go in the opposite direction. For two years I visited the Roubles home every weekend to play with Martha Jane.

Dr and Mrs Cave
My Sabbath school teacher was the wife of Dr Cave, a lady from Trinidad. The Caves wished to open a nursing home in their home village and so they came to Edinburgh to take a British degree. The nursing home was opened in Port of Spain and became a hospital. On their death it was given to the church. Drs Bull (from Leamington) served there in '50's and Dr Bertie Dunlop (my friend from Edinurgh) in the 1960's (he later went to the church hospital in Hong Kong).

I loved Mrs Cave and she loved me and just before they went back home she made me make a solemn promise to be a missionary and love the Lord and treasure my Bible. At 93 years, I am still observing that oath given to a lovely lady. The Cave's are mentioned in the Battle Creek Pioneer book. I felt greatly honoured to know them. He was a very interesting speaker who frequently took the Sabbath service. The church members all appreciated his contribution to their Biblical knowledge. Because of the influence of Mrs Cave, I was ready to go to Stanborough College at the age of nearly 15 year.

Chapter 5

COLLEGE DAYS

Going to Stanborough Park Adventist College with suitable gifts from the church, from parents and from friends. We were now entering a new era of our lives. It seemed a long journey (nearly the whole day) on the Royal Scot and as we steamed into Euston Station 8 hours later we were met by the ebullient Willie Lennox, another Scot who was anxious to introduce us to our new lifestyle.

Everything seemed very strange in London with the underground trains. The bus journey to Stanborough Park was locally known as 'heaven's gates' by the conductors. **Matron Gwen Brown** met us and allocated us separate rooms, possibly to encourage us to integrate with other students. Apart from **Willie Lennox** we were the only students from Scotland. I remember my amazement as I noted the age of most of the other students. To me they seemed very old. Communal living was also a bit of a culture shock. I shared a room with a girl from Hereford and a lady (she appeared ancient) although she may have been in her late '20s she seemed a lot older than me (she came from Southampton). Neither finished the student course of studies. The day I arrived they both had good intentions. Many others dropped out on the way due to financial problems.

My New School (College)

I was soon to learn the routine. The dining room was set out with tables for four students, two male and two female. Each student was allocated a place for one week. I had **Leslie Emerson**, who later became the Editor of the Present Truth at my table and I think Mary Campbell, a Scot working at the Granose. She was from Glasgow. I know I felt very young beside them. Leslie Emerson had already been working in the editorial department of a Sheffield paper for some time.

80

Mary Campbell was approaching 30 (she served as secretary to most of the presidents in her time). The College custom was to change table companions every Friday evening. Friday evening then became a very important and exciting day. Knowing with whom you had to sit at table for another week could be fearsome or it could be a pleasure. It was one way of becoming acquainted with the other students. Interest in the opposite sex was frowned on according to the College Brochure 1925. This was a very gentle way to introduce students to the rule relating to friendship with the opposite sex. This restriction must be understood in the context of the 1920s, although I do think it was a little outdated.

The student's day started at 6 am. by the ringing of a very loud bell. This was my first shock. The ringing of a bell controlled all the movements during the day. The Breakfast at 7 am, was usually not a very interesting meal, of porridge, and stewed dried fruit. Not being a great lover of porridge, it did not appeal to me very much. Lunch was at 1 pm. and supper at 5 pm. At every meal the Matron sat at a corner table in the dining room and was able to view most of what was happening. Too much frivolity was censured. **Miss Brown** left the following year to marry **Dr Hargreaves** an eye specialist who was practising in Persia, at an Adventist hospital, which he had established. Eye problems were very prevalent. Then the following year we had a matron named Mrs Howard. She sat in the same corner seat, where she was always on the look-out for rule breakers. No doubt due to her ever wandering eye, an interesting puzzle question was being asked by the student body during her administration. "Why is Mrs Howard like an isthmus?" Answer: "Because her neck stretches out to sea."

The afternoon was allocated to manual work. Most of the students had to work to earn money as a contribution towards their fees, which were £26 per year. The garden, the farm or the Granose Factory were areas where money could be earned. I was allocated to work at the Granose. This I found rather tedious and soul destroying. Packing Granose biscuits on a continuous line in a noisy factory for 41/2 hours per day, for which I was paid 41/2 d per hour, this was the biggest problem I had yet to confront in my life! I did not last there for many weeks. I think I had to earn up to £15 towards my year's fees. At the low rate at which we were paid it would mean more than 700 hours of misery (packing biscuits was a boring task). This was not only a culture shock it was nearly a 'knock-out' blow for me.
I was soon transferred to kitchen work and household duties, which

were more amenable to me. To begin with, it involved dish washing and vegetable preparation on a big scale. This was more acceptable. We enjoyed conversation and could move around. Work could be started immediately after breakfast and be done in between lectures, and in the afternoon. The work need not be done in an unbroken 41/2 hour session. This was possibly a better introduction to the tedious job of work into which I was being catapulted in my new way of life.

Study Periods
At the class registration I mostly entered for third year studies. Many of the new students at Stanborough College in 1925 had no secondary education and started with first year classes. I found myself sitting in classes, not with students of my own age, but with students who seemed to me to be very old. However, I quickly fitted into this new regime. From that year's registration, 1925, there are no students still alive.

I was now to experience a new mental approach to life. I was no longer being taught like a child, I was being lectured to like an adult. No longer did I sit in class and expect to be 'spoon fed'. I had to start to think for myself, to do my own research and particularly, to use my time to advantage. The Principal was George W. Baird, an Irishman, of great charm. He was not only the Principal, he also lectured on history. Although I had become fascinated with history at Leith Academy, George Baird touched another vein in my powers of perception. This appeal from both my history teachers has affected my thinking and ultimately my perceptions throughout life for which I will be forever grateful. Now, in my 90th, year I am still enjoying and following my ancient history. Bible study featured largely in our studies. This I greatly enjoyed. Instead of sitting back and listening as a child as I had done in church, I was now being directed to read against the background of ancient history, to understand the problems the writers of the Bible were addressing. To my impressionable young mind, all this seemed very thought provoking and exciting. It was my first big mental growing experience.

Being in a missionary college, there was a constant flow of visitors from various parts of the world. This introduced me to worldwide problems. It helped to relieve the tedium and pressure of constant study. Some of these visitors came merely to study English. Many of them were stopping for a short time in transit, to and from mission fields. We had quite a few interesting visitors throughout my four years at College and they were influential in making geography important to me.

A large extended family in Baghdad sent three of their young people over to Stanborough College to learn English. Years later, when we lived in London we entertained a member of that family in our home after the end of the 2nd World War. He came over to London to buy and sell. They owned a large Departmental store in Baghdad. He visited our home one Sabbath when we enjoyed entertaining him. When saying goodbye, he presented us with a gift of crystallised fruits such as we had never seen during the wartime days. They could have been the type of goods he was selling to London stores. They were so delicious, we were almost afraid to eat them. The thrill of receiving such a wonderful gift after the deprivation of the war years has been a lasting memory. Years later, during a war in that country in the 1960s, we saw on a worldwide Christmas Programme, some of our friends were singing carols in their church at Baghdad.

We had more than one student from Japan. I was friendly with one who was a very good tennis player. Nearly all the college visitors came from European countries. This was an experience rich in international relationships. I was friendly with a very beautiful German girl whose father was a local president in the church in Germany. She had long thick plaits of hair, just like the picture of a Gretchen. Her wonderful deep alto voice entertained us frequently in church. I shared a room on one occasion with a pretty ginger haired girl from Denmark. I had a lovely Norwegian friend, Kurt Johnson, who during the 2nd World War became a secret agent and engaged in secretly taking escapees through a route in northern Norway to reach the Allies. Eventually the Germans caught him and shot him on the spot. Then there was **Hans Mainenardie**, a Swiss boy, whose father had a watch making business. During one winter, when we went ice-skating, we lost him for quite a long time, when we were on our way home. Years later, I read of his exploits in one of our church papers. Then there was **Unto Rohe** from Finland who was very friendly with our group. He eventually worked in the General Conference office for some time. His son became a treasurer at Newbold College, Bracknell. I caught up with the family after the war.

There were the scores of missionaries in transit from and to mission stations, in the far-flung parts of the globe. This enriched my education. During my last year at college, a German student was there to learn English. His mother had been amongst the early German workers in the church. He eventually went to the Far East as a missionary and was caught up as a Japanese prisoner of war. During the time spent under these degrading circumstances, he taught himself Hebrew. On his return to freedom, he graduated from Washington Missionary College with my brother-in-law, **Will Hyde**. In later years he became one of our most notable archaeologists. His name was **Siegfried Horn**. The world was becoming like an open book to me, telling me of what had happened in places which had just been place names on the map in my geography lessons. These places were now peopled with my own personal experience of meeting people from many countries. I was beginning to realise that what had happened in one country could have an effect on another part of the world. The world was becoming a global village and the church was playing its part.

Pastor and Mrs Dr Stahl had left California as self-supporting missionaries at the beginning of the 20th century. It was at a time when many people in the church did not think we had more than a few years left until the 'Coming of the Lord'. Dr Stahl and his wife had gone to Peru to take 'The message'. Soon after their arrival in Peru he visited the Inca Indians. Being faced with the language problem, he eventually devised a teaching method similar to the 'look and say' method which was the first means of opening up education to these ancient peoples. The Peruvian Government recognised his ability and was happy to use his knowledge as an answer to their national educational problems with the Incas (his story is in the Book of Pioneers). The Stahl's were at college in my second year. They occupied two rooms on the boys' side of the college building and brought quite an international colour to the college. It must be mentioned that the boys' and girls' living quarters were separated by locked doors and never the twain should meet. The door was only unlocked to let the male students into the chapel in the evening for study hour. This was a constant reminder of the statement in the college brochure that students were accepted at Stanborough Park College to study, and those who had other intentions would be better to stay away. This was treated rather lightly in my day, by many of the students and although the two sexes only met in close proximity in the dining room or classroom, it was expecting rather a lot for single young people not to cast an eye at the opposite sex occasionally. Despite rules most young people eventually had girlfriends or boyfriends by the end of the year.

The breaking of this rule happened largely on a Sunday when many students equipped with 100 Present Truth and Good Health magazines took a train from Watford Junction to London, at a cost of

1/1d return, to sell books and earn the much needed money for fees. This became not only a day out - it was a means of making money far from the halls of learning. There were many friendships made and developed into life-long relationships during the Sunday canvassing adventure.

Although the building was called a college, not all the staff had a degree. The only lecturers with degrees were **Mrs Dr McClements**, nee Miss Cummings (Science), **Miss Binns** (French) and **Mr Jack Ford** with a Science degree. The rest of the staff, I think, were often one step ahead of the pupils on numerous occasions. This was a period of controversy in religious studies. Since the time of Darwin, there had been much controversy reigning throughout the theological world. In the Bible teaching at Stanborough College, the teachers, although sincere, did not have a very wide theological background. They were possibly strong on church history. They were limited in the use of ancient languages at that period, and although an attempt was made at discussion, the approach to the Scripture was church orientated. We were to a large extent reading the Bible as it had been interpreted through the ages. Any reference to current thinking, if not discouraged, was not given much attention. Theology became indoctrination. This must be judged by the time in which we lived and not by present day conditions in education. It was a difficult period socially, educationally and for religion.

One lasting memory I have of the Friday night chapel services was to hear singing by so many good voices and this was a new experience. Having grown up in a small church, I was entranced to hear well over a hundred voices singing in harmony. This was a new experience for me. There were numerous individual singers who could contribute to worship in song. I had a friend, **Connie Langford**, whose sister **Sidora** worked at the Press. They were from Cambridge. Their voices blended in beautiful harmony. Connie always pronounced my name with a prolonged A A-alice. She eventually married Dad's (George Bell) special friend Gilbert Lewis from Cardiff and they went out to Kenya in the late 1920s as missionaries. He is remembered for his work in the translation of the New Testament into the local Swahili dialect. The British and Foreign Bible Society accepted this translation. Then there was **Rose Essery** from Newport, Monmouthshire. Her lovely Welsh voice was a delight. She sang duets with **George Rodgers** whom she eventually married. They found themselves caught up with the Japanese when travelling to India in the Second World War. They came back from the prison camp looking like living skeletons. **Dr Harrower**, a British-American (who had been a member of Holloway church, London, before going to U.S.A. to study medicine) met them as they returned as prisoners of war. Dr Harrower clothed them, and was responsible for their return to health and their re-establishment in the Canadian S.D.A. Hospital, Toronto. Dr Harrower, had been so poor when he left London (the Elder of Holloway church, Brother Vince gave him his last meal and a few shillings before he left for the boat at Southampton). When he became a doctor and eventually a millionaire, he devised a cure for anaemia, which was based on the use of liver. He became very generous to the church. We saw Rose shortly before she died, and she sang specially for my husband (George Bell), 'The Holy City', a song she had sung when they were young people in Newport, Monmouth, church.

Friday night was also 'Gospel Worker's night'. It was really a test bed to develop public speakers. I seemed to get chosen during my first year to give the talk. I had never done such a thing before. I spoke on Esther. Years later I was asked to speak in a Canadian church when we were travelling in Canada in 1976. The church was somewhere in B.C. where an expatriate, who had known me in college came up to me to remind me of what I had spoken about all these years ago when I must have been 16.

George McCready Price was Principal during my second year at college. He was the notable world Adventist who lectured and wrote on Creation or Evolution during the '20s. The previous year he had been a speaker at a debate in the Royal Albert Hall, London, on the current topic of Creation or Evolution. He did not come off very well in the debate. I recall him as a gruff man, who had a delightful wife. During one Week of Prayer when we were about to have a day of fasting, he was seen coming up the drive to Holy Row (a row of cottages opposite the Granose Food Factory) with a bag of about two dozen oranges, it was suggested for his fast. Fortunately, he was called back to the States, after a year as a not too successful Principal. Then George McCready Price was replaced with another American, W.E. Wood. He had been to Australia where he was a great success. He only lasted a year at Stanborough College. Although he was not highly appreciated at Stanborough, he was very highly respected at Southern Missionary College, U.S.A. where buildings were named after him. I think people can do well in one place and be a failure in another place.

During the college summer recess (May to September), students were encouraged to go out selling books (which had been printed at the Press). This had a three-fold advantage. It was a means of teaching the Bible to people who were visited by the student colporteurs. Then the students earned money to pay for their fees and the Press was able to function. The money the students collected had to be forwarded to the Press to provide the scholarship, which was offered according to the value of the books sold. Students had to live during these summer months, and pay for their accommodation. As they sold the books, half of the money belonged to the Press. They had to pay for transport, accommodation and food, leaving very little money for future college fees. There were occasions when students had sold the required number of books but did not have enough money deposited at the Press in order to claim the scholarship. I have heard frightful tales of poverty endured by young students, who were living on a starvation diet in their desperation to earn a scholarship. I had a friend, **Beulah Brookes**, (her mother was a Bible worker and her father had been a missionary). She told the sorry tale of living on 5/- per week, on a diet of bread and dates). She managed to return to college. Life was very hard in those early days. Many real sacrifices were made for the privilege of an education. At that time there was, according to the rules, a stipulation that before graduation the graduate was expected to have spent one summer out canvassing. This was difficult for the person who found canvassing almost impossible. Then after graduation it was essential to serve for two years as an intern before permission to marry was granted.

According to the requirements for a Bible worker's diploma at that time, it was a three-year course, after the preliminary educational course. I should have graduated at the end of my third year, but it was thought by the faculty that I was too young to graduate and was advised to take additional studies, which included the entire Ministerial course except for Hebrew. This I did and graduated at eighteen years. My graduation class was unique in as much as there were only two graduates that year; **Arthur Vine** and myself. He went to the mission field in West Africa and I went to Scotland.

People I met at Stanborough College
I went to College in 1925, which was quite a culture shock. I was not quite 15 years old and for some years I had been reading the popular girls magazines about fun and problems at boarding schools. Stanborough College bore no relationship to the Girl's Own Paper. There were just over 100 students. I was nearly 15 and there were only six or seven students near my age group. The remainder were

16 and over and nearer 30 years of age; so I thought they were all very old, in fact ancient. Most of them had to work to earn money to pay their fees, which were £26 per year. Work was paid for at 4 ½ p per hour (6d). At meal times all these old people seemed to be dressed in the dirty old clothes they used for their work. I worked in the garden, the laundry, the farm, the kitchen and the college building.

I had to work a few hours per week towards my fees. At the 'Granose' food factory packing biscuits, I was paid 4 1/2d per hour, and had never been so bored in all my life. I soon transferred from there to the College kitchen, which was a little more interesting. Here I met with a **lady of German origin,** who had been interned on the Isle of Man for the four years of war in a prison camp. When she spoke, which was not often, she revealed a very restricted difficult life that, although restricted was tolerable, but only just. She was interned as a teenager and I guess found it difficult to understand why she was there. I felt very sorry for her. Some of the best years of her life had gone without any reasonable answer that she could understand. Frugal living was difficult, but not cruel; her lack of freedom was her big problem. I used to balance some of the tales she shared with me with the tales of the returned prisoners of war. For instance, my Uncle Frank had come home from a prisoner of war camp in very bad physical condition (she was quite healthy but miserable), which affected him for the rest of his life. He became very introspective. He visited us soon after his return looking very gaunt and ill.

I think he had come up from Sunderland at my mother's request to collect revolvers from our camphor wood chest, which my mother was afraid to touch. I imagine they came into my father's possession during his artillery training just before his last voyage. They terrified my mother. I imagine she thought they were lethal if touched. She could not get them out of the house quickly enough.

College eventually became a very invigorating experience for me. Again, I had a wonderful history teacher called **George Baird**, an Irishman to whom I instantly related to because of his teaching which I was seeing from a different angle. He showed me intervention of God in historical events. He also related to me; I expect because he could see how he was influencing me. In later years as family friends we visited each other. His son **Kelvin** was at university in London and visited usLily and Rupert regularly. He married **Maura**, the daughter of one our close friends, Madgwick. They eventually emigrated to New Zealand and we still keep in contact. June has visited them in New Zealand.

We played netball and tennis at college which I enjoyed. At that time there were two boys there from Iraq (Persia), from the **Hasso and Sato families.** They were sent to England to perfect their English and I often enjoyed tennis with them. They were very good at it. I really did not hear of them again until 1949 or 1950 when we were living in London. The Hasso family owned a large departmental store in Baghdad. The uncle of the family was in London on business and we met him at the Holloway church and I invited him to lunch on a number of Sabbaths. On his last visit, he arrived with a large box of crystallized fruits such as we had never seen for years. Our eyes just goggled at them as though they had come from outer space. They were possibly what he was selling to Selfridges (up market department store) and other large stores. Sweets at that time were on ration and were of an indifferent quality and we were given a great luxury, which made it an everlasting memory.

Some years later, during the war between Iraq and Tehran, we heard the Adventist choir in Baghdad sing in our Christmas programme on the radio and wondered if there was anyone there we knew. Then 2002, a friend in the States, **Larry Gerraty**, who was Principal of La Sierra College, was invited to take part in a wedding of one of the fourth generation Hasso's. They were able to get him a visa for Baghdad. He was the only American on the plane to Baghdad, but was treated very courteously by many of the Iraqi's on the plane. Speaking to some of the church members he learned that as a Christian church they enjoyed quite a lot of liberty, and that Sadam's wife visited the church each Christmas with flowers and a financial gift and they wondered how much liberty they would have under another regime. The church is fairly centrally situated and is very attractive.

For me living with so many older people was quite a privilege after a very quiet home life. Listening to and not entering into conversation with my senior peers was a new privilege. I had grown up in an atmosphere where youngsters did not enter the conversation of their elders. The college dining room was provided with tables to accommodate four persons, two women two men. Our only opportunity of meeting the opposite sex was at the dining room table, so that became rather an interesting experience for me. At my first table there was a mature student from Sheffield who had been an editor of a local paper (**Leslie Emmerson** who eventually became editor of 'Present Truth') and a mature lady from Glasgow who worked in the Granose office. I do not recall the other students. Maybe he, like me, was rather shy and did not easily enter into conversation. Each Friday evening the matron changed the table lists, so that made Friday evening a very social time of great expectation to some students and hope or despair to others. I think I soon lost my shyness. One unusual student was an old **retired sea captain** who used to like speaking to me because my father was seafaring. He was at college just to learn more about the Bible. Years later, when he met us, he told George how he admired my energy. As a young student whenever he was up early in the morning, I was always up before him. He liked to talk to me about his sea adventures, knowing my father had been seafaring. We had lots of interesting conversations, which must have been at the table; it would have been frowned upon otherwise. Fortunately, there were a few students in my age group only, 5 or 7.

Mary Ford

My special friend was Mary Ford. Her father was a pioneer member of the Welsh mission, an outstanding old gentleman with a long white beard. I remember him expounding stories to me of Wales during the time of the Welsh revival. The story that made an indelible impression on me was the one about a rather eccentric old Welshman who was very impressed with the Old Testament and the importance of sacrifice. He went up on the hill behind the Pontypridd, and offered sacrifices on the 'day of atonement'. It became the talk of the valleys. Then, when his son died, he erected a stone in the cemetery, but he did not put the boy's name on the stone to identify who was buried there. He must have had a dispute with his son and so that he would not enjoy eternity, he withheld his son's name from the place where he was buried. This was an Egyptian idea. He had possibly heard of the Egyptian belief that at the place of burial the name of the person must be recorded and remembered so that the person would be able to live throughout eternity. The identifying and remembering the place of burial, would ensure the right to eternity. This was an ancient Egyptian belief. The naming and identifying a person's place of burial, would be ensure a place in eternity. He must have been a most peculiar mixed up individual. Although even today many people still unknowingly practise the custom of inscribing the name on the tombstone where the loved one is buried, very few know why they do it. This custom is still practised by many people in cemeteries throughout the Christian world at the anniversary of the death; it is customary to visit the place of burial and leave flowers.

Every year, at the cenotaph in London, as a nation we remember the names of the dead from the first and the second world wars, and all the wars since then. We even repeat the customary address on the cenotaphs, "We shall remember them". The origin of the custom goes back to Egypt 5,000 years ago. In Nigeria and the South Sea Islands people still audibly remember the names of the dead and at New Year they recite their genealogy. Yvonne, our adopted daughter who worked as a missionary in Nigeria attended a ceremony each New Year, when the family would meet and recite their family history for the last 20 generations. In respect to Yvonne, they included our family. This was a very ancient custom. There are accounts of genealogies in the Bible. King Herod thought he was half a Jew. When he discovered that his genealogy did not prove his Jewish heritage, he had all the genealogies in the temple records destroyed. He, however, did not reckon with the long memories of ancient Judaism. In Acts, Paul knew his genealogy and he would claim to be of the tribe of Benjamin.

Nurse Mary Ford

My friend **Mary Ford** eventually became an excellent missionary, first of all at Malamulo Leper hospital, and then in Kenya. There was a custom at that time that any child born with a physical defect was disowned by the family and left to die. Mary rescued 15 of these rejected babies and cared for them in her office until she could find parents to adopt them. Before she permanently returned to Wales, she still had a little boy who had a squint in his eye. She had been unfortunate in not finding him new parents. In the Hull church I had told his story in the Sabbath School about Auntie Mary's little boy who needed parents. A very saintly old member gave me £5 to send to Auntie Mary and as she left the hospital in Kenya on permanent return, she took the child down to Nairobi where he had the squint treated. One of the local native ministers adopted the little boy. When we lived in Wales, Mary was paying for the education of three of her children and before she died she heard that one of her Malamulo boys had been ordained into the ministry.

Mary never was a brilliant student when she was at college, but she was a wonderful missionary. Her treatment of leprosy patients and abandoned children was phenomenal. She was a wonderful person to know. In her last few months of her life she refused to go back into a hospital just outside Pontypridd because of the lack of care she had received there the previous year. She was lovingly cared for by **Anthea Fielding** and others. I was grateful to Anthea for her loving tender care of my friend. Mary had given her life for others. She is remembered with much affection by all who knew her.

The Hayes family
College to me was a wonderful experience where I made lifelong friendships. I was friendly with the Hayes family. They had a big bakery at Edgware. They, like many others at the beginning of the 20th century, had emigrated from Germany to London and changed their name from Heisse to Hayes. Father Hayes expanded his business at the end of WW1. Then, when his wife became ill he took her to South Africa for a health cure. At this time he sent his two girls to Stanborough Park College where they boarded. This was on the recommendation of an Adventist lady in the village where they lived. The two families remained lifelong friends.

The Hyde family
They became our 'shirt tail' relations, when my husband George's elder sister Dorothy married William Hyde (one of the sons of father Hyde). Old father Hyde changed his name from Heide to Hyde. He had a small bakery and 13 children – a baker's dozen. When he became an Adventist he sold the bakery and became the baker for the Granose Food Company.

Dr Harrower
Dr Harrower was a member of the Holloway London church when he

decided to go to Loma Linda and become a doctor. On his acceptance at the medical school he sold all his earthly goods to pay the fares for himself and his wife. This meant that he left London penniless (all this money paid for their fares). Elder Vince of the Holloway church gave him his last meal and 2/6d (12.5p). In California he and his wife worked until he had enough money to start the medical course. He became a doctor and in his mature years he became famous for the development of a cure for anaemia. He developed a tablet made of chewed up liver which was widely known and used and he eventually became a millionaire as a result of this venture.

His beloved daughter fell in love with Bob Haining a brilliant young medical student and the elder brother of Vi (George's sister-in-law). When the marriage was accepted, Dr Harrower bought a house in the late '20s in Glendale for father and mother Haining. The Haining's paid a monthly mortgage on this for years in the belief that the house would eventually be theirs. After the death of father Haining and the death of Dr Harrower, the Harrower estate raised the monthly rent beyond mother Haining's ability to pay. The dispute about the ownership of the house went on for years with much acrimony between the families. Vi and the younger sisters never signed an acceptance document stating the house belonged to the Harrower estate and was Harrower property. Agnes (Vi's younger sister) and Bob, who were both affluent, thought it was not worth the dispute (by this time Dr Harrower's daughter was married with children and the inheritance was in the charge of estate managers, and the money from the income was for the daughter's children.

Dr Harrower was reputed to have been influential in Bob Haining's rise in the medical world, although it was thought by many that Bob was brilliant and merited the favours bestowed on him. He eventually became known as a good heart surgeon. After the death of Dr Harrower's wife he married a third generation Vince lady. He was also responsible for contributing to some of the Vince family's education. He was generous in contribution to the Church Hospital in Toronto, Canada, where they became established. Bob Haining met George and Rose Rodgers (Essery) off the boat at Los Angeles on their return from Japanese captivity. They were looking like walking skeletons. He lavishly provided for them, arranging for them to work at the Toronto hospital. The Harrower's were reputed to have contributed to many needy causes

As a wealthy man, in the '20s he was very much of an extrovert. He was always generous to those who had been friends in his day of poverty. On his numerous visits to Britain, he did not forget his old friends. I do not recall if he bought the house at Rickmansworth where Eddie and Vi, lived or if he just rented it. He was over here most summers, a fact which everybody seemed to know.

He was one of the early London church members who was inspired with the new groups in America and Germany propagating 'Diet and Exercise' to promote health. There were several institutions, slightly prior to Kellogg, who propagated an enthusiasm for institutions to promote good health diet, and exercise. He opened a Sanitarium at Battle Creek and a nearby a food factory producing a whole breakfast food ready to eat. This was at a time when advertising campaigns were being devised as a means to sell goods helped by establishing a successful transport system. All these factors came together; doctors, sanitariums, exercise clinics, advertising and transport. The health message was not unique to Dr Kellogg, but he capitalized on it. **Dr Kellogg**, with his Cornflakes, was part of a movement into which Dr Harrower stepped. He was one of the groups founded in America.

Chapter 6

After graduation:- Seven years as a Bible worker

Uddingston, Glasgow

I graduated 1929 during a time when I had measles. I should have graduated the previous year, but it was felt by the faculty that I was rather young for the work, so I stayed the extra year and did Greek and other ministerial subjects. Although I was annoyed, I have been lastingly thankful for that part of my education. My graduation class only submitted two graduates, Arthur Vine and myself. He went to West Africa and I went to Scotland to work with Lamont Murdoch at a tent meeting at Uddingston, just outside of Glasgow. I found a room in a two-room Glasgow flat. I had the second room and the use of the kitchen, which was about 6-7 feet square. In it there was a sink, and a gas stove. The lady was a widow with two children. I had not been there long before the flat was visited by the police. The lady's husband had been killed in an accident and once a month she had to go to Hamilton Town Hall (the county town) to collect her insurance money. On her return home she put the money in a dresser drawer and later in the afternoon, when she went to get money to do the shopping, the money was gone. I arrived while the police were there and was interviewed by them. Being a stranger and the only one who had a key to the flat, it was rather alarming. However, they eventually dispensed with me when the little boy of 11-12 years confessed he had taken the money and was so frightened when he saw the police being sent for he put his mother's month's money down the toilet and pulled the chain.

Life in 1930's Uddingston had some memories. At weekends I went into Glasgow on a famous Glasgow tram car, which charged 2d (less than 1p) for the 14 mile journey from Uddingston to Paisley. There, in the church, I was invited to lunch with the **Howard family** who lived in a three-room flat at Ibrox. The mother, Katie, came from Newcastle and her husband was a colporteur (door to door salesman of religious books) in Dundee and he only appeared occasionally. He sent a little money home, some weeks 10/- and some weeks nothing. Katie's mother was as generous as her income would allow. One room in this three-room flat was let out to a lady for 7/6d (37.5p) per week. How that money fed three children and provided hospitality, only the Lord knows. The children were, Bernard, a bright but quiet boy of 11 years, James, an attractive quiet dark-haired child and Georgie, a beautiful fair haired child of 2 years. I soon learned to love that family.

Come the summer, 2 students, the Brown brothers arrived to canvas (sell religious books) in Glasgow to earn money for their college fees. They occupied another room in this little flat and the family lived and slept in the kitchen. That was life in the '30's.

Hiking had just become a popular leisure occupation, which had been encouraged by Hitler in Germany (physical development was good for youth). They even had a song to sing, when the miles seemed long. In Sheffield, the Brown's had become smitten with this modern idea of hiking, living near some attractive moor land and hill country. In Glasgow, they organized our walking expeditions. We went from a train station called Milngavie (pronounced Mulguy) to the Highlands, a short journey. Arthur and I had a very happy friendship. This was a delightful experience. I had only once before been hiking outside of Edinburgh with James and Alice Gulland. It made us feel very daring and modern.

My visits to the Howard family became the one bright spot in the week. I often went on a Friday night when we could be 8 around the supper table. How she fed us all, considering her very limited means, has always impressed me. She was able to share out of the little she had and infect all with her outgoing, jolly personality in spite of her state of poverty; which did not completely oppress or depress her. Only occasionally I saw a tear, being held back as long as possible. She had been two years at college, where she had been friendly with the Arthur Maxwell family (of Bedtime Story fame) before she married. There, I think, she developed the ability to speak in public. This I very much admired. She was occasionally invited to speak at some of the local churches fellowship mid-week meetings. Now I possibly look back on what I admired in her silent charitable influence which has rubbed off on my life. Throughout the years I have, like Katie, been able to entertain on practically nothing, and of course in recent years I have had a long period of public speaking, not only at church, but in men's and women's secular clubs. At 93 years of age I still do that (2003).

Another vivid memory was of an old coloured gentleman who stood up to thank the Lord for his intervention, which had made it possible for him to attend the Conference. He described and demonstrated his dilemma that morning when he was in the process of dressing. He could not fasten the button on his trousers and he said:

The button came off my trousers, and I didn't know what to do to keep them up, so I offered a quick and frantic prayer and while I was praying my daughter arrived and solved the problem.

I bought a sewing machine with the first salary I ever received, which was £2.2.0 (£2.10p). A little later I bought a gramophone. I think I had to pay for them by monthly instalments. This custom had recently become popular. They were my pride and joy.

My introduction to Bible work that summer was to help **Lamont Murdoch** with a tent meeting that was in the summer months, on a small plot of vacant land in the village. We appointed a funny little toothless man, named **Ferguson**, to be a watchman. He was so proud of the job, he lorded it over anyone who came near the tent, just like a policeman. The tent was quite an attraction in the neighbourhood. I think the only large marquees previously seen had been circus marquees. This was for religious services. Our watchman had a constant battle going with the local children. To begin with, the more he tried to keep them at a distance, the more they teased him. They were a constant nightmare to our little watchman until we got organised and had attractions for the children. They then became part of the unit. Many in the immediate neighbourhood attended the services, so I soon became acquainted with the local people.

Another meeting was conducted at the Hamilton Town Hall at the beginning of September. This required me to travel by bus or bicycle about eight or nine miles between the two places. Both of these districts had been mining areas. This was at the time of the Great Depression of the 1930s. The mines were in the process of closing down and financially it was a difficult period just before 'the Great Depression'. Many of the men were unemployed for the first time in their working life. All they knew was mining. There was an air of despondency in the district. The people were poor; they had little hope of work. Apart from it being a national financial depression, the people had very little to which they could look forward.

The best part of the week was the weekend. I think I was so busy during the week either walking or cycling everywhere, I did not notice the passing time. This was for me the first time I was alone in a strange district. On Sabbath I went by tram to Glasgow. This became the highlight of my week. This was quite a relaxation. Our church building was fairly central. It was on a street parallel to Sauchiehall Street in Glasgow. It had belonged to the Germans before the First

World War (there was a large German population in Glasgow before the war; and there were practically none after the war, so the church was sold in1930). It was an attractive building, raised slightly above the level of the road. As I met the membership, I found some of the members to be real characters. I remember well the Logan family. **Mr. Logan** had a sweetie factory. He was a typical blustering Irishman whose family, the previous generation, had 'crossed the water' at the time of the Irish potato famine. He was always eating sweeties, even in church, and all children near him were well supplied with sweets. From time to time his business went bankrupt. His business had many ups and downs, but eventually he became successful. He changed the business from sweets to agriculture. He started out with a poultry farm - chickens and eventually followed by cows. Before long, the war started and the country was in need of home produced food. Financial success came his way. I met him again later when his business was good and he was able to afford to send nearly all his sons to College. The last time I saw him he was living in the lap of luxury and driving a big car.

Another family in the Glasgow Church was **Mr. Bleasbys'**. He was a dentist. He would greet visitors by asking them if they knew how to cure bloodlessness. He claimed to have a cure for anaemia by the drinking of the juice made from sieved grated beetroot! He was the second elder of the church with a Mr. Barr. His son went to Egypt as a missionary. **Mr Barr** was the first elder and always referred to his son as 'Our Andrie'. I shall never forget the time when we had a visit from a Canadian evangelist. Mr. Barr approached him saying, "Will I come up and pray for you Pastor"? "No" said the eminent evangelist, "I can pray for myself". Neither of the two elders mounted the rostrum with the Canadian evangelist that Sabbath, (these two elders were in constant conflict with each other and found it very difficult to share their duties). During the visit of this Canadian his, daughter won a competition, giving her a holiday in Switzerland. This caused much criticism amongst some of the older members. I seem to recollect they thought she had taken part in a gambling orgy to win the money.

It was here in Glasgow Sabbath School that I taught the children of **the Elias, Mawdsley and Lennox** families in my class. They were all very bright teenagers. At one of the social gatherings, according to Ken Elias's memory, I was in a play with him, which, according to Scottish law, I was married to him. It was a dangerous thing to do in Scotland. According to ancient law, marriage could be performed anywhere in Scotland by an act of promise and it became valid.

My first visit to Loch Lomond was with the church. In those days people did not travel far. I was fascinated and thrilled with the awesome beauty of the hills, the loch and especially with the village of Luss, with its little flower-covered cottages, nestling by the lakeside.

It was in Glasgow that I made my lifelong friendship with the **Howard family**. I became friendly with Katie Howard. Her husband was a colporteur and was away in Dundee most of the time. She had three little boys, whom I came to love. Bernard, a boy of 11 years, was a bright child. His mother was well known for her hospitality. Bernard was used to greeting and entertaining her visitors. He began by bringing all his school work for me to see and discuss. James, the next child, was a beautiful boy aged 8 with a winning smile, but was rather reticent, maybe because of his elder brother, who was inclined to take the initiative, and then there was little Georgie, a beautiful fair haired two-year-old. Katie was one of the most hospitable people I have ever met. She opened her heart and house to all comers. With her husband away, she was glad of company. He was not contributing much to the family finances and she had a very difficult time financially. They lived in a flat with 3 rooms in Ibrox, and like many other people in those days on a very limited income. She always seemed to have at least one or more lodgers. Her colporteur husband earned so very little. Some weeks he did not send any money home at all. While I was there she had **the two Brown brothers** from college, who were canvassing in Glasgow in one bedroom and a lady in another bedroom. The Howard family must all have slept in the kitchen and the sitting room. I frequently went over on a Friday evening when we all had a lovely friendly evening together when the problems and poverty of the week were forgotten in friendship and fellowship. Usually I spent Sabbath with them and would meet again on Sunday morning for one of our walking expeditions to the Minlgavie hills or Loch Lomond. In the previous fifteen or twenty years, hill walking had become a popular recreation with the general public. It was a recreation which had gradually become popular in Germany with the rise of Hitler who called his nation to develop healthy bodies. Fit to fulfil the plans he had for his nation with activities in the open air, this was the 'in thing'. In Germany a new song became popular. Singing and walking went well together:

> I love to go a-hiking among the hills so green
> And when I go a-hiking with a knapsack on my back.

It was while I was in Glasgow that Dad (George Bell) and I renewed our friendship. We had met again at a Conference at Holloway

Church, London. He had been working in the N.B.C. leading the publishing work, but realised he ought to finish his studies, so he had returned to College. We spent some time together during the Conference and he encouraged and persuaded me to return with him on his motorbike as far as Rugby, so that we could have another day together, before I went back to Scotland. I could then do the rest of the journey on the night train. The following day he had to attend the wedding of **Nancy Murdoch and Stanley Bull**. It was a very big wedding for that time with six bridesmaids and six grooms-men.

At the end of that College year **Dad (George Bell)** went to Portadown, Ireland to canvas. He lived in the home of one of the Ulster policemen. I used to have a picture of him in the R.U.C. uniform. At the end of the summer we met on the Clyde at the Glasgow docks. We often recalled this meeting. I was wearing a pink skirt and a teddy-bear jacket, which immediately caught his eye. This was really the beginning of our courtship. We had been writing for some months, and we had our first holiday together in Edinburgh. This was spent, going to the Portobello baths, Port Seaton, the Pentland Hills etc. He had been one of my 'college-group'. We were called 'The Lambs'. The group consisted of our Shepherdess - Lucy Clarke and Edric was the Shepherd. The other boys were, Harry Smith, Harry Davis, but I can't remember the other one. The girls were Frances, Lillian, Mary, Rosa Anthony and I. The boys were all a few years older than we were and as a group we were not noticed, as we would have been, if we had been in pairs. There were about ten of us. During my third year George had been asked to become Field Mission Secretary for North England Conference. He didn't have any particular girl attachments but he belonged to our Lambs.

During this period I was living at Motherwell, on the outskirts of Glasgow and spent quite a bit of time at Falkirk and Glasgow. One of my vivid memories of Glasgow was the number of Italian cafés there were around the city, where young people could go in for a cup of coffee and sit all evening. They also sold mushy peas. The Italians were also noted for their ice cream. (They opened up chip shops all over Scotland). A fish and chip supper cost 1/-. They did not mind keeping the shop open when all other shops were closed. It was an Italian custom. When we went to Italy in the '50s we realised that they were doing in Scotland what was customary at home. It was at Glasgow I had my first perm (1931). It had just been developed using a very primitive machine.

During my second year I worked at Falkirk, and lived in Edinburgh, travelling to Falkirk by bus. Memories of that year are rather vague. It was the year of my 21st birthday. I celebrated it at home when quite a group of my friends came over from Glasgow to celebrate.

Wales

I was then transferred to Wales to work with **George King**. This was quite the most memorable part of my Bible work. I helped at the Barry Dock Meeting and lived at **the Carter's** house at Cadoxton. They were another very hospitable family. The mother was a very strong Christian lady with a heart of gold. She had a three-storey house perched on the edge of a cliff, with a worked-out quarry below. I shall always remember, shortly after I arrived, the occupant of the gypsy caravan died. She was the queen of the gypsies. There was a very big funeral, when everything in the caravan was burnt. She had many pieces of very expensive beautiful china. It was all destroyed. I just could not understand it. That was not the only thing that amazed me. We had a church member who fed the pigeons every day in front of the Town Hall. Her name was **Penny**. I used to visit her mother, who had a parrot who prayed exactly like old Pastor Meredith. Years before, old Pastor Meredith used to visit this old lady and before leaving the house he would pray in his typical Welsh accent. He never lost his Welsh 'hwyl'. The parrot prayed just like Pastor Meredith with the Welsh 'hwyl'.

I lived with the **Carter family** in Barry. My years in Wales were a waiting period for George to complete his education before we could get married. It was 1932 and I was introduced to the different characteristics of the Welsh nation. When I arrived in Wales, it was in the midst of a deep depression. Nearly all the mines had closed and there was no alternative employment. I shall never forget visiting a row of ex-miners who lived in a cottage with 2 rooms. All the families existed on 27/6d (£1.35p) per week from which they had to provide food and shelter for a man, his wife and children. They had to pay for rent and light; fortunately, fortunately coal was free. One day I visited them on a Thursday, and this was the day before their allowance was due. When the children arrived home from school and there was not a slice of bread in the house. I went out and bought a loaf of bread and ½ lb margarine. That family is indelibly imprinted on my memory. They knew real poverty. I greatly admired the Quakers', they bought pieces of land near the Welsh villages and provided vegetable seeds to any man who would grow them. Throughout this dreadful and depressing time the Welsh Mail Voice Choirs flourished. They were a nation who sang their way through poverty and distress. I still have a vivid memory of an old Welsh lady sitting on her rocking chair and beside her the caged green parrot. During our visit, she told me of the weekly visits of **Pastor Meredith**, who eventually became the President of the British Union of Adventist churches. He had always spoken to her in the Welsh language. He was known to have said that the language of heaven was Welsh. How did he know that? Well his logical reply was God always heard and answered his prayers. As I visited her on one occasion, the parrot began to speak in Welsh, complete with the Welsh 'hwel', just as he had heard Pastor Meredith.

Before I arrived at Barry, Mrs Carter's kindness had been extended to **an old sailor** who had had his leg amputated who had no home. He always reminded me of Long John Silver. She took him in and cared for him till he died. He did not always appreciate her kindness. He had a little room next to mine. He had no relatives and no friends. His one and only friend was Mrs Carter. In the basement of her house **Charlie Cook and his wife Lillian** lived. Charlie did colporteur work. It was about the only work available in the 1930's for those who did not work on the Sabbath (Saturday). They had their first baby Arthur while I lived there. Mr Carter worked on the railway. He was a good man. He attended church whenever he was not at work and eventually Dad (my husband, George Bell) baptised him when we went to Cardiff.

Opposite Cadoxton house was a farm, where the farmer made all kinds of home-made beer. This was another thing that amazed me. Many of the Welsh people in those days made their own ginger beer with yeast. He had large vats on the floor of his parlour with numerous kinds of wine brewing, potato, parsnip, elderberry, dandelion, frothing away. He also made regular visits to the pub, so I do not know when he would drink all of his liquid refreshment.

Shortly before my arrival in Wales, George King had been appointed to be president of the Welsh Mission. The big excitement was that he bought his first car for £100. Most of us were still on bicycles or buses.

These were fun years. The children, **Peggy, Bernie and Bert Carter** visited me regularly in my room. They owned a bull dog named Budge, almost as broad as he was long. He wobbled and he dribbled. I often took him out on the country roads on a Sunday morning. If anyone passed me, they always gave me a wide berth, the width of the road. It was the sight of this fierce looking bulldog called Budge that frightened all passers-by. He was not true to his looks he was very soft old thing.

I am told that I regularly made date balls that attracted the Carter children into my room. Besides date balls, I seemed to teach them quite a lot about the Bible during their visits. A big and long-remembered event by the Carter children was when George Bell, (my fiancé) came to visit me. The Carter children had great fun with his style of 'hide and seek'. It was climbing up a ladder from the garden and in through a bedroom window. I do not know how we did not have an accident. They all still remember the thrill and excitement of such fun never before experienced. To this day, they all recall it. Peggy still looks back on my stay in her home with great pleasure. Of all the people her mother entertained throughout the years, I was the only one who wrote a letter of sympathy to her when her Mum died. Bernie, who now lives in Australia, tells me I taught her more than anyone else about the Bible and Bert remembers my date balls.

I moved to Merthyr, to work with **Will Nicholson** and lived with a Welsh family who, years before, had a baker's shop in Merthyr. It was at the time that granddad Bell (George's Father) had the skin factory there. The local people could still remember the skin factory. They were my first true link with the past. They belonged to the period before modernism swept throughout the land. In their early days the family had attended church every night of the week except Monday. Sunday they made three visits to church. Tuesday was the Men's meeting, and Wednesday was a Prayer meeting, Thursday Choir, Saturday a social meeting. Every day was a church day.

When I arrived in Merthyr, I visited an old lady (church member) who remembered George shortly after the family came back from South America (after the tragic death of George Bell Senior). Mrs Bell hired a house in Gwaelod y-Garth just up from the hospital. It was there where they lived before they went to South America and when she returned she went back to the place where she had good neighbours and friends. They all attended the Methodist Church. With no income she took over the house at No. 29 Gwaelod-y-arth and let rooms (everybody in this story seemed to let a room). The lady who applied for the room was a **Miss Living**. She was a Bible worker for Frank Powell. The First World War was still on. Food was scarce. Frank Powell was able to get Mother Bell a sack of potatoes, which made him an instant success. She attended his meetings and joined the church. Young George was a boy of 11 or 12. He went to his first English speaking school. In South America, there were 17 languages spoken in the school. He could do matriculation Maths but could not write much English. This was always a big handicap to him. He sat in a class in the local school where he was a very big boy among little boys. It could not have been easy! Dorothy (his eldest sister) had been to school and could read before going to South America and so she was able to build on that education. Irene (his youngest sister) started school after coming to Wales and so did Eddie (his youngest brother). George came off worst with his education. Mrs Buchanan (their friends in Punta Arenus in South America) sent their children home to Edinburgh for their education. Mrs Bell wanted to keep her family with her – George was a very good worker.

The Merthyr story would be incomplete without the tale of George's visit to a little old Welsh lady called **Mrs Evans**. Not long after their return Miss Living had taken the family to church and Mrs Evans asked them to call and visit her. She lived at Upper Pant (up the mountain from Merthyr). In her living room she had an old grandfather clock that was not working. George, a boy of eleven or twelve, was determined he would like to repair it. Mrs Evans was horrified at the thought. Although, it did not work, it was very special to her. The clock had been in the family for a few generations. She was a little in awe and nervous about the family who had come from South America and was afraid to deter him. George set to and after a while got the clock which had been silent for a number of years was ticking and chiming. That was not the end of the story. Years later when I went to Merthyr I visited Mrs Evans and after brief introductions when she learned of my relationship with George, out came the whole story. She related how she felt sick with fear at what this young child could or would do to their precious grandfather clock. Although she had not heard or seen them for years my arrival brought it all vividly back to her. I encountered a few of his adventures as I travelled around the principality.

Also worked at Newport, Monmouthshire where I lived with **the Dixon family**. He was a policeman. They had two little boys, who were great fun. One of them phoned me years later in the 1980s, and again when there was a problem in the family. While here I lived two doors from **the Edward's family**. They had just come home from the Mission field in Nigeria. When they rented their first house, and they had no furniture.. They had an allowance from the church, which merely bought beds and table and chairs. They were on a very low income and had great difficulty in making ends meet. How they managed to live I will never know. No one was ever invited into the home (it was poverty-stricken!). I never heard them complain. We were very good friends. When we went out walking I was amazed at Zela's ability to recognise what was edible in the hedgerows. She was from Zagreb in Yugoslavia. When we went to Yugoslavia in the 1950's or 1960's wherever we travelled we saw the village women gathering herbs by the wayside for the dinner table. Then I understood where she acquired her ability. Some of the vegetables we had at the hotel were from the hedgerows.

We often reminisced on College days. She had been sent to one of our German colleges to learn German and then to Stanborough College to learn English. There she met her husband, a boy from Hull, Fred Edwards. When he set his eyes on her he determined he would marry her. At the end of the College year she went back home to Zagreb. Fred, with a friend, cycled down to Zagreb in the summer after they had finished doing their canvassing. Fred a tall, fair, handsome and quiet; his friend was much older with a rather off-putting manner. When they went to church, the members were asking "which one is it?" (The other boy was rather unusual). The family were fairly affluent and his father was a director for Singer sewing machines in Yugoslavia. Her sister had married a Swede who owned a chocolate factory. By marrying Fred they could only look forward to a very poor income. Her parents seemed to accept her choice. After they married they went out to West Africa.

I remember one story they told me about a miraculous escape they had in Africa some time before they left to come back to Britain. They were late in returning home one night from a distant destination on a dirt track road. The only light they had was from the car and from the stars. Suddenly the car stopped. It seemed for no apparent reason. The day had been long and hot and Fred was tired. He did not have the energy left to get out in the darkness to find out what was wrong. They decided to sleep where they were and wait till morning when they could see and identify the cause of the breakdown. On wakening with daylight, Fred got out of the car and was amazed to see the front wheels of the car just inches away from a precipice. The car had no mechanical problem. They could not help believing that an angel had caused their unexpected stop in the darkness of the African night.
Newport Church had a special meaning to me because it was where Dad (George Bell) had grown up as a youth. He had helped to dig the foundations of the church. Some of his special friends came from

Newport. **Mother Bell** (Hannah Bland Townley Bell) had willingly contributed money for the building of the church, which she should have been reserving for her family's education. With little or no knowledge of business, she bought a shop on the Caerleon Road near a church member. The shop was like a general store. She bought badly (old stock) and had to sell cheaply. Her business adventure was a bit of a disaster. The often, repeated family story is told about Irene. All the children had to contribute help in the house or shop each day. Mother Bell had grown up at the end of the 19th century when children were expected to physically help in the home and in the business. Irene, a clever girl, was at Newport High School and was thrilled at all she was learning. She regularly arrived home from school with lots of homework. Books she had to read, essays she had to write. Mother Bell did not understand or appreciate the importance of education. Indelibly on her mind was the story she had heard when she lived as a girl in Lancaster, of the poor man who with little or no means became the wealthiest man in the city. She would not marry her husband until he had saved a £100. The family were brought up with the story of this man. He built a hospital in memory of his wife. She always recalled this story – he had started with little or nothing and became the wealthiest man in the city (there is a monument in Lancaster today to prove it). In her mind, she thought that what one man could do, everyone else would be able to do. Education was not part of the programme. She never did comprehend that he was unusual and unique. What she did not appreciate, was that every ambitious man could not be as successful. In her day all children were expected to contribute to the family financially and physically. They had done so in her day, and they must do so today.

One day, on coming home from school, Irene was told she had to scrub the shop floor, before she could do any homework. She was literally led to the floor with a bucket of water and the scrubbing brush. The traditional record is that she landed on her back on the floor with her long legs kicking in the air and her voice screaming in indignation; "I will not scrub this floor!" She was not going to scrub any floors. She never lived that event down in the family history. It came up quite regularly as the family recalled their early struggles.

Here again one of Dad's (George Bell) misdemeanours caught up with me. There was in the church a lad called Arthur Brooks about Dad's age. They were life-long friends. He went to America, worked his way through a medicine degree, and then went to Cambodia as a missionary. We kept in touch with him until he died. Like all early

106

teenagers, they were up to tricks. Between them they arranged the forms in the room where the church met for worship in such a way, that when someone sat down at one end, the whole row collapsed. George Bell used to tell of the quick retreat they made as the elder chased them downstairs.

There was always a wonderful group of young people in the Newport Church. It was a joy to meet with them. One of the interesting old members was **Sister Essery**. She was a very good Bible student and she taught a Sabbath School lesson until just before she died. Her daughter, Rose, had a lovely soprano voice. She belonged to the young people's group who grew up with Dad. She was a special friend of Irene. She married George Rodgers.

My first swimming lesson was with her sister, Anne. As a child I had never been allowed to go near the sea. My mother had a horror of the sea, which was understandable. She would tell us "there are sharks in the sea, and if they get near you they can swallow you up". Years later, when my brother George came home from New Zealand, he told me that when he swam under the water, mentally he could still see sharks. I was 21 when I had my first swimming lessons. One morning a week, Anne and I would go to the Baths and I eventually swam a breadth. I felt Dad was such a good swimmer I had to be able to enjoy the water with him.

Then there was **Florrie Pope** and her daughters Betty and Winnie, rather beautiful girls with good singing voices (Betty married Eddie Dunlop). Their Mum and Dad owned a motorbike with a sidecar and on Sunday's they travelled around the Welsh countryside. I joined them on more than one occasion. I have a vivid memory when we went to the Wye Valley, seeing a field of cowslips for the first time. (They have nearly vanished now). Florrie did very beautiful needlework and exhibited at Eisteddfods.

During the summer when I worked in Wales we were expected to do so much ingathering (collecting money for mission-work). Usually, another Bible worker and I would go across the Bristol Channel to Somerset and Devon on the boat. And on one occasion a man threw himself overboard on our return journey. The boat had to turn round to find him. It was quite an event. We went to Somerset and Devon for a month or five weeks each summer to collect money for missions.

In this way I soon grew acquainted with and enjoyed many of the country towns of Devon and Cornwall. Although ingathering sounds a depressing job, we made light of it. I was accompanied by **Violet Ward** (nee Mrs Watts) and **Claudia Eyre** (nee Murdoch) and **Bessie Buck** (nee Lethbridge). We were expected to collect so much money, by visiting the shops in these country towns. Often, when we knew we had more than reached our quota, we would do a little sightseeing in the afternoon.   At weekends I became acquainted with two members who lived in the country, one at Fivehead, where we went on the Sabbath, and her sister-in-law who lived near a canal at Creech St Michael. Her house was on the side of a canal and she kept ducks. It was here I tasted duck for dinner for the first time. I can recall the taste of the lovely stuffing she made. These were very good days. When we visited Silver Street, Braunton, a lady gave me a very big donation. Every time I went through the village in years to come I remembered that donation. Another thing that impressed me was the fuchsia growing wild in the hedges and the lovely old village of Lee. I was amused when I was in Ilfracombe, when an undertaker man saw the books I was selling. He made the comment about good health. He was very adamant, he would not give money for anything to do with the subject of good health, saying: "I do not want people to have good health, I want them to die". He must have been having a hard time! Much of this took place when the world was experiencing 'the Great Depression'.

Chapter 7

YEARS OF MINISTRY

Just before my marriage in 1937 I resigned as a paid Bible worker and became a wife and an unpaid Bible worker. George had worked with **Jack Howard** after his first year out of College and while in East Anglia he renewed his friendship with **Leslie Hardinge**, an Anglo Indian boy whose hobby was furniture making.   Seeing what his friend could achieve, George determined to do likewise. When I was informed of this grandiose idea, I naturally questioned him on previous experience. Well what have you already made?   The answer was a hen house. I did not think much of a hen house as a recommendation for 'fine furniture'. I was naive enough to believe that he could do it, or was I foolhardy. I gave my blessing and hoped for the best. Only time would tell.

George did his second year as an intern at Ilford, London, working with **Clifford Reeves** in quite a big campaign.   On arrival, he rented two rooms. He made a contract with the landlady to have permission to be able to do some woodwork in his room. In those days, working people were not as affluent as they are today.   She was glad to get a lodger on any terms. Unfortunately she did not really know what she was in for.   George had determined to make his own furniture. He had seen what could be accomplished.   The 'furniture making bug' bit George in a big way as he realised we could have a much more unique style of furniture if he made it himself.   He haunted the 'high class' furniture shops in London where he saw good class modern designs.   He visited the Building Museum to inspect unusual woods.   He visited the wood yards in the dock area to examine the various unusual woods coming into the country.   This research resulted in him making a dining suite, and a bedroom suite, in his hired room before we got married. In faith I was prepared to accept the idea and furniture making proceeded, early in the morning and late at night.   When I visited the bed-sit in November the skeleton of our dining room furniture was in commendable shape.

We were married at the Scotia Hotel, George Street, in Edinburgh on the 2nd September 1937 by **Pastor Morrison**.   Bessie Buck was our bridesmaid and my cousin Phemia's husband was the best man.   Our new life together began, by borrowing camping equipment from the Madgwick family (a tent to camp in during the honeymoon).   By borrowing an old car, a 'Morris Oxford' was well past its 'sell-by' date from Eddie (George's brother) and off we went for better or for worse.

After the wedding breakfast we had left the fashionable hotel in a taxi, traditionally decorated by the Dunlop boys with tin cans and old shoes. The tradition of the shoes is very ancient. The shoe symbolised the land the woman brought with her to the marriage. In the Book of Ruth, Boaz receives the shoe as a symbol of the land Ruth owned. In the museum where Tutankhamun lies, his wife's shoe lies beside him in the coffin symbolising she was claiming him in eternity. The other tradition we observed was the throwing out of a handful of coins to the children waiting near the car of the bride and bridegroom, about to leave the reception. Whenever there is a wedding in Scotland children congregate in the hope of 'a pour out,' the coins thrown out by the bridegroom symbolise his financial ability. The taxi took us as far as Corstorphine, to pick up our ancient borrowed car. We progressed to the north, passing Linlithgow, an ancient town where Mary Queen of Scots was born, then on to Bannockburn and Stirling, so rich in Scottish history and early 'nationalism'. Mr and Mrs George R. Bell spent the first night of their married life in a borrowed tent and were travelling in a borrowed car. On the first morning of their life together George went out to the farm to buy milk and eggs for breakfast, after which we were off on the first day together to enjoy the beauty of Scotland. The ancient car nevertheless served us well as we progressed up hill and down dale. Then before we realised it we were suddenly confronted with the River Tay sparkling in the distance, and in the bend there was the delightful city of Perth, reputed to be the smallest city in Britain lying between two inches (an inch is a lake). On the first day of our married life my interest in archaeology was confirmed as we visited the Roman settlement on the top of Kinnoull Hill. Then passing near Scone, the ancient capital of Scotland where the Scottish Kings had their seat of authority in ancient times; and where 'the stone of Destiny'; had rested for years, before it was stolen and taken to Westminster. (It is reputed to be the stone on which Jacob laid his head on the night he left home, but this can't be true!). Tradition also tells us Pontius Pilot was born here. That is just possible; his father was a governor of north Britain. It was not long before we passed the wall of tall beech trees, which are kept trimmed vertically.

They had been planted, as I recall, by Bonnie Prince Charlie's men who were on their way to the '45 Rebellion. Then up through Glen Shee which caused us to ponder on the ability of our borrowed car taking the steep hill bends, which have now been re-made and levelled off. We were now amidst dramatic mountain scenery. On our arrival at Braemar, we discovered to our amazement that we had just ascended the highest road in Great Britain. On one of the steep hairpin bends, we had seen a Bentley stuck on the side of the road and our ancient car glided by. This was the Dee Valley and it has gained in popularity since Queen Victoria made her residence at Balmoral. The countryside here is such that it compels you to stop and stand and stare. Here the Cairngorms stand majestically guarding the Dee valley.

We were out for twelve days, during which time we paid an unforgettable journey to Skye. When we camped at Kyle of Lochalsh, it was in the garden of a very hospitable lady, who when we arrived, was making pancakes. She gave me my first lesson in pancake making, which was to stand me in good stead in the years that lay ahead. Skye is indescribable in its beauty, whatever the weather. You travel on roads that are sometimes not much more than dirt tracks. The mountains frequently have a collar of cloud around them, with a rugged peak protruding above the

George and Alice's wedding 1937

cloud. We met many gypsies driving cars, but what had happened to their caravans? We saw cottages with doors hardly high enough to enter and a few black houses where the peat fire smouldered, sending forth an aroma drifting across the road. Dunvegan was just full of folklore, with its bottlenecked dungeon. Apparently an old laird had a wife who was troublesome to him. He built a dungeon into which he put his troublesome wife. The dungeon only had a bottleneck entrance. This meant, once she was in, she could not get out. He was gracious enough to put food down to her (such charity!). In the castle, the MacLeods still proudly display the flag to visitors. It was said that the flag had been left by the good fairy. The fairy had predicted that the MacLeod family would face times of great danger in the future. The fairy flag could be flown on only three occasions to save them from complete devastation. On two occasions the promise of the fairy has been fulfilled. As the fairy flag is now displayed to visitors, they are told that only one more promise remains. They live in fear of that final destruction when the flag can never again be used to save them. We left the castle wondering what that doom would be.

We had my Mother come with us for our last two days of the honeymoon. We wished to give her a break and indicate to her that although she had parted with me, it was not a final break. She could still join with us. This was greatly appreciated.

On arrival in London, we expected that the South England Conference would have appointed George to his new place of work. This had not happened. We were eventually told that we were appointed to Wimbledon. We tried for 6 weeks to get accommodation there at a rent that was not too prohibitive. We were only permitted to spend a certain percentage of our salary on rent. We found nothing! Then we heard that Pastor Bacon who was at Bournemouth, found the climate unsuitable for his health, so we went to Bournemouth for our first appointment. That was a very good move. The weather that September and early October was like an Indian summer. Before moving, George took a group of canvassers out every Sunday canvassing. I went with them. The only thing I recall was one of the North London church members who were with us always chose the shady side of the street and I was left with the sunny side, it was a very hot day. I met him years later and I recalled his selfish act. We went out canvassing every Sunday to earn much needed money for our new home.

Bournemouth 1937- 41
We were fortunate to find a house at Parkstone. The committee suggested that George conduct his first effort at Poole. We found a new house at Parkstone. It was in a cul-de-sac. We felt very fortunate; the rent was 21/- (£1.15) per week. The house could have been bought for £550. To furnish it we owned one carpet, which I had bought when in Wales, a dining room suite and a bedroom suite made by George. We had Pickfords bring my piano, a small desk, and two leather easy chairs from Edinburgh. I had bought material for curtains

at Lewis's in Kensington, and when we entered our first home, it was nearly completely furnished. So much of it had been self-made. It was a thrill and we both felt very fortunate.

Life was really beginning in our new home. We found living in Bournemouth quite a new experience. It was a holiday town, the climate was mellow, and the days of sunshine in late autumn were delightfully warm. After the Sabbath services we would walk along the beach from Sandbanks in either direction. That was a rare treat. On Christmas day the weather was so mild we had the dining room French doors wide open. By contrast, in early January we had several inches of snow, a quick contrast. On our first Christmas day we were invited to the Benfield's for lunch. They were a generous family and George had known them in the days when he was in charge of the colporteurs. To do this we cycled from Parkstone to Winton, possibly five miles, to celebrate our first Christmas.

Life together in the ministry had to be lived on one salary. Out of that we had to send 10/- (50p) per week to Grandma Bell. She had no income. I think she may have had the 10/- (50p) a week national pension. It was still a custom for the boys of the family to help support their widowed mother. This was a custom going back 2 or 3 millennia. It was a time when married women did not go out to work. This made our living very frugal. It was a time when the wives of the Adventist ministry were expected to help with the church work. I was a qualified experienced Bible worker with years of experience so I really did full time Bible work in the church for two years until the twins were born. The Conference did not even pay my bus fares. They were prepared to pay an illiterate man his travel expenses on the Sabbath, if he went out preaching, but I had to cycle or pay my own fares. This was a difficult time as I was not a good cyclist.

In those days every penny had to be counted. I had to estimate every penny I spent before I went shopping. In Parkstone the International Stores provided a book with every item priced. On a Thursday I would sit down and decide what I could buy for 5/- (25p). That left me with a little money for fruit, vegetables and bread. I made a lot of pancakes, in those days. I also did quite a lot of entertaining. How, I do not know. We had quite a lot of apples given to us from church members. I made a lot of marmalade and even made jam with carrots. I made a lot of soup. One incident we laughed at for many a long day happened one Friday afternoon when coming home from the shops. By mistake I left a parcel of marrowbones in the baker's shop. When I realised my

113

problem I went back to the bakers to try to retrieve the parcel. The baker's shop was quite near. In front of quite a number of customers I asked if the parcel had been found. "O yes", said the assistant. "A bag of dog bones was left behind!" I was glad to collect the precious bones and from that time George claimed to be fed on dog-bone soup.

One vivid memory that very difficult year was on a Sabbath when George had invited five visitors he had known in Birmingham, to have tea with us that afternoon. I hurriedly made a salad tea, and we waited and waited and waited and the visitors did not turn up, so we began our own tea and just as we were finishing, the visitors arrived. I had to rush the dirty dishes out to the kitchen and remake a new salad before I could appear to greet them. We entertained most Sabbaths. I really do not know how I did it.

This first year our responsibilities were for Bournemouth, Poole, Salisbury and Weymouth. George's travelling allowance was 5/- per week. To visit Salisbury cost him a whole week's allowance. It was similar when visiting Weymouth, consequently he often hitch hiked to Sabbath appointments at these isolated groups and of course he also had to go about once a month visiting the members in these isolated groups. On one Sabbath when he was at Salisbury, he was not home by 11 pm. I walked up to the main road in the dark hoping to meet him off the last bus – but there was no George. I was nearly frantic with anxiety. In he rolled at nearly 1 am. That was our worst experience. Hitch hiking to save 5/- (25p) but at what a cost!

We held a small campaign at Poole that winter. In order to advertise the meetings, bills had to be distributed. I did not mind doing that, I had done that in Scotland and Wales many a time. The crunch came when George wanted me to push an advertising barrow along the main street, with his photo and topic of the lecture on it. I objected in no uncertain terms. It became one of our laughable memories throughout the years. It was the only time I can recall when I did not co-operate with him in his work. I think he eventually pushed the barrow himself. From the Poole campaign we had a baptism and a memorable wedding.

One old man who came along to church set his eyes on an old maiden lady who attended the services. She had not been married before. The marriage was not too successful, but it was the wedding that was memorable. Not yet being ordained, George asked his friend Pastor Joyce (father) to substitute for him. To begin with we had a lady

114

organist, who was also a teacher of music. Instead of a limited section of the wedding march being played, as the bride came in, she played the whole piece. This left the congregation standing for some time waiting for the March to be completed. When the legal responses were being made, the old man could not quite hear what Pastor Joyce was saying. This legal section has to be word perfect in the presence of the presiding minister. He was asked to repeat:' I plight thee my troth'. Pastor Joyce repeated the phrase at least three times. His reply was: "I slight thee" or "I flight thee" or "I blight thee", before he was shown the phrase in print. "Oh!" he said: "I plight thee my troth". Then, to make matters worse, when they had to kneel on a hassock for the blessing, he rolled off the hassock and had to be helped up. By this time an audible titter could be heard throughout the congregation.

For our first year's ministry at the Bournemouth church we had **father Vine** as elder. He was wonderfully good for a young minister just starting in the work. He guided George gently through some of the pitfalls that can occur when a young man is dealing with old church members for the first time. We have always retained a very high respect for him and remembered him with gratitude. Another family we remember with gratitude is the Wills family. He was an insurance agent, not always at church, but his wife and two daughters were always there. Knowing our state of penury, they offered us the use of all their camping gear. They also offered to take us to the place of our choosing which was Durdle Door. We stayed for a fortnight and then they brought us home again. That was real generosity and a never-to-be-forgotten kindness. It was a wonderful break and no responsibilities and we were able to explore the countryside. We gathered wild mushrooms and came back and cooked them, and for dad it brought back memories of Punta Arenas when these were the only vegetables available. We had mushrooms every day.

The following autumn (1938) was the first time we were parted. It was felt that I ought to spend a little time with my mother. Before I left, I wrote George a note for him to read in my absence. This I did at Christmas and birthdays. I found them all after his funeral in his desk, he must have treasured them. I immediately destroyed them. Now I am sorry.

I'll be thinking all the time of you, and you alone.
For the greatest happiness I have known, I owe to you.
Clearly now I see the joy, the comfort you have given me.

115

You have filled the whole of my space.

My brother **George** had gone to New Zealand when I was at College. Then, in my Bible worker years, I was away from home. Now we were liable to move anywhere in Britain. We knew how lonely my mother must be. We greatly appreciated all she had done to help us settle comfortably in our new home. I was usually home once in the year. It was decided I should go to Scotland that autumn. I travelled by coach from Bournemouth to Edinburgh. It was a long journey. While in Edinburgh we visited a national exhibition at Glasgow. In the exhibition there was a stand advertising the 'Queen Mary,' the biggest passenger liner at that time. It exhibited a realistic replica of the smoke room on the Queen Mary, which was lined with peroba wood. I spoke to the salesman and was telling him about my dining room suite, which was made of an even more beautifully patterned peroba wood than the example on the panelling which had been chosen by the makers of the Queen Mary to exhibit the best that could be bought. The demonstrator then told me that this wood was so scarce, that if it had been made of solid wood instead of veneer, it would have denuded the forests of the world for a hundred years to come.

One amusing memory of that first year was caused by the presence of some aspidistra plants in the church. A member of the church committee took exception to them. They had been donated by one of the members. At this particular period they had become rather old fashioned and an article of fun, due to Gracie Field's comic song about the 'biggest aspidistra in the world'. The church was heated with gas radiators. A few of the members were anxious to get rid of these plants without causing offence. George had a bright idea. They were all placed on the windowsills above the gas radiator, and eventually they died a natural death, without offending anyone.

The first summer we were in Bournemouth we were asked to help with the Young People's Camp at Woolacombe in North Devon. Only one camp had been held the previous year at Blue Anchor in north Somerset. It was famous for being the first Young People's Camp and infamous for the activity of getting all the campers to roll in the mud, as a health giving activity. A Mrs Druitt wife, of a doctor, conducted this activity. It was never repeated. Camping was quite a new venture. Pastor Warland was the Young Peoples leader for the 1938 Camp. 120 young people attended at Woolacombe. The tents were round army style-tents and cooking was done on trench fires. Toilets consisted of a hole in the ground, which had to be re-dug several times

116

during the camp. Only sacking gave them a covering. This was camping at its most primitive. I had a limited budget per person to feed all these youngsters and I had little or no experience. They say fools step in where angels fear to tread. I think I must have been not only ignorant, but also very courageous to attempt the task.

Although this task was awesome, I have good memories of the fortnight. I also have horrifying memories of that fortnight and the night I got an earwig in my ear. It felt as big as an elephant. I remember laughing at one of the Watson boys. They had just returned from Kenya where their father was a missionary. They had been used to living in the wild open spaces. Woolacombe introduced them to 'an all white group of young people'. Climbing up the flagpole was not much different to climbing a tree. Here they had an appreciative laughing audience and a very irate **Pastor Warland**.

The Devonshire cream teas at such places as Clovelly, that lovely little village, were memorable. At the end of the fortnight it was wonderful to go to the baths at Ilfracombe and relax in a hot bath. It was such a relief!

The story of that camp has become part of our 'family tales'. One of our concerns was with the Peacock boys (they eventually became good church elders). The two boys had cycled all the way from Coventry to Woolacombe on a hot summer day. On arrival, dirty streams of perspiration decorated their faces. When they presented themselves to Pastor Warland, he was most indignant; they had not yet paid their fees. This fault was eventually accounted for, but I was so sorry for them in their apparent penury.

Still in Bournemouth, the girls (Jill and June) were born 16th June 1939 and the outbreak of the Second World War was 2nd September. They were premature (7 month babies) and very small, but fully formed. Jill was 3lbs 12 oz., and June a breach 2 lbs 14 oz. I had not been expecting twins, so their arrival even surprised the doctor. It was arranged I should have the baby at the hospital at a cost of £5 per week (which was nearly two weeks salary). Bournemouth had many old people, so there were many deaths. The Pastor or Vicar received a payment from the undertaker for conducting funerals. Funeral fees paid for my stay in hospital. The dead paid for the living. Some weeks previously, I had taken up a special offer to have a newspaper for 6 weeks. It provided a special insurance. This was very fortunate. After the birth of the twins, a friend asked us if we had taken this paper with

117

its insurance. In the contract was a clause against the birth of twins. This brought in enough cash to pay for the hospital fee.

Dorothy, George's sister, was on furlough from Africa. Will had gone to Washington D.C. to finish his degree. We were expecting Dorothy to visit us at the time of the birth. George did not inform her, before she came, of the birth of twins, lest it should make her defer her visit. When she arrived at the station, she enquired about my state of health and was told 'twins'. She did not turn a hair, or turn round and go home but stayed with us until I was able to cope on my own. Because the babies were under weight, the hospital would not have allowed us to come out at the end of a fortnight (which would have cost more money), but seeing we had a trained midwife staying with us, we all came home at the appointed time. We could not have afforded extra time in the hospital.

Dorothy was with us for six weeks. Her little girl Anne was nearly a year old and was not increasing in weight, which was very worrying. At a visit to the baby clinic, she was told to go home, buy some veal bones and vegetables and make veal bone soup for the child. That week Anne put on 3 or 4 lbs. Dorothy stayed with us until I was able to care for the girls on my own. I very vividly recall one day she greeted me with: "I am going down to the beach for the day, and you must learn to do everything yourself". I thought she was very cruel, but I had to become independent. My independence came that day. In August George went to the South England Conference in London. He phoned me one day to say he was being ordained to the ministry on the Sabbath. Dorothy said: "You must go to London. You can't miss George's ordination". I will care for the babies. I was able to go to London for that special occasion. Will came home by sea, in September from the States. There was no air travel at that time. He, with Leslie Emerson, arrived safely at the end of September. We did not know of their journey until they arrived at Southampton.

Jill and June in 1941

We moved to Weymouth that autumn, to our third house in less than three years. The babies were still very small. Life was difficult. Peggy Vine's mother, **Mrs** Graves, kindly helped us during the move. She was always very kind.

We had Olive Davies as a Bible worker. From time to time she went off sick and I had to arrange to make her visits. This was acceptable until we met her out in Weymouth, while I was caring for two small children and doing her work. I also had Grandma Bell to care for. Through no fault of her own, Grandma Bell became quite a responsibility to the family. She had become a widow out in Punta Arenas and came home with four children, and a piano and not very much money. After visiting some relations she decided to make her home at Merthyr Tydfil, South Wales, where she had lived before going to South America. Here she had made good friends in the Methodist Church who welcomed her home. She rented a house in Gwaelod y Garth. Before going out to Punta Arenas Dorothy had already begun her education. George and Irene had not started school. Eddie was born out in Punta Arenas. When the Bell family came home, Dorothy could read and do arithmetic. George had been to a school where 17 languages were spoken. He became very proficient at Maths but could not write or read much English. Eddie had not started school. Life in Merthyr required a difficult adjustment from all the family, particularly for George. Social Security was in its infancy, and money was a big problem for the 'Bell' family. Grandma Bell let out one of the rooms in her house in Merthyr to a Miss Living, who was a Bible worker for Frank Powell, an Adventist Evangelist. Within the process of time the family became Adventists. Because of the shortage of money and with four children to educate Grandma Bell bought a business in Newport, Monmouthshire. In the process of time Dorothy went to Watford and became a nurse. Irene did exceptionally well at school and became a tutor to an ambassadors children and George had finished his limited schooling. Eddie went to school. At Newport, a new church was built. George, who was a big strong lad, helped to dig the foundations and Grandma Bell gave generously of

119

her money for the church building. This impoverished her with the result she had little money left to live on and educate the family. The custom at this time was that parents spent what they had on their children and when the children began to work, they were responsible for the parents. George was sent up to New Cumnock to work on the Murdoch farm, in the anticipation that he would learn farming. Grandma Bell was not a businesswoman. The shop she had was not a financial success and was eventually sold. She learned the lesson, that not everybody with a little money was a financial success. Grandma Bell moved to Sheepcote Villas at Watford with a widow's pension and very little money. As the children gradually started to work they were expected to contribute to their mother's keep. When I married George, he earned £2.10s (£2.05p) per week, we had to contribute 10/- (50p) per week to Grandma Bell. Our salary was equivalent to that earned by a dustman, the lowest paid worker at that time. This left our finances at a very low level.

Will Hyde, Dorothy's husband, maintained, that Mrs Bell was her sons responsibility. This was a generally accepted opinion of the older generation at that time. This idea goes back for millenniums. Irene's husband also adopted this attitude. There was just George and Eddie to support their impoverished mother. When Dorothy was home on furlough, she would take over the care of her mother. Irene would send her mother an occasional gift.

By the time we arrived in Weymouth, Grandma Bell, who was living at Watford, was having problems in the home where she had accommodation. She was not just the easiest person to live with. Irene tried to fix her up with Eddie at Watford. Vi would not have her on any account. Irene was in desperation and contacted George insisting that their Mother was his responsibility. I felt under obligation to have her. At that time I had to constantly learn to forget and forgive, then concede to agree. It was a very difficult experience. As I had never had difficulty in getting on with people wherever I had lived, I felt confident I could and would manage. We do not know our own weaknesses until put to the test. After six or seven months I was just about at the end of my tether. It was wartime. I had two children under 12 months. I had to help George with Bible work. Grandma Bell made everything twice as difficult. She interfered with the cooking; she interfered with what we could listen to on the radio and interfered with practically everything in the house. I did not know where things were from day to day. George tried to counsel with her, but I do not think she heard what he said and I had reached a very low ebb! We compromised and hired a room in a bungalow in a house opposite. She only came over lunch time and went back between 7-8 pm. Both Dorothy and Irene told me I was very brave to even try living with her (they were her daughters). We had problems with her until she died. That is another story. I always remember repeating the prayer, "Dear Lord please make me good, and do not forget to make me nice". I came across a saying recently: "To dwell above with saints we love, well surely that is glory. To dwell below with saints we know, well that's another story". That was very appropriate for my year in Weymouth. She stayed with us until we moved to Parley Cross, when she moved back temporarily to Stanborough Park.

Weymouth was a very vulnerable place at the beginning of the war. It was a naval dockyard, and bombs were targeted at the naval dock. Bombers also came over night after night on their way to Bristol. We were right under the bombers regular nightly route. Our house was next door to that of a young married woman, whose husband was on night shift. Every night, the twins slept under the table and we were under the stairs. We had our neighbour and her little girl in at night to sleep at our house for company. They were very appreciative. I cannot recall where they slept, but it meant she was not alone.

Although it was wartime, the beaches had not yet been closed to the public. At thirteen months old, we had June actually swimming, like a little dog, in the sea. People from the beach came down to see this tiny child actually swimming unaided.

George had to make visits to Bournemouth at least twice a week. As his train would approach the Weymouth station at night, he would be looking out of the window to see if our house was still standing. Towards the end of this year we had a little car. Although petrol was in short supply, we had a petrol allowance. I can recall a soldier trying to sell us petrol. We dared not accept his offer. Army petrol was coloured pink. Any civilian caught with army petrol was very heavily fined. On one occasion we had been over to Bournemouth for the day and were returning home after dark, in our little car. The twins were asleep at the back. There was only the light of the moon. No artificial lights as car lights on the car or in the streets. We realised when we were nearly back to Weymouth that our petrol tank was nearly empty. We did not know if we would manage to get home that night. It was very nerve wracking. The planes were flying above us. We were travelling by the light of the moon. When we arrived home, the petrol tank was dry. We realised we had come home on the wings of a prayer.

The garden of our Weymouth house supplied nearly all the vegetables we required that year. We have never again used so much beetroot. Our young neighbour used to say: there is always a good cooking smell when I come in here at night. There were no freezers. We bottled fruit and vegetables. Work was constant. On one occasion we had ½ an egg each per ration book. I gave one egg to Grandma Bell, thinking she could enjoy an egg. It was impossible to buy eggs. She used the precious egg to wash her hair. I was mildly furious.

The fourth year of our ministry we moved back to the Bournemouth district of Parley Cross, a few miles from Winton, to conduct a campaign at the Y.M.C.A. Winton. Here at Parley Cross we had a house in half an acre of garden, which had been a market garden, so it was well matured. We grew all the vegetables we needed. In the summer we took some of the biggest and best up the lane to a church member who was a gardener to show Charley Proudly, our produce. The carrots were 2 1/2 lbs in weight. We had a pumpkin 48 lbs in weight. Charlie Proudly turned to us and said "Pastor Bell you will never again grow such vegetables". He was perfectly right, we never did. It was that summer that George decided that because we had a house with plenty of land and there was no Young People's Camp because it was wartime, that we should at least have a camp for the local young people. He organised a 'week's camp' in our garden. We borrowed some empty Nissen huts from a farm down the lane. They were the sleeping quarters for the boys. We filled Hessian sacks with hay for the beds. The girls slept in tents in the garden. I cooked in my kitchen with the help of two church members. The Y.M.C.A. gave us margarine and jam. We could buy basic necessities. Our garden supplied most of the vegetables. We had the local young people and a small group came from Stanborough Park. We had well over twenty campers. The twins were two years old. With it being wartime, there was nothing much the campers could buy with their holiday money at the local village shop except potato crisps. They shared them with the twins, and this caused them to get diarrhoea. It became necessary to make an announcement: "Please do not feed the twins". We managed a camp concert at the end of the holiday during which time I vividly recall that in the middle of one of the acts, the telephone wires in front of the house were covered with most of the birds of the immediate neighbourhood. The cause of the trouble was the presence of an owl. The birds alerted all the other birds in the neighbourhood and they ganged up on the intruder to meet the threat.

Food in wartime was a big problem. Apart from all the gifts of food we received, we still needed money to feed the group. A small charge was made of 10/- (50p) per camper for the holiday. If more than two children came from one family, we charged 7/6d (37.5p). If three came from a family the fee was 5/- (25p) each, and if more than three the others did not pay at all. When we finished I had 1/- left over. Asking what I should do with the 1/- (5p). George told me: put it in the gas meter!

Brighton and Hove (1941-45)

Hove SDA Church

We moved to Hove to a house at the foot of the South Downs, which was in a delightful position, especially for afternoon walks. On the front door of the house was a metal cylinder containing 'The Law' (Deut. 6:4-9) which indicated that the house belonged to a Jew! During our years there we cared for Brighton, Folkestone, Hastings and Worthing, plus the isolated district. Unfortunately we were again in a direct line for bombing raids from France. Many of our sleeping hours were spent in an Anderson shelter. This was a flat iron sheet surrounded by iron mesh. It was like a cage. This was where we spent many nights. Life was getting more difficult. The twins were growing up. They had a nice little playmate next door, whose mother played the piano very well. Her husband was a soldier. We could hear her playing the piano every night I soon got friendly with a Channel Island lady who had a little boy. She worked locally, so we took her little boy with us on our afternoon walks on the South Downs. They

123

were still beautiful and untouched. Now some of it is built upon. I frequently recall the natural 'dew ponds' we saw as we walked on the Downs. Sometimes we met a shepherd who was happy to explain to us the importance of 'Down herbage', which is so good and important for the sheep, particularly in the springtime. The Downs afforded a distant view of Sussex, which was a restful contrast to the current problems of the day.

During this period of our ministry George was frequently away at least one day a week sometimes more. He travelled mostly by bus or train, which was not very reliable, sometimes he would cycle. He visited Eastbourne at least once a month, sometimes more. Eastbourne station was out of bounds for trains. It was only 22 miles from France. Beachy Head was near and a very visible landmark for young German pilots. The result was the grass grew up on the Eastbourne station platform. Passengers had to walk from west of the station to the east of the station to get a connection, when travelling to Hastings. Most weeks I had to take the Prayer Meeting (afternoon) in Brighton. We seldom went out in the dark. I had a regular Sabbath school class and sometimes the Sabbath Morning sermon. At church, June was seated with an old lady who really loved her and Jill went to a younger member, (she was her Sabbath School teacher). They both looked forward to this. It was a special outing in the week. I cared for a number of George's duties. It was at this time we had a visit from Pastor Harker, who had written a number of the hymns in the hymn book. He heard me speaking to the children and as the next copy of the Children's Sabbath School lesson book had not arrived from America, he persuaded me that I was capable of writing the children's quarterly lesson book. This I did.

It was during this wartime period when food and transport were a problem that we had to make some adjustment nearly every day. Most Sabbaths we walked to church or went on bicycles. One Sabbath we had a soldier visitor from church to lunch. He was newly arrived from Canada. His name was **Roland Neufeld**. He had just arrived in Scotland the previous week and was very home sick. This was the first time he had really been far away from home. He was stationed at Beachy Head. His work was on the early radar system. By way of conversation I asked if he had any brothers or sisters. "Yes" said he, "I have 23". I thought he possibly belonged to a small Canadian church and was accounting for the brothers and sisters in his little church at home, but no! He was the youngest of 23 children. His father was of Dutch extraction and had married three times and

Roland was the youngest of the third family. Years later during our visit to America in 1976, I kept asking the question whenever we went to church: "Is there anyone here called Roland Neufeld?" Eventually, at Pacific Union College one Sabbath, my brother-in-law asked the man in front of us at church: have you ever heard of Roland Neufeld? "I am Roland Neufeld" he said. We had a wonderful reunion. He was a raw recruit from Canada when he arrived in England. He soon made himself at home and when he was transferred to the London district, he got friendly with a girl in the Holloway church and married her.

Another memorable event was due to one of our army visitors. Every Sabbath lunch we had our traditional rice pudding. Rice in Britain soon became unobtainable, and it was with great ceremony we ate our last rice pudding until the end of the war. This 'last time' happened on a number of occasions. This was possible because during the last year or two we had parcels of rice arriving from America, Canada and New Zealand. More than one of our lunch guests must have written home, telling their parents about these children in Hove who were eating their last rice pudding. Rice is still a memorable dish in our household.

In our Hove garden we had two or three hens. They were good layers. The girls used to go out to collect eggs before breakfast and sing:

> Chick, chick, chick, chick, chicken,
> Lay a little egg for me,
> Chick, chick, chick, chick chicken lay one for my tea.
> I haven't had an egg since Easter,
> And now it's half past three.
> Chick, chick, chick, chick, chicken lay a little egg for me.

We also had two 'kaki Campbell' ducks. They were very good regular layers and not being in water, the egg yolk did not have a strong taste. Eventually we had bees and they supplied the needed sugar. For a while a friend had given the girls a snow-white (pedigree?) rabbit. When it was mated, we had a motley group of babies. As they grew up, we gave them to a bus driver neighbour a few houses up the road for his dinner plate. All essential foods were in very short supply, which we bought with the use of ration books. I had two vegetarian ration books and two meat books. This gave me more cheese (instead of meat) with which to cook. Daily on the radio we had a short talk from the radio doctor to encourage good health. Recipes were given on how to use what we had to the best advantage. Some recipes were helpful and some pretty dreadful. At the Hove church was an elder (who had

125

an allotment) called John Deanne. Mr Deanne was able to supply me with fruit, gooseberries, gooseberries and more gooseberries, which I bottled. I paid him whatever he asked. It was usually over the top, but it supplied us with fruit throughout the year. I bottled the gooseberries (but I had no sugar to make jam). Years later, when we were in Canada, we attended a Camp meeting at Calgary. When we arrived we were parked beside a big Winnebago. The driver got out saying to us: "I'm John Deanne, pleased to meet you". We told him we came from England: "My grandfather lived in England" he informed us. We asked where he came from? "Brighton", said he. He was the grandson of our old elder. This was such a coincidence.

During that difficult time of rationing, I managed to provide two wedding receptions for members (one a Bible worker). A question I was always asked was how do you do it? I do not know. It must have been a little bit of magic and imagination.

During our stay in Hove, we were fortunate enough to have two very memorable holidays in a gypsy caravan in Derbyshire. George had been up to Newbold to visit a farmer friend, Todd Murdoch. He came back with two beehives and the information that Todd had bought a gypsy caravan for £5. His little family had been to the Lickey Hills near Birmingham in it for a holiday (holidays during the war were almost unknown, except to relatives). Being friends, we asked if we could borrow a horse and the caravan. Petrol was not only scarce but it was impossible to obtain by this time. We had no car. The first time we used it, we invited our friends, the Rupert Madgwick family, to join us in our borrowed gypsy caravan. We would use the caravan and they would have their own tents. The big brown trunk was used to transport our bedding and other essentials. The second time we used it was quite an adventure. We had Jill with her leg in plaster and in an invalid chair and Euan (Alistair) a baby in a pram. We sent the trunk by rail to Rugby, a week in advance to be sure of it getting there on time. With the help of a farm cart, our luggage was transferred from Rugby Station to the farm.

On the first caravan holiday, we began by going by train to London, changing to Kings Cross and going to Rugby. Due to the scarcity of all edibles, we took with us two week's meat supply, which we were to cook on arrival. Alas and alas, one of the farm dogs found it before the meat could be cooked. It was goodbye meat. For this trip I had made 500 ginger biscuits. They were safely stored in a tin box and were our one luxury during the fortnight.

126

The typical gypsy caravan was fitted with two double beds, one bed up aloft and one bed below at the end of the caravan. Near the roof was a little window. The kitchen area had a metal stove, which was heated with coal. A metal chimney went through the roof which allowed the smoke to escape. On the roof was a little window about six inches deep. One damp day when we had an invasion of flies, June climbed up and systematically killed as many flies as she could. There is a picture of this event somewhere to prove it. On the front of the van was the driving bench where we had a typical patchwork rug. Two of us sat on this bench as we drove through the quiet country lanes of Derbyshire singing all the horsy songs we could think of:

Horsey, horsey don't you stop
Just let your feet go clippity, clop.
The whip goes swoosh and the wheels go round
Cheerio we're homeward bound.

All we lacked were the clothes pegs to sell. The older ones had turns to sit on the front seat facing the hindquarters of a horse. The younger ones (at one time we were fourteen) cycled. Dad brought his bike, but it never left the back of the caravan. He and Lily were the capable drivers (Lily had been brought up in rural Ireland). George had control of the horse when the hills were very steep and there was more than one steep hill on our route. There were times when we all had to push from the back. It was arranged that everyone in the party had a turn on the front seat. We had more than one interesting episode as we went along. The girls, especially June, enjoyed going out with George first thing in the morning to collect Mary, the mare. She looked so small as she carried a bowl of oats to Mary. On one occasion a gypsy approached us. He recognised a good horse when he saw one and he tried to bargain with us for Mary. She was a good mare prepared to pull anything. She had a willing heart. On another occasion the police approached us. They were looking for unwanted visitors to the country who may be spies. We did not have any difficulty with their visit. When we pulled up in the main thoroughfare of Harrogate the passers-by did not approve of our outfit. I think we might have looked like gypsies (they had a bad reputation for stealing).

Each evening we had to find a farm where we could park for the night. Then, first thing in the morning, the girls took pleasure in going out with a bowl of oats to bring in Mary the horse and hitch her up to the caravan. The children looked so tiny beside the big heavy mare. It was memorable as far as holidays go.

On our second year with the gypsy caravan we were on our own. At a traffic stop in the Main Street in Derby, we were recognised by a church member. As we stopped to hail him, we heard a voice saying: "Pastor Bell, of all the people in England you are the only one who would be doing this". He was a man called Charlie Kelly. He was a very good colporteur. We eventually gave him a lift to his home and had lunch and a good laugh with the family.

The next year, when the caravan had been sold, we went back to the farm and borrowed a flat wagon. George bent some metal bands and covered the wagon with tarpaulin. So we made our journey in a covered wagon. This was our last gypsy caravan holiday. It was the third year of the war and once again we were on the road with primitive facilities. With this lowly contraption, the 'covered wagon,' we went towards Stratford on-Avon. On the way we stopped at our friends the Billie Murdoch's family, who joined us for a day as gypsies on the road. Years later I met up with their oldest girl at Loma Linda. This was one event she remembered as a child in England, travelling in a covered wagon with the Bells. That day she had new white socks and to her horror she had dirtied her new socks. She did not often get new socks, new socks were special and they had to be bought with coupons, so she felt it was quite a tragedy when her new white socks were soiled. It brought tears to a little girl's eyes. That night we had difficulty getting a caravan site. Stratford was partially open to holiday visitors, and when a covered wagon pulled up at a caravan site, the owners did not want to have a gypsy family on their site. It was degrading. Wherever we went they thought we were gypsies. Eventually we found a good site on a farm.

Alistair Euan with dogs in 1946

After the war we were offered the Madgwick's bungalow in East Anglia. I felt by that time that I had sat behind the hindquarters of a horse long enough and would like something more civilised. We got it. We had a respectable bungalow and quite a lot of rain to contend with. Dad said: "If this is a civilised holiday, give me the hindquarters of a horse".

During this time, we had become responsible for Irene (George's sister) and her two dogs Betsy and Mary, a Wire Hair Terrier and a West Highland Terrier respectively. They were quite an added responsibility. When we went out as a family anywhere, where dogs were not permitted, such as London Zoo or Madam Tausauds, or other comparable places, I was left outside holding the dogs while the family did their sightseeing. It was quite a chore. Irene's husband, Sidney Pullinger a Colonel in the Royal Engineers, had been killed in an accident as he was returning from Persia (Iran). One of his responsibilities was the laying of the oil pipeline to the Mediterranean. When he heard of his wife's illness he came home on compassionate leave and unfortunately the plane went into a mountain at Shannon, Ireland. (See the appendix for his war record). We became responsible for Irene until the time of her death. She had a complete breakdown. Eddie would take no responsibility for her at all. He brought her straight down to us. Dorothy was in Africa and could do nothing. She was George's sister and he was responsible for her.

We kept her as long as we possibly could. I was pregnant with Euan (Alistair Euan)* and the doctor eventually insisted we hospitalise her. It was a difficult decision. George visited her regularly until she died. It was a very sad end for such a brilliant girl. That year was very difficult. I wondered if it would ever end. After the baby was born I had a very difficult two months. George had to constantly visit Irene.

129

He made quick visits to Lancaster to place his mother in accommodation there. He found a distant male relative who was prepared to share his house with her. They got on fairly well together. He was very dominating and she gave way to him. How they managed we will never know. Fortunately we had a very good friend of Irene's, Ethel Rata, who became Irene's legal representative and cared for her financial outgoings. That greatly helped. As the bells of the old year rang out that year, we both heaved a sigh and hoped we would never again have such a difficult time. No problem lasts forever. During this time we met a teenage girl called Anita, who was trying to cope with her terrible domestic problems. We took her into our home. She stayed with us for six or seven years.

Then in the spring of 1945, we were asked to go to London and look after the churches in Holloway, Wood Green and Edmonton. This came as an interesting and challenging change. It would at least bring different problems.

* Note from the editor. All my mothers friends called him Euan and all dads friends called him Alistair which became shortened to Ali.

THE LONDON YEARS 1945-50

Leaving Hove we were often reminded of W.H. Davies when he said:

> What is this life if full and care,
> We have no time to stand and stare.

We never had much time to stand and stare, but London was quite a different proposition. What of the future? We had worked long hours at Hove, with little time to ourselves. We had faced insurmountable problems. How different was London going to be? We shall see what we shall see in the big city.

We rented a house with five bedrooms in Cranley Gardens and moved with three children, two dogs, 3 pups and **Anita.**

On arrival at the Holloway church, we found the back door of the church had been blown out by war damage and it needed repair. Holloway was one of our central London churches. As a student I had attended the Dedication of the church. I recall sitting by a radiator with my friend Claudia and having lunch with her parents at the interval. Holloway had a good and growing church membership. While at Holloway, we held the 21st Anniversary. We were invited to the 25th

Anniversary and while George was still alive I attended the 50th Anniversary. One memory I often recall was the presence of pigeons on the church roof. If I stood by the door shaking hands with people, I was liable to get pigeon dirt on my hat. Fortunately, an old Jew frequented the district. He was very good at catching pigeons. It was shortly after the hostilities of war and food was still in short supply. I imagine he caught them to make pigeon pie. George encouraged him to centre his attention on the birds around the church. To catch them he attached corn to the end of a string, as the bird ate the corn, he pulled the string and caught the bird. Another memory we had was of the standard of the church committee. When an item was decided on the committee, the members of the committee always observed the sacredness of the decision.

The three churches we had to care for were very different in their membership. A number of business people were the core of the church members at Holloway. Wood Green membership was more a mixed membership and Edmonton members were definitely working-class. They were all good and faithful. It was very noticeable that people travelled across London boundaries to attend the church in which they felt happiest. We were happy to feel that there was a general effort to support all our projects.

Our house in Cranley Gardens was near the famous Highgate Park. During the Black Death a pit was dug in this park that at that time was well outside London. It was filled with lime and the corpses from the Black Death were buried there. Now it was a delightful park area at the end of our road. The house at Cranley Gardens had five bedrooms. By this time we had three children and while at Hove we had taken into our home Anita a teenage girl of 16 years of age. She was with us for seven or eight years and became a member of the family. She found work in the **Manier** Watch Repairing Factory, until she left to go to Bedford, where she married a policeman.

It was near Highgate Station where Dick Whittington, was said to have heard the memorable words: Turn again Whittington, Lord Mayor of London. My travelling in London now was done mostly by bus or underground, but shortly after arriving we were able to acquire Irene's car, a Hillman Minx car. It was in her garage and was almost in new condition. This was a great advantage for George.

The unforgettable year was 1947. The house was old, the rooms were large with high ceilings and we had practically no heating. The

131

electricity was turned off about 10a.m to conserve the national supply. Coal had been in short supply because many miners had gone into the army. The winter was so cold with the constant snow and frost over a five or six week period. It became difficult to move coal from the Coal mines to the large cities. It became a national disaster. We kept the kitchen heated, but the rest of the house was freezing. The caretaker at the Holloway Church, **Mr Crutwell** managed to get us half a bag of coal. I do not know where he got it, or how. He brought it to us. He was such a little man. I shall never forget him or his kindness. Some of that precious coal we used one weekend when we had visitors from Australia who were in transit to America, and were living at the Strand Hotel. They were in church in the morning blue with cold. I invited them back to warm them up a little, while we burnt some of our precious coal. We all sat as closely as possible around the fire. We sat close together and breathing out a little heat as we used some of our precious coal with some wood we had collected from Highgate We all sat as near the fire as possible to keep warm that afternoon. I met them years later at Pacific Union College. They had never forgotten that afternoon.

While in Holloway George revived the Colporteur (book sales) work in North London. He collected members from around our three churches and led them out each Sunday, usually to the East End of London, selling Present Truth and Good Health. It became a vigorous group and our caretaker friend Mr. Crutchwell eventually cared for the group for many years to come a job he continued to do faithfully till the end of his life. I cannot express how much he loved Dad. Through the years he always expressed a great love for our family and he passed on to his son the task of keeping in touch with us.

During this period I arranged for all these members who took part in the literature work to have a special social evening. With the help of some of the members we laid out the festive table, such as it had never been seen during the war years. Paint and paper were used to devise decorations. Fifty people were able to enjoy the first special meal since The War. It was a great and much appreciated event and it meant that we were attempting to return to normal. Again how I managed is lost in my memory. I have always had a good imagination for transforming food from its original condition, into something more attractive. We served a three-course meal and the guests called it a banquet. Being autumn I made the drinks from fruits, which were available in the hedges. It was such a wonderful surprise for the guests to enter and see the attractive tables. They gave a gasp of surprise. It became the talk of the churches for many days to come. The Young People's (YP) leader, an Australian called Pastor Minchin had encouraged me to do this for the YP group.

We were able to run very strong Young People groups. Recently the American idea of giving badges for achievement had been introduced and we worked on this idea in the August of the Olympic year an International Camp was conducted at Stanborough Park for which George and I were responsible. The Camp held over 200 campers from around Europe. George had organised the erection of the tents, during a very hot weekend when it was really exhausting. Fortunately he was able to keep his workers going in spite of the heat, and had everything ready on time. The treasurer was so impressed that he generously gave him a present of £10. It had been a terrific job but at the final ceremony George led 48 Master Comrades to be inducted. There had never been such a large group.

Another innovation was a play I had written on the early history of the church. I produced it at the Holloway Church. The local Young People's leader helped in the choosing of the actors. I remember **J.O. (John Oliver)** was James White and the music leader contributed advice on suitable music. This was the first time drama had been used in the church. The only thing approaching drama had been 13th Sabbath Programmes. This play lasted the whole evening (there were a few questions raised about the validity of drama in the church, but it weathered the storm). It was a success story. The Stanborough Park and the Wimbledon churches were quick to follow in my footsteps. On looking back it was possibly very amateurish, but it told a historical story, and was an event that impressed the church members with our church history. The participants enjoyed its preparation and execution. The war had ended, we were in a new era and we began what became a custom. A little later I wrote a programme on Hymns giving details of the authors and their background. Several churches borrowed this copy from me. In moving the manuscripts have been lost!

By this time we had acquired the Hillman car out of Irene's garage. Petrol was becoming more easily obtainable, and we needed a garage as there was none attached to the house. Shortly after moving to Cranley Gardens, George noticed in the road behind our garden there was a row of garages. One garage had cobwebs on the padlock. This indicated to him that the garage was not being used. This district had been built in the era of the horse and carriage. We were able to acquire

133

the rental of the garage. For the first time we had a telephone, which was not a complete blessing as we had one particular member who worked a night shifts. As he finished his shift he would phone at any time after 6 am. This was not always appreciated.

Both dogs had pups before we moved to London. We kept the two original dogs and one of each of the pups. The young dogs were called Spot and Dinkie. The girls each claimed one of the young dogs. The girls went to a little junior school, two roads away. The nearness of the school was suitable, but at the time all schools suffered from a lack of teachers. There was a national shortage of teachers. An attempt to deal with the situation was made by encouraging people returning from war to apply for a 'one year' crash course in teaching. For a number of years this created great difficulties throughout the country. There was a lack of continuity in teaching staff and the quality of education left much to be desired. This affected the girls education. There were terms when they had at least two sometimes three new teachers. This was inevitable. Many teachers had been drafted into the army. With the war at an end, a quick course of one year was offered, to tide over the country's educational problems and new recruits to teaching were being employed with little or no experience. Although It was a very difficult situation, it could not have been avoided. We just had to do as things would do with us.

Every half term we took advantage of the nearness to so many interesting places in London. We visited places like the zoo, Madame Tausauds, the museums, particularly the science museum at West Kensington, which was always a great success with the moveable demonstrations. Nearly every afternoon, when the girls came out of school, Euan and I would meet them and we would take the four dogs up to Highgate Park for a run. To do this we had to cross a busy main road at the top of Cranley Gardens at a pedestrian crossing. The people in the nursing home behind the crossing noticed that our dogs had learned the kerb drill. 'Stop, Look, Listen, and Cross'. There was however a never to be forgotten day. Usually when we entered the Park we let the dogs off the lead. They usually ran off in great excitement at being off the lead and in an open space. On this particular day there was in the distance a lady sitting on a bench and was busily knitting (nearly everybody did knitting those days). She had a pram with baby in it. Now knitting wool was a precious commodity at that time. It could only be bought with clothing coupons. The tragedy then occurred. Spot, our young Wire Hair Fox Terrier ran up to this lady's pram, it was similar to Euan's little pram. The lady sprang up to keep this strange dog off her baby. Spot got tangled up in her precious knitting wool, which was really irreplaceable. By this time I had arrived full of apologies the tragedy had happened. Money was no use in such a situation. The replacement of clothing coupons was more important. They could not be bought. I was distraught, ashamed, confused. How the poor lady felt can only be imagined. With lots of apologies I departed. After extracting ourselves from that embarrassing incident, we went off, including the dogs, humiliated and ashamed. They knew something terrible had happened. The problems of the day were not yet over. As if that was not enough there was more to come. Further along into the park, the two young dogs started to fight. They knocked the stick out of the hand of an old gentleman. Here was another set of apologies. I had by now had more than enough. Putting the four dogs on the leads we cut short the walk and began to make for home. We were out of the wood but not out of trouble. I had to control four dogs and two children and Euan in the pram while waiting for a suitable time to cross a busy main road. We were all tense. The dogs had been disgraceful the children were full of suggestions. I expect Spot had been chastised and was not her usual obedient self. At this main road crossing Spot sprang from her lead and ran across the main road and down the road facing the crossing. We all had to follow in quick pursuit. We distinctly saw her enter one of the gardens, but could not tell which one. It was rather far off to identify. By now we were all in a state of frenzy trying to retrieve a very disobedient animal. Looking into the garden we thought she had entered we caught no sight of her. Some workmen a few houses away suggested another garden, again there was no sign of her there. Then we all began calling her. We did wonder if the workmen were hiding her. Then suddenly the disgraceful Spot, crept towards us in a very subdued and cringing attitude of submission. In her doggy way she was admitting her disobedience. We were all very angry with her, but pleased to see her at last. A very subdued family of Mum, three children and four dogs hastily made for home. I was determined not to take three children and four dogs to the Park again. My cup of anguish was full and running over.

On another occasion we lost Spot in the High Street. In those days pedigree dogs were being stolen and sold for a big price at Petticoat Lane, complete with a spurious pedigree. At the idea of losing Spot we were all decided to go to Petticoat Lane on the following Sunday to try to identify our precious Spot. I phoned the police station to report our lost dog. They asked me to describe the colouring, which I did. Then the officer said: Any other identifying marks. After a moment's thought and hesitation I said: yes. She has a brown horseshoe around her bottom. I could hear a roar at the other end of the line. Anyone seen a wire hair dog with a brown horseshoe round her bottom? We were very pleased to have her returned to us the next day none the worse for her adventure. She was an animal that attracted trouble.

While we lived in London one event that cannot be forgotten was our adventure into puppetry. We make the string puppets with papier-mâché. Then the clothes had to be made so it was quite a big undertaking. Dad made the staging, which was like a Punch and Judy show stand. The girls worked on the puppets. Then we did a show 'Peter and the Wolf', using Greig's music as the background (gramophone records). At the church they performed 'the laughing policeman' to the accompaniment of the gramophone record. It was very successful. Another puppet shows they did was 'Red Riding Hood'. They were asked to go to a number of the churches to do their performance. We also had a pantomime horse, (made with sacking, and big enough for two of the young people to get inside. This was in the days before cassettes and sound production.

Dad had two or three Evangelistic Meetings each year, which meant he was never off the road. It was very hard going. We saw so little of him. He always remembered me telling him on one occasion, that he was a bed and breakfast husband. We were able to get Anita to stay with the children some evenings, so that I could enjoy some free time. It became a custom after the Sunday service, for some of the Holloway Young People to go up to Hyde Park Corner where they enjoyed joining in the debates going on there. I remember Anita stayed home one summer Sunday evening, releasing me to go up to Hyde Park. It was a rare occasion for us to be out together, so it was very special. We drifted off from the group and as we walked together under the lime trees of the embankment, we watched and listened to the noisy starlings returning to their roost from their day's feeding in the countryside (10 - 12 miles away). Each evening near the close of the day they winged their way home chattering as they flew to find a roost in the trees of the London parks. While enjoying this natural spectacle we walked towards Westminster Bridge. Then standing in the golden glow of evening light as the sky was gradually reddening. I recall repeating to George the words of the Wordsworth's poem, 'On Standing on Westminster Bridge'. We were standing on the bridge not in the morning hue. But in a sunset glow and I was saying:

Earth hath not anything to show more fair,

136

Dull would be the soul, who could pass by,
A sight so touching in majesty
The city now doth like a garment wear
The beauty of the morning, silent bear
Ships, towers, domes, theatres and temples lie
All bright and glittering in the smokeless air.

Never did sun shine more beautifully
In his first splendour, valley, rock and hill,
Ne'er saw I never felt a calm so deep!
The river glideth at its own sweet will;
And all that mighty heart is lying still.

As the sun was slowly setting George said 'Say it again'. This is one of memorable and lasting impressions of London experienced at the close of day and not in the first morning light. We shared in this picturesque rare experience at sunset together.

With having *Anita with us in London, we were able leave her in charge of the family and join the Madgwicks for my first foreign travel. We went to Italy. Not many people travelled to the continent before the war. Foreign travel was just opening up to the multitudes. This was very special to me being the first time I had ventured abroad. The winter prior to this great event I was fortunate enough to have been able to attend a series of lectures at a College in Drury Lane. The lectures were on Italy. The lecturer was an Italian, who had the eye of an artist. He illustrated his lectures with pictures of famous buildings and places in Italy. He saw not only the building but also the surrounding beauty of the landscape. Without doubt from that time I began to see the beauty of the countryside in a way I had never seen it. I look back on these lectures with great thankfulness. I had learned to open my eyes in a new way. I began to see beauty I had never seen before.

*Anita was a homeless teanager who we took into our home for a few years.

The holiday in Italy was a great event for me as it was my first time abroad. Crossing the Channel was a great adventure. At that time there were no roll, roll off ferries. It was exciting to see the car being hooked up aloft to be put on the Dover ferry. To me it seemed a marvellous event. Then our first night in Paris in the Sacre Coeur district was a shock. Seeing for the first time a French toilet was hilarious. We stayed in a hotel, at Via Reggia, in Italy. I was then able to look through a telescope, for the first time and see the moons around Jupiter. This was an experience of wonder for me! Florence was the place where I enjoyed the culmination of my year's lectures. To see the beautiful baptistery doors for the first time. To enter the cathedral and see Michael Angelo's lovely Pieta and paintings conveying in art a three-dimensional beauty. We walked across the ancient medieval bridge over the Arno, resplendent with shops, sparkling with the jewellers. The art was an overwhelming experience. Florence was like travelling through time. I never tired of visiting museums and art galleries.

Then in Rome, we visited St. Peter's and the Vatican, enjoying its ancient beauty and wealth. Then, I heard George say to an American, who was viewing everything according to her guidebook. "Oh I do not use a guidebook, my wife knows it all." This was an exaggeration! Then it was like a dream come true, to walk the Apian Way, to saunter through the Via Sacre, to see the Archway depicting the sacred vessels of the Jerusalem Temple and seeing Pompeii as it was 2,000 years ago. That was almost unbelievable. I had read of its ancient beauty but never imagined I would ever see the actual paintings. Then there was the visit to Capri. I was developing a new aspect of history, which has since influenced my life and opened my eyes in an unforgettable way. I can never be the same again. I grew up quite a little during that continental tour.

While still in London we placed our tent at Bognor Regis. It was not too far from London. It had an attractive sandy beach with lovely surroundings. Before Euan went to school we enjoyed most of the summer there. The girls visited us for the weekend. Some weekends George came down with Rupert and the boys. We let the Minchin family use it in the month of September, before we took the tent down. Another summer we had the tent down between Sandbanks and Swanage. That was a delightful location. To get there we had to cross a ferry, which could be quite an event. We parked in the garden of a vicarage. The vicar's wife had a similar family to ours, which made our residence there very friendly. It was here the girls had whooping cough. We went home for a few days eventually returning to camp at the Lorna Doone farm, Somerset (so as not to spread the whooping cough to the other family). I shall never forget commenting on the creamy colour of the milk on this farm. George then took me to the cowsheds, where I saw cows knee deep in manure, which possibly accounted for the colour of the milk

READING 1950-52

After five years in London we moved to Reading. It was shortly after we arrived at Reading that we were able to have our first new car, a Ford Prefect. The church arranged a business deal with the government for the transaction of sterling for dollars, so that the ministry could buy a limited number of cars. We were eligible for one of them. At that time cars were unobtainable on the British market. The day we collected our first new car, Euan climbed on the bonnet. It was not appreciated. Although the car was new, it had no heating as heating system had not yet been installed in small cars so when travelling in the winter we carried hot water bottles with us.

The house we had in Reading was at a position on the map where we had an Oxford postmark. Although the house paid rates to Reading (Berks); the children had to attend a country school two miles away in Oxfordshire. One great benefit of this was that it had a permanent teaching staff. This made all the difference. This also gave me freedom during the day to travel with George when he was visiting members.

On arrival in the Reading church the head deaconess took us proudly round their fairly new church. We did not have many church buildings in those days. I was amazed on entering the vestry to see on the vestry floor a very well worn rug. I asked the deaconess if she had such a dilapidated worn rug in her back kitchen. She got the message and I never saw the rug again. She had a very well furnished house. She was a good church worker and before we left Reading she gave Jill her violin, which was eventually given to a little Chinese girl, who became a concert pianist.

It was in the garden of our house at Hilltop Road, that Dad built our first caravan with the help of Euan who was 5 years old. He bought the chassis and built on top. The task was colossal. I seem to remember there were over 400 screws to be screwed in. I bought a mechanical screwdriver for George's birthday to make the work easier (it was a tool recently on the market). The caravan was built mostly very early in the morning. With the caravan we went down to the South Coast, almost opposite the Isle of Wight for holidays. I well remember one very wet Sabbath when we could not get out, so I started reading the Pilgrims Progress to keep us all occupied. I do not think I have ever been forgiven for that. On another occasion we had a visit from the Stokes family. Their eldest boy had missed out on his education because they had been on Mission Service in West Africa. He was not doing well at school but he started looking through one of the encyclopaedias I kept in the van and became inspired with the engineering pages, so much so that it sparked off something in his thinking and his school work improved. His parents saw a quick change in his attitude towards school.

One evening after a very stormy night when we visited the beach to have a look at the damage the storm had done. We found the beautifully made yacht, which the previous day had been ready to sail round the world. It had come out into the Channel and was caught in the storm. It had set out from the Isle of Wight in a storm when it suffered a break in its rudder. With no control, it was blown up onto our beach a complete wreck. Just one thing wrong had made it into a wreck. It lacked a rudder. These were very happy days! The children spent many happy hours scrambling in and out of the boat.

About this time I remember on one occasion I was having visitors to lunch, and lo and behold the cat from next door got into the kitchen and stole one of my precious pieces of fish. This called for a quick re-think.

While in Reading George ran a very successful campaign in Swindon. It meant a thirty-mile journey to and fro twice a week. The journey took him over the Downs, which were often in the fog. He used to take a church member over with him to help with the ushering but travelling in the fog she became sick. I could not leave the children because by this time Anita was married. He soon had to find a replacement. It was here in Reading that George started marquetry for the first time. He had had ambitions to do this for years but could not get started until I saw a special knife and equipment in a craft shop and bought the primitive little set which introduced him to the craft of marquetry. He was then able to do it in a big way. He traced his own pictures. To make his pattern he used a needle he made holes in the paper, then he dropped charcoal through the holes. Arundel Castle was his early attempt after that he did Godshill, Isle of Wight. He did most of the marquetry as a relaxation when he returned home from Swindon about 10 pm at night. Driving through the fog was quite a strain. He did his marquetry to relax before going to bed. He entered his marquetry pictures in the Three Counties Show and got First Prize for the Godshill picture.

It was while we were in Reading the girls swam the breadth of the

Thames. They attended a little village school at Sonning Common and were much happier there than at the London School.

CARDIFF 1952-55

From Reading we went to Cardiff and the journey there was a journey we would like to forget. While the furniture removers were packing the furniture and books one of the removal men was a chain smoker. George pointed out the danger to him, but he was not prepared to stop smoking. While we were in our empty house in Cardiff awaiting the van, a policeman arrived to advise us that there had been a fire in the furniture van and it was parked in a car park at Ross on Wye. We will always remember that place. Even now every time we pass Ross on Wye, I recall that dreadful day. Apparently a motorcyclist travelling behind the van saw the smoke coming out from the back of the van. He increased his speed and alerted the driver who pulled in at a nearly empty a car park, and called the fire engines. We spent the night in a hotel in Cardiff before going back to Ross on Wye. June was poorly with lead poisoning having drunk water in the night (the hotel had lead piping). In areas with lead piping it was wise to run some water before pouring it into a glass for drinking. When nearly there, we could see half burnt items of furniture etc. scattered on the roadside and we knew we were about to see the furniture van. It was really pathetic. George was anxious to rescue his bees. He lost two of the hives. We disposed of the dead bees in the car park and arranged to receive the charred remains of our furniture the next day. We lost all our bedding and much of the older furniture but George's dining room and bedroom furniture was intact.

The next day we had to come to terms with the problem. We bought beds for the children. My double interior spring hair mattress (from Knockando) was saved. It had been made from the horsehair collected from the farm at Knockando. Before I was married we had it sent to a factory where the original horsehair was made into an interior spring mattress, but it was a Scottish size bed not the normal English size, so we had to think of buying a new double bed. We slept on a mattress on the floor for four or five months until the insurance was settled. A difficulty arose with the insurance. We could only claim £500 insurance from the furniture removers. That was a maximum. This was the first time we had not taken out a personal insurance when moving. We pointed out to the assessor that one of the packers had been chain smoking when he was packing our books. He advised us to forget it. We would not have been able to claim anything if it was known that a dangerous light had been taken onto the van. We had

141

to make the best of a bad job. It was at this time that year Grandma (Alice Anderson) came back from New Zealand after visiting her son, my brother. She stayed with us until we went to Liverpool. She did not like the constant moving on to new towns because it was difficult to make new friends. Understandably she was able to buy a flat in a tenement block in Comely Bank, Edinburgh, which was not far from the Botanical Gardens. Amazingly she was able to make contact with some of her old friends in the area.

Cardiff was a return to my old stomping ground. When we went around the churches in South Wales, on more than one occasion Dad was introduced to the membership as Miss Anderson's husband. Cardiff was a good time for church work. We ran our campaigns in the church and were fortunate enough to be able to invite some of the most famous Welsh choirs to sing for us on a Sunday evening. This was quite a wonderful experience getting to know the best singers in South Wales. At school some of the children's hymns and prayers were in Welsh.

By this time we had the beehives in the garden but when a neighbour suffered from a bee sting a new place had to be found. From then on, all the hives were on the hills north of Cardiff or on an allotment nearby. The back garden in Whitchurch where we lived was not a very convenient place to keep the bees. Although our neighbour had said that he loved all animals. He loved bees until one of them stung him. The farmer was pleased to have the hives. We used to laugh when he spoke about his daughter who was married to an army man called Colonel 'Orpen Smelly'. His father-in-law always referred to him as 'Awful Smelly'. The bees did very well on the Welsh hills.

When the next move was made to Liverpool, the removal men refused to move the hives. When the removers were shown the certificate that included the bees, they replied that they did not move wild animals. Dad and June had to install the hives on the removal van themselves. While we were in Cardiff Dad slipped and got badly stung with over 40 stings. He nearly collapsed and June had to sit and extract each sting without letting the venom escape. George gave instruction that if he passed out June was to ring the emergency services. From that time on a packet of capsules for injections were always kept inside one of the hives.

While in Cardiff Dad built a dinghy and we bought an outboard motor for it. The caravan was put on the Gower at Oxwich Bay. This suited

142

our growing family very well. Oxwich was noted for its beauty. It had a long sandy beach. It was good for sailing. It was good for fishing. The church developed the South England Young Peoples Camping Site in the village. This suited us very well and occupied our limited leisure time. The first year we were at Cardiff, **Pastor Johnston** the Young Peoples Leader (Youth leader) was ill. We were requested at a few days notice to set up a camp in a field at the end of a lane at Oxwich and organise the camp. Our caravan became one of five caravans in the field next to the Camp. This delightful camp site was isolated and nearby a good long sandy safe beach. Access by bus was three times a week. Oxwich became our holiday site for the next three years. The village was quaint and the beach was long, an ideal place for recreation!

Two events helped to make our visits there interesting. The first year we were there, we found a wreck at the end of the peninsula. We also found a lobster pot lying on the beach. It had been washed up in a storm. We regularly placed the lobster pot near the wreck and one summer caught sixteen Lobster and crabs. Having become friends with the William's family who owned the beach café, they were pleased to be the recipients of the lobsters, where they were used for the 'fresh lobster teas' in the chafe. The lobsters were a great success. We also took to fishing and one summer when shoals of mackerel were in the bay. That summer we caught over 700 mackerel. In the early 1960s Oxwich had a bus service on a Saturday and Sunday. During the week the bus only ran on two days, one bus in and one bus out on a Wednesday. So we had lots of visitors down at the weekend and very few mid- week visitors. The weekend when we had our big catch of fish was soon observed by the visitors to the beach. When the beach people saw us approaching the beach after a fishing expedition, many of them came towards us and were anxious to buy some of our catch. We managed to sell all our mackerel at 2d (1p) each. They sold like hot cakes. In fact one lady became rather angry with me when she accosted me saying: "You have sold out every time I come down". In the evenings when the crowds had gone home, the children would go along the beach with a sledge contraption which they had made, picking up empty bottles for which they got a 1d or 2d (1p) at the cafe The girls worked at the café most summers and earned 10/ (50p) a week. It became a lucrative holiday place for the Bell family. With our unexpected earnings from mackerel, George and I had a weekend on our own at St David's. Who should pull up in the car park beside us at St David's but our friends, **Frances and Ronnie Bolton**. (my friend France Hayes from college)

While in Cardiff I realised the girls were about to enter Higher education and our financial means were still very limited. Much against George's better judgement I went to a Commercial College to equip myself with an ability to earn money to help with their education. Although I was an efficient Bible worker and had worked throughout my working life for the church, it was worth nothing on the commercial market. I did the (eighteen month) Course in Shorthand and typing in six months by going to the College mornings only. At that time it was not 'the done thing' for a minister's wife to go out to work, so I was definitely going against custom. I was then at the ripe age of 45 years and I was sitting in class with girls of sixteen. I had never really worked in industry before. To make this change possible, each of the children had a household task to perform before going to school. I always remember Willie Lennox laughing at Euan's weekly pay of 6d, for doing the laundry. By this time we had a washing machine. This one was a gift, from Lily Madgwick (when we were in London. They had bought it before the war. It was a big round Canadian model. It occupied quite a lot of space in the small kitchen. It was at this time that we bought a new washing machine and Kenwood food mixer. Since then I have always used a 'Kenwood' and have been completely satisfied with its service.

We had difficulty with education when we moved to Cardiff. The girls went to the local secondary school. From their conversation I gathered that the Welsh children were not very bright. However when I went over to the first 'teachers' meeting I gathered from two teachers I questioned that they were capable of doing more than what was expected from the class. They had been put into the lowest class (F or G). As I spoke to the teachers about their work I gathered they had been placed in a class where there were two places. It was recognised that they were capable of being with a higher group, but there were no available places. The next morning I had an interview with the Headmaster. I expect by this time I was rather irate. He excused himself by telling me that they were in the only class where they had two places. I did not think that was a good enough answer. As the conversation progressed I told him I felt he had robbed my two children of six months education. I was prepared to go to the Educational Office in Cardiff if he did not rectify the mistake. He eventually compromised, saying he would get them transferred to the Grammar School and they were there for a year before we left to go to Liverpool.

LIVERPOOL BIRKENHEAD AND SOUTHPORT 1955-60

I went out to work

With the move to Liverpool I had to get used to working in an entirely different environment. To begin with I had to find office work. Never having worked in an office, I had no references to offer. It was an embarrassing situation, to say the least of it. Eventually after one or two temporary jobs I was accepted at The Merseyside Margarine Factory as a secretary to the Sales Manager. This immediate acceptance happened because the Sales manager was not capable of keeping a secretary for more than a few days. He was what is called in common parlance 'a chauvinistic pig'. For my introduction to office work, I could not have been chosen by anyone worse. However during the few days holiday I had after starting I had a good talk to myself. I determined that I would return to this terrible man and in the process of time I would attempt to have him treat me courteously. It was essential for me to earn money and if this was the only way I had of earning it; I was prepared to try. This learning process happened very gradually during a period between September and Christmas. I made it my business when I was not busy with secretarial work to search through the files and learn as much as I could about the company in which I was working. When the Sales Manager eventually left in February to return to the London Office the Director asked me if I could manage the Sales Department. This involved my doing Secretarial work and caring for the salesmen. I did this willingly, but the Company offered me no additional salary. Altogether I was there for five years. When the manager of the Invoice office left I took over that responsibility. When the Despatch man left I took over his job. Eventually I was doing three men's work and that of the secretary, and I loved it. It was decided I was worth three men and a girl. This was the first time I could not engage in church work and it left George feeling very lonely and out on a limb. He rejoiced at my successful secular work but missed my organising hand. I found the experience of working in industry, a cultural shock. I saw for the first time what the workers were like. I could not understand why anyone would wish to work slowly. Like my father I had always done things quickly. To observe staff take a long period of time to begin to work was not in my nature. They dawdled over their work. They spent an inordinate amount of time in the toilet and they took days off, presumably sick, when they ought to have been at work. I had always been taught to be worthy of any payment I received. Maybe this trend went back to my maternal grandfather, who had been a manager at a Paper Mill in Sunderland. Shortly after he took over the managing of the Paper Mill, the men went on strike. He did not approve of strikes. He adamantly stated that men ought to be paid a fair day's wage for a fair day's work. My maternal grandmother, who had never had any contact with men on strike was shocked at having to mix with such people who did not do a good day's work for a good day's pay.   She is reputed to have questioned the wisdom of her husband in bringing his family to live amongst such people. She questioned his wisdom of their recent move to Sunderland by saying: "What a like folks hae ye brought us among?"

Like my grandmother I could not understand this modern way of working. It was not acceptable to me.

George reorganised the Liverpool church to make it more friendly and comfortable. He changed the seating. He used the space upstairs to make a flat for a caretaker. They had the flat in lieu of cleaning. He organised a system, making it possible to send two students to Newbold College (Adventist college), and the first two were John Arthur and Roy Gee. Both of them merited from the investment made. Years later, when we were retired, I found a note book in which the items contributed by the membership were recorded. Memorable was *2/6d (12.5p) from June who was at college, 5/- (25p) from Jill and 5/- (25p) from Margaret Jones; who were both working. We sent it to John, feeling he ought to know the sacrifices made on his behalf. We also cared for the Wallasey and Southport churches. There was a good friendly relationship amongst the members.

John Arthur
John Arthur became a pastor for the Adventist church and served in the UK for the rest of his life. He eventually joined the church administration and did a wonderful work.

John Arthur's work record is as follows:-

1961-63	Church work in the North England Conference
1963-67	Publishing Director for North England and Wales
1967-77	Publishing Director for the British Union
1977-81	Executive Secretary and ADRA Director for the British Union
1981-86	Vice President and ADRA director for the British Union
1986-90	President and ADRA director for the British Union
1990-2001	ADRA Director for the Trans-European Division
2001-2005	Publishing Director for the Trans European Division

146

John was given two awards for his work for humanity:-

1992   The Order of Mother Teresa from the Albanian President
            (this is their highest civilian award)
2006   Order of the British Empire from the Queen

Both of these were for his work with ADRA (the churches aid agency
Adventist Development and Relief Agency).

While at the British Union he ran a 26 week radio programme called
'Who Cares' on Radio Luxenburg. He designed the new logo ADRA
(Adventist Development and Relief Administration) for the church
relief organisation.   This was eventually used by the church world-
wide. When John went to Newbold College he gave up being an
architecture apprentice with the with Cammell Laird shipyard in
Birkenhead.   If he had continued with that he would have eventually
become redundant.   Instead God gave him a wonderful working life
influencing for good many 1,000's of people for this he is eternally
grateful. He called us mother and father. John's father had died
before we knew him and so we were like parent to him. We were very
proud of our son.

On a church outing to Llandudno, we had a **Chinese doctor** with us.
He had recently escaped from China. As a young doctor he had
worked in the Adventist hospital in Shanghai. When the Communist's
took over the country, the church was assured that the hospital work
would continue. It did continue, but one by one the Adventist staff
were expelled. This doctor was the one remaining Adventist doctor
left in the hospital. He thought it would be wise to apply for an exit
visa. This was promised to him on two or three occasions. Near the
time of the exit date the visa would be withdrawn. Eventually a visa
came with an early morning departure for the following morning. The
family had a few hours to get to the airport. When they left their home,
the house looked as though it was still occupied, the breakfast dishes
were still on the table. They arrived at the airport, just in time for the
London departure. Each member of the family was only carrying hand
luggage.   Miraculously they all boarded the plane before the
withdrawal notice arrived.   The doctor had an appointment at the
Liverpool Eye Hospital. He was so grateful. On this coach visit to
Llandudno, he spoke to us about his family, who were living with
relations in Southampton. He had a little girl who had to leave her
violin in her Shanghai home when they escaped. As Jill was no longer
using the violin given to her by Miss Brewer in the Reading church, we

offered the violin to our Chinese friend. Years later when travelling in America, I heard of this little Chinese girl had become a concert pianist. Her brother was the editor of the Chinese 'Signs of the Times'. Many years later we visited him in Southampton, where he entertained us and we drank tea, which had grown in his mother's garden. It was almost colourless, but had a very delicate flavour.

Meeting people returning from Missionary Service

One of our tasks in Liverpool was to meet ships coming in to the docks with visitors from different part of the world, who required help in transit. This introduced us to families from many different countries. Liverpool was the first port of call for ships trading between West Africa and Britain. There was a constant flow of missionaries from West Africa. Usually we just took them home, gave them a meal and arranged transport to their next destination. Occasionally families would arrive who had to remain a few days. One doctor came from Eastern Germany, which was then a Communist country. He was on his way to Burma. He had a new Russian made car. Due to conditions in his home country, everything of value had to be locked. He went with George to see the car into a bonded garage for the intervening week. He was anxious to take all moveable parts to keep them safe. George had great difficulty in persuading him that his car would be safe in the bonded warehouse. From that time onwards Burma needed help and it still needs assistance from the West. I have often given a thought to that missionary and his family.

We shared hospitality with an American doctor's family as they were in transit on their way to Pakistan. He had left his lucrative practice in America and offered six months service to a hospital in Pakistan. They appreciated the help we gave them and as a thank you took us out to a hotel for dinner. This was our first meal in a hotel. Years later shortly before Dad died we had a letter from the doctor's daughter who had noticed what she thought was our address in the Year Book. She mentioned it to her father. He felt sure we were the family who had entertained them and wrote to us. Dad was so delighted to think he had been remembered after all these long years.

Our Caravan

We put our caravan down at Heswall on the Wirrall and used to go down there sometimes at the weekends. At that time there were mud flats in the estuary (now overgrown with grass). In earlier times small ships would sail up as far as Parkgate but now ships use the other side of the estuary to go as far as Queensferry. Some Sabbath afternoons we were able to spend time, either walking on the sea wall or bird watching on the foreshore. The river was tidal and the water went out a long way. Tides had to be watched. It was very easy to be caught by the tide. It was at Heswall that I saw a blue moon. I had taken Euan down to the caravan to do some of his revision. In the early evening on looking outside the door, I noticed that the moon was blue. I thought that I was seeing things so I called a neighbour. It was caused by atmospherics. We were able to entertain **Ken Madgwick** and friends there before he went to New Zealand.

Uncle Jim

My father and his brother Jim married two sisters. Uncle Jim's wife was Bella and after she died Uncle Jim came to England from Canada to visit while we were in Liverpool. This was his first trip back to Britain. When he was a young man my father had paid his fare to New York. It was wonderful to hear his tales of his early days. When he arrived in New York all he had was 6d (2.5p) in his pocket. He started sweeping the streets until he earned money for his train fare to Canada. There he was able to claim land as a pioneer. His life was spent in the great open spaces of Saskatchewan. He claimed a pioneer's piece of land which was as much as could be ploughed, with the use of a horse in one day. His first job was to build a log cabin in which to live. When that was ready, he invited Grandma Anderson's youngest sister Bella Anderson, to go out and join him in Canada. She married him on arrival. They set up their home at Meota. Their courting days had started in Sunderland, when the Thomson family had moved back to Sunderland from Portobello. It was a good marriage. They had to work very hard to change the wilderness into good agricultural land. They had three children, two girls and one boy called Jim. On this visit from Uncle Jim we were all wide eyed as he recounted the story of his son, (my cousin Jim), who loved fishing. When he was quite a big boy he wanted to go fishing on the ice. His mother made him a warm outfit out of rabbit skins for this task, thus clothed he would go up North to fish. We were told that he would sit over a hole on the ice and get an abundant catch of fish. He would send his catch by rail to the nearest town. Their home was in the log cabin, and the children had to be sent to boarding school. Boarding schools were situated in a central position, suitable for the education of children from many of these out-lying farms. They usually attended on a weekly basis. Their up-bringing was like that of many other families. The neighbours in the next farm were a French family with whom they were very friendly. People living during these pioneer days had to be very self-sufficient, making what they wore and growing what their own food. They would go to the town possibly once a month.

When the children were about ten or eleven they moved from Meota. Uncle Jim changed from a farmer to a garage proprietor. He had the town garage. Eventually he became the town mayor. When he visited us in Liverpool this was his first visit home. Young Jim now had children of his own. A grandson of Jim's was not only a clever boy, but he played in the junior national ice hockey league, and he went to Harvard University. We have copy of a newspaper article about him in our family archives.

When Dad was preaching in the afternoon at Southport, we would get out of the car at Ainsdale and walk along the beach for the few miles into Southport to meet dad after the service. I remember seeing what looked like a large swollen man's hand in the water.

It was here poor Spot (the Wire Hair dog) had her last accident and died. She ran into the path of a passing car. We were very worried lest Spot's death would affect Jill who was about to do her G.C.E. exams After leaving school Jill went into a solicitors office before going to College in London to do a Teacher's training course. June went from school to College to do her teacher's training. When Jill and June finished school and went to College, they both worked in a small maternity hospital at Southport.

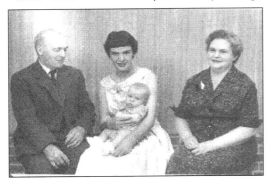

Jim Anderson with 3 generations of his family

All the money I was earning was used for the children's education. Euan (Alistair) was at Sherry's College (a private school) and June was at teacher training college. Jill was at college and then she had a job as a secretary to a solicitor. Anything left over money was saved for a deposit on a house at our next move. It was fortunate I had gone out to learn how to work in the outside world because it was a very expensive time bringing up three children. Euan was at the age where he had suddenly started to grow and frequently had to have new trousers. The girls were at College. We needed every penny I could earn.

Apart from visitors from abroad we met many of our own missionaries in transit. From time to time I meet people who have said to me: 'you had entertained us in Liverpool as we were returning home home'. We may have long since forgotten them because we entertained so many people!

HULL, GRIMSBY and ULCEBY 1960-65

We had arranged to buy a house on our next move, which was to Hull. We took over the house that the previous minister had used. It belonged to the North England Conference and was in Victoria Avenue. We moved into this Victorian house with four bedrooms. Jill was in London, June was teaching at a local school and Euan was a pupil at the grammar school. I had got a job at Reckitt & Colman's. George's district stretched over the river to Ulceby and Grimsby. This meant he had to make regular crossings on the ferry. The local Hull church was on the main road, in a small building but quite central.

YVONNE EURICK

It was here we became acquainted with Yvonne Eurick, who while sitting on a bench at Torquay met a local Hull church member. This member approached her with Voice of Prophecy (V.O.P.) literature. In the following conversation Yvonne revealed that she was a nurse in a Hull hospital and that she had belonged to the Adventist church when living in Georgetown British Guyana. She was given both the church and our address and was able to communicate with us. When she got back to Hull she was doing a midwifery course and when George heard about this ex Adventist and looked her up at the hospital. She occasionally came to church, and we invited her home to lunch with us and before long she became a pre-eminent member of the family. Yvonne had been brought up by an Adventist lady, called Aunt Ruby, in Georgetown, Guyana. Her mother had died when she was either two or three years old. At the age of 16 she had rebelled against Aunt Ruby and like other young people she wanted to go to Britain. This was allowed and she set off with £10 and with the London address of a relative of Aunt Ruby's, who had no interest in her. To earn money she worked at the Salvation Army Home and then Lyons Corner House until she was old enough to enter nursing at the age of 18. She found us when she was doing her nurse's Maternity course, five or six years later. Yvonne came back into the church and became a permanent member of our house and at that time she began to call me Mum (Ma).

After five years we left Hull and Francis and Margaret Robinson took over the responsibility of caring for Yvonne. She made her permanent home with us although still working in Hull. Eventually Margaret, Francis and Yvonne applied for Mission work at the same time. Only Yvonne was chosen. We saw her off to Ghana, with a very limited supply of essentials to work at Kwahu Mission Hospital near Nkawkaw in Ghana with Doctor John and Dr Ruth Lennox. Her luggage was so limited I had to insist that she added quite a few essential items to her supplies. I did not think one saucepan, and one cup saucer and plate, were sufficient enough knowing she would not be able to buy much in Ghana. When we took her to Heathrow Airport we met a Division representative, who was there to see her off. When she had gone they divulged to us that the Ghana Mission had renounced her appointment. They permitted her to go, in the hope that some work would be found for her on arrival. She worked in the hospital under Doctor John Lennox as administrator and Mrs Spall as matron. The directors of the mission must have known that there was a possibility that the hospital would be taken over by the Government sooner or later. This must have been the reason why they attempted to revoke her appointment. This did not take place until her second tour. When the hospital was taken over by the government, Yvonne and Mrs Spall had to arrange for the hand-over of all equipment to the Government. They both returned home on furlough. That year Yvonne was desperately thin, and utterly and totally exhausted. I had to feed her up with all the nourishing food I could get her to take to renew her energy, so that she could return to her new appointment in Nigeria.

Her return to Africa was to Jengre, near Jos in Northern Nigeria. This was the station where the **John Hyde's** family had ministered in the 1930s. They had arrived there when there was no mission work in Northern Nigeria. Years later when Louie Hyde was an old lady she told me her life story. They had arrived on a Friday night at Jengre, in the midst of a tropical storm. They pitched their tent that first night during a deluge. The next morning they had to hang up all their possessions to dry. Young **John Hyde** would be about 12 years old. It was Sabbath morning so they sang hymns and had the Sabbath School lesson. While this was progressing, they were being observed and they could see eyes staring at them through the foliage of the trees. Eventually four or five almost naked locals emerged, wanting to know how to read out of the books they were using (they had seen friends reading, when they went into the big city and they wanted to do likewise). This was a challenge to John Hyde (Will Hyde's brother). He had been working as a missionary for several years in Southern

Nigeria and felt that when natives were being baptised into the church and they should be able to read. They became Christians by the hearing of the Word only; but with no knowledge of how to read Scripture. John (Father John) believed they ought to be able to read Scripture if they were to understand the Bible. Being the type of person he was, he made a big issue of his idea of teaching. He was diplomatically advised or encouraged to go north to Jengre. This was his opportunity to put into practice what he had been propagating for some time. These four men, who viewed the missionary family through the flap in the tent, became his guinea pigs. Now he had his opportunity to test his theory by some practical work. He was really in the forefront of a fairly new movement in education. I do not know if he had ever heard of the look and say method of teaching children to read. However that was the method he used. He had used it successfully with his young son, John. Before long he had these four native men were reading simple words as a result of his experiment. He used the Gospel of John, as 'a reader', which is notable for its use of small words Within a very short time, he had these four men, who had absolutely no educational background were beginning to read from the Gospel of John. He had been inspired with this new teaching method. Young John was now, 11 or 12 years of age. Most of his education until now had taken place in Africa, under the tutelage of his father. He was up to standard educationally with children of his age in England. Father John Hyde's built a house and a mission and eventually a hospital at Jengre. It was to this house and this hospital that Yvonne found herself in the late sixties. The son John Hyde became a doctor and returned as a missionary.

After serving there for another tour, Yvonne came home with the sad news that the Jengre hospital, like the one where she had served in Ghana, had to be handed over to the Government. This was a big problem. She did not know if she would be able to return to Africa. She had done two tours in Jengre hospital. Was this to be the end of her missionary work? Before leaving Jengre however Yvonne and **Dr. Inga Kalman** went around the villages interviewing the chiefs to find out if they would like to support a regular clinic for mothers and children (1-5 years of age) in their village. The answer was 'Yes'. Inga and Yvonne decided they would like to introduce this type of medical work into the villages.

During Yvonne's furlough she went up to Liverpool and did a course at the Hospital for Tropical Medicine to acquaint herself with the latest methods on child welfare in the tropics. The most important feature was to control diarrhoea, which was endemic. A large proportion of children's deaths in Nigeria were preventable by a very simple cheap remedy. After the children became sick they soon became dehydrated and within days they would die. To begin this work a car would be necessary, so Yvonne had to learn to drive. That was not without its problems. Yvonne had passed her driving test but she was not confident. June gave Yvonne extra driving lessons before her return to Nigeria where she had to buy a car. During her years in Africa she had lived very economically, so money was not a problem (one missionary told me she lived like a native, with a minimum of furniture and very simple local food). The first car was an ordinary saloon model which was not very suitable for the rough dirt roads but it was suitable for Yvonne to drive. To begin with the chiefs made little shelters for the clinics. In the process of time money was raised from the Norwegian and the British Governments for this project and a four wheel drive Toyota minibus was bought to transport staff and medicines to the villages. The WHO (World Health Organisation) provided a gas fridge for storing the medicines. Then more substantial clinics and small churches began to be built. These clinics became very popular. The mothers were given a health lecture and a Bible story and then the children and mothers were treated. The clinics became popular and productive and the good health news spread quickly throughout the district. North Nigeria is a Moslem area, but our church had a strong presence in the district as a direct result of the work started by the 'Hyde's' all those years before. What Nurse Yvonne and Doctor Inga did was greatly appreciated by the whole district. When Doctor Inga eventually returned to the UK this left Yvonne in full charge of the driving and acted as the doctor. Eventually Yvonne had a local man **Timothy Kakwi** to do the driving. She also had a young **Dr Jon Marc** join her for few years and he loved driving on the dirt roads (I think he thought he was rally driving). By this time they had the Toyota.

Yvonne always had a great respect for our family and on one occasion she said to the girls, 'As long as I live, I will never be able to thank Ma enough for what she has done for me'. Yvonne treated me as a respected Mother. On one memorable occasion Yvonne came to me in some distress and we had one of our little chats. She began: Ma, I do not feel I am fit to be a missionary. This problem was due to her early relationship with **Aunt Ruby**. She had left Georgetown, Guyana and Aunt Ruby because of a youthful conflict of ideas and interests. Now years later as her Christian experience had developed a guilt complex developed. The problem was that although she had acted according to her culture and she had regularly and sometimes with

154

difficulty dutifully sent back part of her salary to Aunt Ruby (although I do not think Aunt Ruby was in need of it), in her heart Yvonne still retained a deep hatred for the way Aunt Ruby had treated her. She was a lady who had been kind enough in her own way, according to culture and custom. She had taken this motherless child and cared for her and eventually brought her up to teenage years. Yvonne had developed this hatred as a teenager (possibly like many another of her age) and now many years later it was surfacing. This hatred was interfering with her dedication as a missionary.

We sat down quietly at the fireside for a whole afternoon and talked this problem out. I felt there was a solution. She had to face up to it. She was about to attend the churches General Conference at Atlantic City, U.S.A, as a delegate, and I suggested that while at Atlantic City, she should fly down to Guyana and meet Aunt Ruby and in this way I felt Aunt Ruby might not be the ogre Yvonne had imagined. This she did and Aunt Ruby greeted her with all the love affection and kindness that she had always felt towards her as a little child. They got on famously together. Aunt Ruby was delighted that she had become a missionary. She made her the benefactor of her will, and insisted that at her death Yvonne should return to Guyana to bury her decently. She even gave instructions on the clothes in which she should be buried. Some years later Yvonne returned home for the funeral and fulfilled her duties.

We have spoken to many missionaries about our Yvonne and they all tell the same tale. The local people accepted her in quite a different way to their acceptance of white missionaries. She was evidently different in appearance to the Nigerians, but she was black and not white. The hospital nurses would comply with Yvonne's requests willingly, when they would have shown resistance to the requests of a white missionary. Yvonne lived very simply. To a large extent she lived on the local basic foods. Her home had a minimum of furniture. She was paid as a European, and spent her surplus money helping in the education of promising Nigerians. All this was obvious to the local people. She silently communicated with them by the life she led. Christians and Muslims heard the story of Jesus in her day-to-day life. Many a time I was in touch with Blackwell's in Oxford, buying books for Nigerian nurses who were doing a hospital course and lacked essential books. She financially helped one young man, called Johanna through his degree at the University. I am told even the beggars of the district came to her door and were never turned away. The request could be simple, often only, 'a cup of cold water Sister

Please'. When Yvonne was eventually killed in a car accident the whole district came out to her funeral. I was told the whole village walked around the church for a whole day saying: 'Goodbye Sister'. The local army Colonel was in charge of the procession and he respected her contribution to the district and he personally arranged the Order of Service on the day of her funeral. The stone we had erected was a free gift to her memory. The inscription I requested was: 'She touched us all with love'. Yvonne is one of the bright stars in our crown.

Alice and George's 25th wedding anniversary

The house
We hoped to be able to pay for the house quickly. I had to continue the work I had started in Liverpool and then in Hull where I was employed at Reckitt & Colman's. The money I earned that was not spent on education, went towards paying for the house in Hull. The plan was to have a house free of debt for our retirement. We still had the expense of Euan's education to consider but by this time he was at Hull Grammar School and then he went on to Newbold College.

My purse was stolen
While in Hull it became the custom for George to meet me on a Friday at lunchtime to do the shopping. On one occasion while we were in the market I had money stolen from my handbag. I had just been paid

156

my weekly wage. While examining fruit at a stall, I recalled a lady hustling me at a fruit stall as she pointed out an exceptionally good price on some fruit. Shortly after this interlude I realised my purse had been stolen. After reporting the loss to the market police I was asked if I would recognise this woman. Of course, as she touched me I had turned towards her. The policeman took me to the local police station where I had to answer numerous questions and to look at pages of criminal's photographs. Then we returned to the market. While I walked round, the policeman kept me in his sight. In a very short time I recognised the same lady, doing to another shopper exactly the same thing she had done to me. I alerted the policeman of her presence. The officer saw her doing the same thing to another customer and arrested her. When the court case came up she had a solicitor who accused us of pouncing on a poor old woman. The solicitor misrepresented what I had said when he spoke. Not knowing the rules of the court I intervened and re-stated my case. The magistrate told me I was not allowed to speak. The old lady was dismissed but the police officer told us as we left the station, there was no doubt she was guilty. Apparently these petty thieves do not work alone. They usually have an accomplice who relieves them of the stolen money almost immediately. When caught there is no evidence on them and the same solicitor always takes up their case.

The churches new house policy
In Hull we had the opportunity to buy our first house. The church realised the ministers needed somewhere to live on their retirement and they introduced a new scheme giving a house allowance which enabled people to take out a mortgage to purchase their own house. We moved into the church house and then purchased it with a mortgage in order to pay for the house within10 years.

My work at Recketts and Coleman
On arrival in Hull I really had to take whatever job was offered to me. I knew my age militated against me. I had attended an interview where I had stated: I do not wish to be accepted or rejected because of my age but because of my ability. At Recketts I sat in a large office beside **Madeline**, with whom I became very friendly. The work at Recketts was repetitive and not as interesting compared to Liverpool, but it earned me the money with which to pay for the house and help with the family expenses. Madeline became a close friend of the family. Some of her friends became my friends. June was now teaching and to start with she cycled to school but in her third year she changed to a school 7 miles from the house and she bought a Lambretta motor

scooter. Her first 2 years in Hull were at schools that were nearer to the house. There were times when she gave me a lift to work on the back of her Lambretta (motor scooter). Otherwise I travelled to work on the bus. On the bus journeys I met a regular traveller to Recketts. We got talking morning after morning. Her name was **Audrey** and she was Christian Scientist, so we had a lot to talk about. Her job was to edit a monthly magazine for the factory. When she heard my daughters went out walking on the Yorkshire Moors and they slept at hostels, it made an immediate appeal to her, and she joined them in some of their adventures and soon became a friend of the family. It transformed her life. Audrey now lives on the Yorkshire Moors near Malton and still enjoys walking. Madeleine lives on the Island of Mull. She married a man called McClean and his family came from Mull, where they eventually retired. We had our 25th Wedding Anniversary while in Hull when we entertained all the church members in our garden for the celebration.

Crossing the river Humber

Two of the churches were on the other side of the river Humber. Dad had to use the ferry regularly. When he went over there for the day, June would drive him to the ferry in the morning. He caught the train and hitched a lift to make his visits (there was no convenient bus service). In the evening he would phone before he got on the ferry for the return journey and we had to meet him at the docks in the evening. He became quite well known to the sailors who called him 'Sunny Boy'. Ulceby was one of the first Adventist church to be established in England. There was just a small community there in the late 1960's. It was just a small country district.

Ulceby and the Marshall family and David

Ulceby church was one of the early churches to be established in the U.K. The Marshall family had been represented since its earliest inauguration. Sometime after we arrived, David the youngest member of the family was the Sabbath School secretary. Dad heard him read a very well written report and was impressed with his ability. He had just done his 11 plus and was being transferred to the local school at Scunthorpe where the options were in the scientific line. He wished to do classics. Dad went to the Grammar school at Scunthorpe in the hope of getting him a transfer to Grimsby (which was really outside his area). It was not a normal move but after a bit of a hassle it was arranged. To do this David had a daily walk of over a mile to the station. He then had to take the train to Grimsby. After school there was the return journey. Dad had impressed upon David that he had to do well. His parents reported that when he came home from school, he went straight up to his room to do homework. He did very well with his 'O' levels and 'A' levels and had an offer from offer of a place at Hull University which he accepted. Though out his life David was hard working and he had a wonderful life working in the church. He married Anita, a young lady in Hull to whom we gave Bible studies. She worked in a solicitor's office.   On one occasion I asked Anita about her ambitions. She said she would like to write a book and she did. When Yvonne was killed in a car accident in Nigeria it was Anita wrote a book about her life.

David Marshall and his life's work

1965-8	Student at Hull University 2:1 Honours in History and Politics
1978	Graduate of Hull University Doctor of Philosophy
1968-79	Head of History at Stanborough Park School
1979-2011	Editor of Stanborough Press Ltd
1981	Ordained as a Minister

David pays credit to the following people:-

Pastor George Bell, who acted as a wise uncle and advisor, enabling him to move from the Secondary Modern school to a College of further Education, and also encouraging him in his studies and career. David reports that without this help he, like his friend at school would have gone to work for the Scunthorpe steel works, but God had other plans for him.

He also pays credit to the Headmaster of Stanborough School, **Hugh Dutton** for arranging the time table to allow him to go to London one day a week to do research for his doctorate.

David became an ordained as a Pastor of the Seventh day Adventist Church partly because of work as Religious Affairs staff sponsor while he was at the Stanborough Park School and also for his part in founding of the Hemel Hempstead church.

Ministers' wives
Minister's wives come in for quite a lot of criticism in some churches. I had just two reminiscences. One from Mrs Kent who said to me a few years before she died: I always remembered you as an example of a good minister's wife. When you came into church, you sat down quietly with your Bible in prayer until the service started. Then there

159

was the comment from Margaret Robertson in a letter on my 90th birthday. She recalled that on one Sabbath when I heard that the speaker for the morning service could not attend the service. I quietly without a fuss disappeared into the vestry with my Bible for a few minutes and then appeared and gave an excellent sermon.

Ingathering (the Adventist church charity collection for missions which is now called ADRA)

One memorable experience took place during the Ingathering. George was collecting for Ingathering around the Dock area. He noticed in a number of the warehouses, stacks of sacks bearing the same logo. On enquiring what the sacks contained, he was told they all contained peanuts. Apparently a few years previously many of the turkeys in East Anglia had been dying. Their feed was supplemented with peanuts. On laboratory inspection it was discovered that if the small germ seed in the peanut became damp, it became cancerous. This fungal infection was the cause of the death of thousands of the turkeys. From that time onwards, samples of all peanuts coming into the country had to be sent to Liverpool for inspection before they could be released.

Our five years in Hull

George always felt we were at the end of the line but it was a fruitful time and we made good friends. I made time to attend local literary lectures. They were really enjoyable. At lunchtime, I often went with Audrey to the Art Gallery. The church grew while we were there. Jill completed her teaching, Euan met Doreene and he went to Newbold College. June had her first teaching job. It was also the place where I remember two extremes of weather. One for being the worst fog we have ever experienced. One evening June did not get home till 8 pm. Then there was the winter when the snow was on the ground for six weeks and the sea froze. Some country districts had to have food dropped by a helicopter and Hull although inland it is on an estuary facing east and any weather coming from Russia hit Hull first. We didn't need summer clothes, as it never or very or rarely got warm. We were now getting near retirement age with only 5 more years to go, when we were invited to go to Erdington, West Midlands.

Sutton Coldfield in the West Midlands 1965 and onwards

Our churches were Erdington, West Bromwich Langley and Walsall. This was our last move before retirement was to Sutton Coldfield, West Midlands. This meant selling our house in Hull. It took at least

160

six weeks to find a buyer, as finding a buyer was quite a problem. I was left behind to sell the house, while Dad and the girls (Jill and June) moved into our new home in Sutton Coldfield with a minimum of furniture. We only had a further five years before retirement. Euan was at Newbold College and the girls (Jill and June) both found employment in the same school in Walsall. They decided this was to be their last move. They had been moving all their lives and were constantly leaving friends behind. They had had enough! We had the care of the Erdington church, an almost new and mostly white church where the elder looked upon the building and contents as if it was his own private possession.

West Bromwich

After a year we were asked to care for West Bromwich (mainly Caribbean and some Indian members). They met in a Unitarian church building which to put it mildly was dilapidated and filthy. The entrance to the room where we met was through a corridor (full of old newspapers, waiting to be re-cycled). I felt it was almost sacrilege to worship under such conditions. A local church member had offered a piece of land for a new church building. It was the width of two houses. Not a very promising piece of land on which to build a church and without any planning permission. This became an almost insurmountable problem that seemed to go on forever. Paul Belton an architect had drawn the plans and permission for his plan to fit into this narrow space had been rejected. After submitting the plans three times and having them rejected three times, we were beginning to think no church would be built on that plot. When Dad was in the Planning Office one day a little man sidled up to him, whispering: "Write to Whitehall" and with that he disappeared. This we did and in a remarkably short time a letter came back requiring us to re-submit, the plan and if it was rejected, Whitehall would intervene on our behalf. We could hardly believe it. Eventually we found out that the man who helped us had seen and was impressed with the Adventist Church in China before the war. We still had Paul Belton's architect plan and a very small piece of land!

Permission was granted and we were faced with the prospect of raising the money. Before the church could be built I had made 100s of lbs of jam and marmalade. There is a limit to how much jam can be sold by one small church; and I eventually discovered a very good money making device. I decided to paste shells onto jars and bottles and sell them. By doing this I could create attractive presents for Christmas. They cost me very little to produce only a lot of hard work.

161

On one occasion while in Spain, we brought more than half a hundred weight of shells back home. That gives some indication of the numbers of jars and bottles I had to collect and decorate. Many of the church members worked in hospitals and were able to sell them there. Then I had to find a suitable variety of flowers, which could be dried and preserved. This gave me the idea of making floral pictures with dried flowers on scarlet and royal blue card as calendars. June grew dried flowers in the garden. This also became a good money making venture which required very little expenditure. Dad compared concerts and this was another good way of adding to the building fund. It was in this way the money was raised for the West Bromwich Church. The Church was built, furnished and dedicated in good time (1971). I also made the kneeling stools for the platform using 13 different early Christian symbols. Grandma Anderson's oak dining room chairs were refurbished by Dad for the platform. Dad made the pulpit and communion table. It was in this way we left our mark on the church. After Dad's death, instead of giving flowers many people gave money, which was used to put in a modern pulpit to his memory.

Poem written in honour of Pastor & Mrs G R Bell by the elder of the West Bromwich Church:

> Our Pastor's name is G R Bell
> And really he's done so well
> The hours of service he has given
> To help us on our way to heaven.
>
> Has really been too much for him
> He's done it all without a whim
> And now he ought to take it slow
> And let another have a go.
>
> While here with us he's been our guide
> It hasn't been an easy ride
> He's had his share of troubles too
> Helped on of course by me and you.
>
> But he's a man who's true as steel
> And so he's made us all to feel
> That whether old or may be young
> Our first step is the bottom rung.
>
> From that we climb another one

And that's the way that we go on
May be we'll stumble even fall
Just like the man whose name was Paul.

Now G R's given of his best
And really he should take a rest
And leave the work for younger men
There's lots of scope for bright young men.

His wife she too has laboured long
And always mingled with the throng
She's very talented indeed
And always there in case of need.

If teaching she is just the tops
Of course she pulls out all the stops
There isn't one she can't pull out
She's not the one to boast and shout.

Did I hear you say marmalade?
The pounds and pounds that she has made
For here she'd earn the accolade
There's nothing better ever made.

And with a needle boy oh boy
She gives people so much joy
To see the things that she has made
Makes people envious in the trade.

Confections too are really good
I wish that I could do as good
All this she takes into her stride
And doesn't puff herself with pride.

There's much, much more I'd like to say
But as it's near the close of day
Just please accept our heartfelt thanks
For having all here in your ranks.

And may our Father keep you well
Until in heaven you go do dwell
There to tell of battles fought
There to tell of victories won.

Walsall
After two years we relinquished the Erdington church and we took on responsibility for Walsall. This was another church which met in rented premises with limited facilities. The members met in a local church hall. The membership was encouraged to develop their church building fund, so that when a suitable building was available they would have money to buy. The congregation consisted of ordinary working people with big families and small personal finances. I organised sales of work but this did not bring in much money. Dad suggested to the congregation that they give two offerings on Sabbath. The second one was to be half a crown (12.5 p) towards a new church building. More than one member thought he was asking for too much money for the church. Then I had to start all over again making marmalade and jam. I must have made hundreds of pounds of marmalade for the members to sell around their friends.   I then resorted once again to the shell vases and the floral calendars. Dad's effort developed when he saw a picture of Christ in one of the annual calendars. He collected out-of-date calendars and he made frames for the picture of Christ and sold them, mostly to the Indian members.

Walsall church was eventually purchased from the Methodists, while we were on our six month tour of U.S.A. The building was in a bad state of repair. It required a lot of alteration, to make it into a suitable place of worship for the Walsall Members. They have kept it in a very good condition. Money was eventually found and by the time the church was dedicated it was free from debt.

Langley Church
George felt very strongly that the Indian members needed an Indian Pastor. He persuaded the church administration to bring an Indian Pastor, and Pastor Massey came from India to serve his community and eventually a new church was built in Langley.

Retirement
At the time of our retirement, the Conference was short of workers and requested us to continue in our ministry although retired and on a pension. The church paid our travelling expenses and our phone bills etc. This we agreed to do this on the understanding that when we wished to go on holiday that was permissible.

Chapter 8

People I have known in my married life

Bournemouth District
I left Wales in 1937 when George and I were married. The 2nd year we were married George had to conduct his first wedding, for a partially deaf old gent to a maiden lady. To begin with the music teacher organist continued to play the Wedding march long after the pair reached the altar. She was determined to show her ability and played the whole piece, leaving the old couple standing in front of the minister, and when the time for the legal responses, the old chappie had difficulty in hearing the exact legal words which had to be repeated.

He said:

> I slight thee my troth. I light thee my troth.

With that he was shown the written word, and he joyfully said:

> Oh yes. I plight thee my troth.

He had difficulty in getting the ring on the right finger. What a dreadful first wedding.

Woolacombe Camp
That summer we were asked to help in the conduct of the second Young People's camp at Woolacombe For details see p97).

Brighton and Hove
We were in Hove during the later years of the Second World War. Not a pleasant experience, sleeping in an Anderson shelter and seeing the plate glass window of a shop sway out and back again as the result of a near-by bomb explosion.

Visitors

A girl from Birmingham
After the war we had a visit from a little girl from Birmingham, and we took her to the sea which was beyond a barbed wire. She had heard lot of bombs falling but had never seen the sea, nor could she imagine what it was like. Her first glance of the English Channel was to ask. "Where does all the water come from?"

165

A doctor soldier

One Sabbath I invited a doctor soldier home for lunch. As we started to talk I learned that he had been serving in India and that his batman had been an Adventist from Northern Nigeria. Will and Dorothy (George's brother in law and sister) worked 20 years in Nigeria and Yvonne our adopted daughter worked 8 years in Nigeria. This batman had requested the privilege of time off on Sabbath to go to church which the doctor thought was rather unusual. This doctor thought it was rather strange and unusual so he started to quiz his batman who was very well versed in the Bible and was able to supplying a very comprehensive answer. Eventually the doctor became convinced of his bat man's biblical knowledge and understanding, and he became a baptised as a member of the Adventist church. Now this man was not merely a doctor, he was the great grandson of Burton, the famous explorer whose explorations followed those of Livingstone in Africa and is commemorated as one of the famous by a statue in the square outside of Westminster Abbey. You will find it almost outside the Methodist church. I remember him each time I pass that way and am pleased to inform anyone with me that I entertained one of his relatives.

Visitor from the Canadian Prairies

Most of my visitors during the war were just ordinary men from ordinary homes. I have often recalled a tall young Canadian from the prairies. I had invited him to lunch. He had just arrived at Glasgow two days previously and felt very lost and homesick. To make conversation I asked:

> Have you any brothers and sisters?
> Yes he replied twenty three.

Thinking I had had been misunderstood, I suggested I was not referring to his church, thinking he maybe thought I was asking about the number in his home church if he came from a small isolated district and wished to know the number of church members. "Oh No said Roland, I am the youngest of 23 children, my father has been married three times!"

During my visit to the States in 1976 I met quite a number of Neufelds as I travelled around.

Soldier visitors and rice puddings

In Hove we entertained soldiers every week. It had long been our custom to have rice pudding for the sweet when we came home from church the Sabbath. On one occasion when we arrived at the rice pudding we lamented over the fact that this would be our last rice pudding until after the war was over, as we could not import rice at that time. We had not reckoned with our American guest whose parents sent a parcel of rice to our family at Hove. This was an experience which was repeated again and again. We had rice from Canada, the States, India, New Zealand and Australia. We never wanted for our regular rice pudding on the Sabbath.

War time weddings

We had two war time weddings in the church and I gave the reception for each of them, surprising the guests at the variety of unusual goodies at the feast. Possibly because I had spread my bread upon the waters and it boomeranged back to me after many days. By the way that advice was literally practiced at one of the Jewish feasts (can't remember at this moment which one).

London

Our arrival at Muswell Hill London our family consisted of Mum and Dad three children (Jill June and Alistair Euan) and a teenager Anita (she lived with us for a few years). We had accumulated on the way 2 dogs and 2 unsold pups, 4 hens and 4 beehives. Not a normal family unit for this part of London. By this time we had Irene's car but no garage. The car had been new at the beginning of the war and had been in a garage at Trowbridge throughout the hostilities and had not been used. Our house had no garage; it had been built when residents had a horse and carriage. When George was walking along the road at the back of our garden, he noticed a row of seven garages. Now at the keyhole of one garage he noticed a number of spiders webs, which indicated to George that it had not been used for some time and we were able to rent it.

The Bees

The bees were a problem, two hives went in the garden, after consulting with next door neighbours (a bee sting is a quick way of becoming bad neighbours); and two hives went on the roof of the Holloway church. Many of the London streets are lined with plane trees, which bees like to visit. Unfortunately the honey is not so attractive to look at because it is the colour of black treacle. In spite of living in a closely built up area we were able to harvest over a

167

hundred pounds of honey per season, which meant we always had a good supply. This was a time when sugar was rationed.

Visitors from Australia
Our visitors in London varied. One week we had two missionaries from Australia who had called in at Norfolk Island because the plane had developed a fault on their return journey. There were very few houses on the island where Europeans could be given temporary accommodation. Our two missionaries were taken to the Governor's house and were surprised to find that George the V1th's brother was the Governor. After breakfast they asked to be excused, because it was their custom to have morning prayers. The Duke said that he would be glad to join them as his grandfather always had a Bible reading and prayers after breakfast.
I also had two Australian missionaries to lunch who had to give accommodation to the two brothers famous in the film business because of some unforeseen circumstance.

Visitor from Papua New Guinea
We shall always remember the young man from Papua New Guinea who stopped off in London on his way to the church General Conference in the States. I had him home to lunch and in our table conversation I learned that years ago his people were cannibals. His father had eaten missionaries. Now when I was at College I recalled we had a visit from a skinny little Welshman who became quite well known in stories of early missionaries. In his younger days he had been a missionary in New Guinea, and there was more than one book describing his escape from the cooking pot. He was well known colloquially as Jonesie. He spoke to us about his early work on the island, and took quite a bit of time discussing the cannibalism that was still occasionally being perpetrated. I think he enjoyed describing the big pan they had for the cooking of the captured white man. When they came to Jonesie they took one look at this skinny specimen of a man; he was so skinny, they did not think he was worth cooking and he escaped the pot and he was able to tell the tale which today seems unbelievable. Our young visitor was the son of a cannibal and he assured us it was not now practised. He had contributed to the American war effort and on arrival in the States he was to be presented with a medal. He was a local lad and knew exactly where the Japanese were; better than the army with all their modern equipment. He had been responsible for leading the Americans to make a big capture of the enemy. His other story was that as a young lad a shark had caught his leg and he had made a spectacular escape

from the jaws of the shark and showed us his scars.

Reading
We were not very long in Reading but my indelible memory is of Miss Brewer a very dignified old lady who had seen better times. She introduced us to the newly built Reading church. When we reached the vestry I was shocked when I saw a very old frayed rug on the floor. Looking at it I asked if she would have had a rug in such a condition in her own house and pointed out that this was the house of God. She instantly picked it up and I never saw it again. A brand new rug replaced the old worn out one was in the vestry.

Liverpool and Missionaries and People in Transit
Liverpool was a busy port in the 1960's. From time to time we had to care for missionaries in transit. On one occasion we were told of a doctor and his family from East Germany who were in transit it to Burma. They arrived with a new Russian car to take to Burma. Our East German doctor realized how fortunate he was to have a new car and arrived with a system of securing any movable parts. He was horrified at the idea of leaving his new car in the garage at the docks. He was sure someone would surely steal some essential parts. George had great difficulty in persuading him that his car would be safe with the Customs.

The Indian family
There was also a family (Mum, Dad and nine children aged from 12 years to 18 months) who arrived from somewhere in the Far East; it was winter and they were clothed for the tropics. They had to meet their family in London but they were in Liverpool. They told the authorities they were Adventist's. The authorities phoned George and asked him to be responsible for them. When he saw their appalling condition, he contacted the church Dorcas society for clothes. They gave what they could, but it was insufficient, so he went with all 11 of them to the Salvation Army who willingly helped with everything but shoes. With a gift of money they all went to the nearest Woolworth's store where they followed with George leading the way, like a long crocodile line of Mum, Dad and all the others to the shoe department. They were all supplied with Wellington boots. They left in their new warm boots and their sandals in a bag. George got in touch with the London family and put them on the coach to London.

An American Doctor and his family in transit for Pakistan

We had benefited from the generosity of American's during the war and when in Liverpool we entertained an American doctor and his family who were on their way to give 6 months service free to a hospital in Pakistan. I was very impressed with such generosity. About 35 years later, we had a letter from an unknown person. It was this doctor. His daughter was a secretary in one of the Adventist American Division offices; and while browsing through a year book she recognized the name G.R. Bell and wondered if it was the family who entertained their family in England on their way to Pakistan. I later learned that a number of American doctors gave 6 or 12 months service free to allow for missionary doctors to have their furlough (holiday).

Chapter 9

RETIREMENT YEARS study and travel

In 1976, my husband and I visited U.S.A. I constantly ran into feminist ideas. I visited churches where the feminist ideas were being discussed and on my return home I read a number of the recently written books on the place of women in the Bible. My new study was a revelation, and I spoke in some of our churches from Edinburgh, Glasgow, Newcastle Liverpool, around the Birmingham area, Plymouth, three in Cornwall and 2 London churches as well as Newbold College. I have spoken to ministers within recent years, some of whom recalled my College lecture. That may be an indication of the interest it created.

Travel

Although we cared for churches after our retirement, we eventually planned to enjoy two or three months each year travelling. We had a caravan, which made travelling in Europe possible. We had been to, Spain, Portugal, Morocco, Italy, Austria, France, Yugoslavia, Greece and some of the islands, staying in hotels and camping or caravanning. This had been a wonderful experience. I enjoyed it all. I had never in my wildest dreams as a youngster ever expected to be able to travel. It was like fulfilling a dream or travelling back in time. Now, as we travelled, we had time to stop long enough to comprehend the background of what we were seeing and not rush from one site to another.

My studies at Birmingham University

I had been to Birmingham University for two years in a part time capacity. It happened this way. Over a number of years I had attended extra mural theology lectures at Birmingham University. There I had the privilege of being able to listen to nationally and internationally known theologians. After the lecture there was frequently an opportunity to ask questions and this I did occasionally. On one occasion **Dr Michael Goulder** approached me on my way out, saying I do not think you were right in what you stated Mrs Bell. I knew what I was quoting so suggested I send him a copy of the quotation. This I did on a number of occasions. Some years later, the Chair of New Testament had given one of these lectures on 'The Essenes'. At question time I made a statement contrary to that of the lecturer's. She was very negative concerning my statement and she did not approve of what I had said. Dr Goulder who was on the platform said to her:

"If Mrs Bell has used a quotation and you question it, you will receive a copy of it during the week." Dad felt so proud of me when I came home that day and told him.

Some-time later Dr Goulder suggested I go into the University to do some under graduate work. At the age of seventy I entered a new era in my life. I questioned the possibility of this new venture with Dad. He graciously said to me: "through all our married life, you have stood by me, worked with me, done much of my Biblical research. I could never have accomplished what I have done without you. Now this is your opportunity and you must take it". It was quite miraculous. It came at a time when we were free of Church responsibilities. It also came at a time when we had the money to make University possible. Unexpectedly Yvonne had made us benefactors of her will and I had the money to pay the fees (sad though it was to lose Yvonne). Apart from the lectures I attended I had the privilege of post graduate study for two years with a Jewish Rabbi and a New Testament lecturer. This has greatly influenced my thinking since. For me it was like putting a magnifying glass over the Bible as it revealed its hidden depths and with this background knowledge I have been able to use it to expand my writing and lectures throughout my retirement years. I was now reading the Old and New Testaments in the context in which they were written. My published books are revelations of the background of Biblical literature.

Note - Alice Bell's daughter, June edited all her writing and produced 2 books one on the OT and the other on the NT. They are obtainable in printed form or as book E- books (see page 169 for details).

Biblical research
I was now reading current archaeological research. This became very exciting especially when I read the report that Schlieman had made of Troy and followed in his footsteps. He was the son of a Lutheran Pastor and as a young growing boy his reading had been the Bible and Homer. He accepted Homer's Odyssey as history. I had read Homer's Odyssey and Iliad in a Rieu translation and found them a mine of information, especially in language and customs. Many people thought them to be fables. Homer wrote in 800 B.C.E. Troy was destroyed 1,200 B.C.E Schlieman became a businessman and travelled in America. By middle age he had become very wealthy and became inspired to use his wealth as he attempted to find Troy. He married a Turkish wife and was granted permission to dig at Troy. The report of his excavation was a very exciting account that really inspired

me to go to Troy. History has always been a fascination to me since my school days. Now we were able to visit Troy and unveil a picture of life as it was lived 3-4 millennia ago.

From Troy we went to Crete, arriving early in the morning. The boat arrived as the local people were just beginning to start their day's work. We booked into at a guest house. George and I started to investigate in the town, so that we could decide on our best plan of action. I found the eating places that the locals frequented, where we were admitted into the kitchen to savour the smells of the food being prepared before we ate. That was a new experience for us!

Ancient Crete enjoyed a high standard of civilisation going back to Minoan times 2,600-1,900 B.C.E. Then in l9th and 20th centuries C.E., archaeologists uncovered large palatial complexes where a high standard of workmanship displayed a unique artistic beauty. The people were knowledgeable in metal and stonework. The island was obviously strong and an important unit commercially in the Near East in the 3rd and 2nd millenniums B.C.E. An Oxford archaeologist, named Evans, who was the son of a wealthy father, was responsible for the early excavation. He had been inspired by Schlieman's work at Troy and Mycene. He was thrilled as he found the remains of a wonderfully constructed palace, including the throne. He had had an important section of it reconstructed, for which he has since been criticised. It was obvious that the civilisation had come to a sudden end. Through the years there has been much speculation as to the cause of that destruction. It is now accepted that the volcanic explosion on the Island affected an extensive area of the Middle East around 1400 B.C.E.

Mycene

On that early visit we also took time to call at Mycene on our way home (we visited it on a number of occasions some years later). Mycene was the centre of civilization that followed the great devastation in 100 BC. It spread over the Greek mainland and islands. The Great Lion Gate had been broken in the Cyclopean wall. The city spread up the hillside. Just outside of the walls was the great Beehive tomb of Agamemnon, who had lain there for centuries with his face covered with a golden mask (now in the Athens Museum). The golden scales, (also in the Athens Museum), were used to symbolically weigh his heart at his final judgement. To enter the citadel through the great Lion Gate was a cultural shock. To climb the city streets and to recall its bloody history was a sobering experience. The mighty men of the past have left the great stonewalls and faces covered with gold in desolation. It was a sobering thought!

Visit to North America

George felt he would like to visit his sister in U.S.A., but I was not very keen. I thought that if I we went it would be rather nice if we could have a comprehensive view of U.S.A. About the time when we made the decision to go, we were due to attend the G.C. Conference at Vienna. There we met quite a number of our friends from different parts of the world. One of them suggested that if we bought a car and trailer, we could make an extended stay and visit a number of friends and places. Hans Kohler, one of George's friends from College days, introduced him to an Adventist General Conference man, a Mr. Lichfield, who would help us to organise the buying of a car and trailer together with insurance. We planned to go 1976.

We left home shortly after breakfast time one May morning. We had lunch with Euan and Doreene. They took us to Heathrow. When Fiona was told that Grandma and Granddad were in that aeroplane in the sky, she thought she would never see us again. We crossed the Atlantic Ocean that afternoon. I remember saying to George, when we were above land: "Columbus would never have believed this". We changed planes at N.Y. for Washington and were met by my friend, Marjorie and Bernard Seton. We stayed with the 'Setons' for several days while we acquired a car and trailer (caravan). The car seemed enormous to us. It was a big Chevelot, with air conditioning. The trailer was small just 14' equipped with gas, water and toilet arrangements. We were soon to be on our great caravan journey, lasting six months and covering between 8,000 to 9,000 miles. The journey started in New England. We were able to visit a number of the early places of habitation, where the pilgrims landed such as Plymouth Rock and the origins of the Civil War, etc. It was a luscious land, very attractive with its little white churches dotted around. Then we were off to Niagara Falls, they were splendid and magnificent. We went over and under The Falls. I will never forget an incident shortly after we arrived. George had to attend to some item on the car at a garage, and I went to post a letter. I was told where the Post Office was and started to walk there. Suddenly I realised I was the only person walking as Americans do not walk further than their car. I was observed by passing motorist and felt so visible almost naked. I was glad and relieved to get back to the cover of the car. From there we progressed to Ottawa to visit Doctor Keith Madgwick and family. They entertained us, not only at church but also around the district. Dad felt so proud one morning in Keith's surgery. He was introduced, to one of his patient's as Pastor Bell was my minister back in the Old Country.

We also had an interesting day with Kath and Andy Mitchell and family in Toronto. They all contributed much to our visit as they showed us their new land.

From Canada we crossed the American border again, visiting Chicago, that great city and the Henry Ford district (Dearborn). It was then across the prairies. That was a long and seemingly unending journey, but very beautiful in its own distinctive way. I remember stopping at a lay-by to read a notice labelled Archaeological Site. I was full of expectation. I thought we were going to see some ancient landmark or excavation. It turned out to be a place where those who were on the westward trek in the late 1700's had stopped.

Buffalo Bill and Yellowstone National Park

Our introduction to civilisation in an urban setting was the area where Buffalo Bill was said to have originated. Then, we went on to Yellowstone National Park. It was our first National Park. Yellowstone was our introduction to the superb giant geysers. They shot up into the air at regular intervals. It was here we saw our first bear which was robbing a dustbin. I drank my first American Soda. As we were crossing a small plain, we saw a family of the ancient 'Shakers' dressed in garments belonging to two centuries ago. They were a group descended from the early settlers to America, who lived in their own settlements. They make furniture in the 'shaker style'. It is of exceptional quality and is very desirable. They do not use modern equipment. They dress as they dressed two hundred years ago and do not seem to feel any embarrassment at being so different from the people around them. They have their own schools and Colleges. I did have the opportunity later in our visit to meet the Principal of one of their colleges. I have always remembered a statement he made: "The main trouble in America today, is that parents are willing to give their children anything that money can buy, but they do not share themselves with their children." A child needs a parent at his own particular time, not at a time convenient to the parent. Yellowstone had been spectacular and memorable! To be fully appreciated, it really has to be seen. At our camp sites we had a visit from bears that was a bit of a shock.

While at Yellowstone we phoned George Emm. They lived at Calgary and invited us to visit the Adventist Camp Meeting with them. The Camp was beautifully situated, well up on a mountainside. It was well equipped to supply the requirements of church members from a large area of the country. Every essential facility was provided, from the

175

hotel and the chalets for the non-campers to the well designed Church, for the Sabbath services and Conference Sessions; to a swimming pool, recreational rooms and a site for tents and trailers. We pulled up our trailer next to the son of Dad's church elder from the Brighton Church - John Deanne. That was quite a co-incidence. He was on his way to Alaska and we were making for Vancouver.

The Rockies
Then it was on through the Rockies, they are so like all the pictures we have seen of them. They are unbelievable and staggeringly beautiful. We gazed up at the almost unbelievable beauty of the snow-capped peaks breaking into the brilliant blue sky, then down to the lake in the valley with its inverted reflection, the sight was so over-whelming; I felt I could not absorb any further beauty. We stopped and stared, drinking in nature in its natural spectacular grandeur, I felt I could hardly breathe. I was in touch with the infinite.

Vancouver
One purpose of visiting Vancouver was to renew friendship with an old college friend, **Claudia Eyre**, now Murdoch. It must be nearly forty years since we met. I telephoned from Calgary, asking her if she recognised my voice. It was very wonderful to able to meet up with Claudia after about 40 years. It was such a meeting. We stayed in their guest house and visited the **Murdoch's (Janet and Johnnie)**. I think Janet loved George. We were also able to visit **Nancy and David Bull** in their log cabin. They had a house in Palm Valley. As a boy Stanley's parents lived in a two up two down house in Watford Town. They became Adventists. On leaving school he went to work at Watford market, as a delivery boy for a stall holder who sold fruit and vegetables. In those days it was possible to have the goods you bought delivered. This was David's first job. He heard of night classes being conducted at Stanborough Press, so he joined the class to extend his education. Eventually he did his matriculation exam. While working in the Press he was asked to go to Egypt and on his return home he did a B.A. at London University, and married Nancy Murdoch. They went to teach in the Church College in Jamaica. He continued to study and eventually did a doctorate (this from a boy without an educational background). He caught the bug of education and was hooked for life.

USA
We crossed the border back to U.S.A. and our caravan was searched at the Customs lest we should be importing bugs from Canadian fruit with which to infect the American fruit. From then on we stayed in the

176

States until November. We visited as many National Parks as possible, starting with Crater Lake. Possibly a site made by an asteroid (which could be partly responsible for the chaos, which wiped out the dinosaurs). As we went south through the forests of The Redwoods, we were amazed at the height, the huge girth of these ancient trees. Some had tunnels cut through them, big enough to allow a car to pass through it. There are now restrictions on felling the redwoods. They are a natural heritage and must be preserved. When we were not in the forests we were on a coast road where from time to time we saw whales.

We made three visits to the Adventist University at Pacific Union College where **Will and Dorothy Hyde** (George's brother in law and sister) lived. After the first visit we travelled south to meet the girls (Jill and June) at Los Angeles and spent some time at **Bessie Lethbridge's** home. We bought a tent for the girls to use while they were with us for a month. We visited Grand Canyon. Jill and June walked right into the canyon and stayed over-night at a lodge along-side the river, before coming back up the next day. Dad went half way down the canyon on a mule which was a very hot journey. We also visited Brice, Zion and Yosemite National Park before returning back to see Will and Dorothy at Pacific Union College with Jill and June who then returned to England.

The return journey home was across the southern desert. This was a wonderful scenic experience. The stark beauty of the desert was unbelievable. Before going down to Florida we stopped off at the mouth of the Mississippi to take a trip on an old fashioned paddle steamer. We stopped for this on a day when a private party had booked the steamer for the day. I managed to be introduced to the Captain, explaining we were only here for the one day. He graciously invited us to join the group, telling us to mix with the crowd as though we were one of them. We were invited onto the Bridge. While talking, I told him that my father had been seafaring. He asked which line? When I told him the Benn line, he said his company entertained men from the Benn line every Christmas. We had an enjoyable and memorable day on the river. Towards October we went south to the Keys in Florida, where we had a trip in a glass bottomed boat to see the coral reefs, then north through the Blue Mountains in the glorious autumn colour of the countryside and it looked as though the countryside was on fire. A sight I have never forgotten! It was when visiting the three early sites of Jamestown, Williamstown and another town that we were shown a film to illustrate the early history. On each of these occasions I found a definite French bias in the production of the film. I interviewed the assistant curator, (who was English). She appreciated my point of view. I repeated this at the other two towns. When visiting a very elegant house near Washington D.C. that had belonged to an early tobacco farmer, I saw in one of the china cases, china that I thought was Chelsea, but it did not have the logo. I asked the lady in charge of the room if it could be identified. She brought a lady from the office with a key to open the case and my assumption was right. About a week later came a climax as we were visiting The Statute of Liberty, before going home. Here in the museum was a collection of the national dresses representing the nations of Europe. They represented the countries of Europe, the ancient lands the persecuted people had left for 'the land of the Free'. The women were depicted in their glorious national dresses. The models represented and displayed the elegant 17th century Empire gowns of France. Scotland was represented by Highland dress. The Irish model was an attractive Irish colleen. Poland, Austria, Denmark and Sweden they were all there, a colourful display. The model representing England was of a lady from the Potteries in a sackcloth dress. I was livid. I was prepared to search out the curator. George prevailed upon me saying that we only had 24 hours in this country so forget it this time. I have regretted my decision ever since!

The sequel to this event happened some years later when we were in Greece. An American was camping on the same site at Tolon. She was in Greece for six months to become acquainted with Greek history (she was the editor of a paper back home). She did not know much Greek history, so occasionally she visited us with her questions concerning the excavations. I had recounted to her my experiences of the strong historical 'French bias' I had witnessed in the introductory films about the early settlers. We had a rainy day when she could not pick oranges and started to read through some of her 'Time' magazines. In an old copy of 'Time' she read about an effort being made by the Ministry of Education to re-write junior school history. The next morning she hastened to tell me the news for which she thought I had been partly responsible. I assured her it was just something waiting to happen.

When we left America after six months of very interesting and informative travel, we were taken to the airport in a yellow cab by an émigré Russian, he was of Jewish extraction. He had represented his country as a wrestler and as a result lived in a certain amount of luxury. He had an attractive flat, plus many other creature comforts, not enjoyed by his countrymen. When it was known that he had a Jewish background and was becoming more Jewish than Russian, he was forced to return to basic Russian living. In the 1960's when there was a Russian resistance movement against progressive Judaism, his position changed. Until this time many Jews had integrated well into the community. About this time in Israel Zionism was becoming strong and there was a call to the Diaspora Jews to return to the land of Israel. Although this young man had never previously shown any interest in his parents' Judaism, he now began to think of his ancestry. He began to ask questions about his fore-bearers, and to learn the history of their struggles throughout the centuries and from where he had come. The story of the Jewish wanderings from land to land intrigued him. When the authorities became aware of his interest in his Judaism, he began to have some of his privileges withheld. He was not always called to travel abroad to wrestle for Russia. His flat was taken from him. He became aware of investigations being made about his private life. This alerted him to the cause of his problem. Having contributed to the esteem of Russia sport in America, he had become known to a few Jewish Americans who were prepared to help him get a visa. These people offered to sponsor him and he obtained a visa to go to America. All this took quite a long time, but eventually he left Russia, never again to return. A Jewish family met him at New York. Eventually he married one of their daughters. This family set him up as a yellow cab driver. As he drove us in a yellow cab to the airport he told us his story. Now he has a son. His son is going to be brought up as an orthodox Jew. It is what his inheritance demanded. Thus ended our American experience!

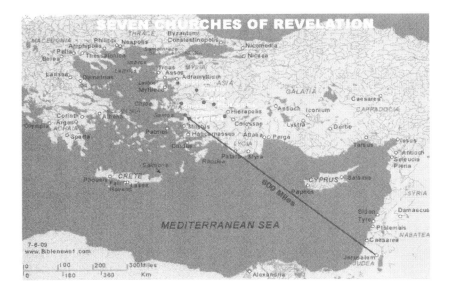

Turkey

This was the beginning of our extended holidays. We planned to cross Europe as quickly as possible. Euan drove us as far as Munich in one day. We left Dover on a night boat and he drove the car and caravan to Munich. He made his return journey on the night train after installing us on a camp site. He must have been exhausted the next day. We were then half way towards Turkey and our first destination of Istanbul. The previous winter I had spent much time on research not only on the geographical grounds but also on the ancient history. On this visit we planned to cover the area covered by the seven churches of John's Revelation.

Istanbul, our first place of call was very exciting. It was our introduction to a completely new civilization. The city had crowded narrow streets, with the human population in strange dress, with its mysterious looking shops and its immense bazaar with its glittering and dazzling products offered by strange looking men, asking exorbitant prices (especially to foreigners). They were usually willing to come down to less than a quarter of the original offer. Then there was the traffic. There may have been traffic laws, but nobody seemed to know them. Every driver had his own law. Then, as we milled around the crowded thoroughfares, we were constantly aware of the numerous mosques with the minarets piercing the skyline.

It was rather thrilling to drive along the Bosphorus and approach the ancient Constantinople, now known as Istanbul, with its almost unbroken walls that had been built to protect the city for well over a millennium. They were bathed in the golden late afternoon sunlight. We both heaved with a sigh of excitement as we anticipated what our experience in the east was going to bring us.

The site where we camped was lapped by the waters of the Bosporus and was organized like a well run European site. We were never again to find anything comparable to it while we were in Turkey. It was equipped to a high standard, with good toilet facilities and, cooking equipment and was organized by the A.A. (Auto-mobile Association). It was conveniently placed for visits to the important sites in the city.

For our itinerary we planned to visit the Santa Sophia, the first Christian church built by Constantine in the 4th century. Constantine was the son of Constantius Chlorus who died at York. His mother was canonized as St Helena. She was a Christian and had influenced her son to become a Christian. In his mature life he promised his mother that if he was successful against Maxentius at Milvan Bridge, he would become a Christian. On the night before the battle he is said to have had a vision, in which he saw in the sky, the form of a cross. He took this as an omen and vowed that if he won the battle, he would become a Christian. The battle was victorious. He was responsible for introducing Christianity to the Empire and brought in an edict of toleration of religion. He was responsible for the building of at least seven churches in Rome and the church of the Holy Sepulchre in Jerusalem. His great victory is commemorated on an Arch in Rome.

Istanbul (Constantinople, Byzantium)
We visited Turkey on three separate occasions, stopping each time at Istanbul, which is a fascinating city. Many buildings belonging to the ancient past are dominated by modern architecture. Walking through Istanbul is like stepping back in time. The city awakes to the sound of the minaret, but lives with the noise of the 20th century. In some parts of the old city it can feel like a journey through the centuries. It can be a marvellous experience but slightly weird and awe-inspiring.

The central mosques of Istanbul belong to 3rd to 5th CE century culture. In the third century Constantine had the Santa Sophia built as a Christian Church built to vie with architecture of Rome. He brought the wealth of this world to enhance the building. The obelisk in the open courtyard is Egyptian. It marked the place in Luxor where in the

13th century B.C.E. a God had spoken, and a temple was eventually built to mark the sacred spot. A decorated pillar stands in the midst of the Santa Sophia. It came from the Temple of Diana in Ephesus where it had once beautified the world famous Temple, in Ephesus, during the time of Paul. Two hundred years later Deodorus, the famous 5th century Caesar enlarged Constantine's Santa Sophia (he also built the small chapel on the top of Mount Sinai) and added the stained glass windows depicting Biblical scenes. At every turn there is a Christian symbol from the past. With the rise of the Muslim's the Santa Sophia was transformed into a mosque. At the other end of the courtyard was the Golden Mosque with its seven minarets. This is the only mosque in the Muslim world with seven minarets. The Santa Sophia and the Golden Mosque create the sky outline of Istanbul.

After entering a number of mosques, we noticed that the faithful Moslem's washed their feet in the pool outside the mosque, before entering for worship. This is an ancient custom going back to very early times. Jews wash their hands before eating, not only for hygienic purposes, but for symbolic cleansing. A similar function of cleansing took place in **the** mikveh (other nations have similar cleansing customs). As worshippers enter the mosque they remove their shoes. When the faithful are assembled, they move forward with hands joined together towards the Umbra, like a brotherhood. Non-Muslim's remain at the back of the mosque during the worship.

When we had the opportunity to visit a home in Istanbul, our feet were washed before entering the house. Our wrists were anointed with perfume, because we were their honoured guests. Customs such as these may be difficult to explain. They belong to the ancient past. As the worshipper enters the mosque, he enters without shoes. The faithful brothers linked arms and walked together towards the ambra as one person, as the sacred word was read. They all knelt together as one person in prayer, symbolizing unity among brethren.

The Muslim's have erected the magnificent Blue Mosque at the far end of the esplanade. Since entering a Muslim country, a recurring question was ever present: Why a minaret and why was the apse decorated like stalagmites? This query took me about six weeks to solve. It was important to the understanding of the land where we were travelling. I must have asked the question to at least twenty people and had no satisfactory response. One day I was fortunate enough to ask a Muslim theologian who went into great detail about the state of crisis that pervaded the country in the 7th century:-

Jewish and Christian monotheism was well known on the Arabian peninsula. Arabs were still polytheistic and in a state of crisis. Trade with East and West had made the city of Mecca wealthy and cosmopolitan. Arabs who were, once, humble and nomadic people were now losing their sense of identity and were adopting alien styles and elitist lifestyles. Old Arab customs were being abandoned and the wealthy distanced themselves from the poor. This was scandalous behaviour under past customs. Muhammad did for the Arabs what Moses did for the Jews.

My informant went on to explain how Muhammad, son of a local trader in Mecca was resting in a cave, in the heat of the day, when he experienced a vision. The Koran was gradually disclosed to him. He woke in the heat of the day, exhausted by trying to absorb all he had heard. He went out and rested under the shade of a palm tree, and when refreshed returned to the cave.

Understanding Muslim architecture was then explained. The apse with the stalactites, represent the cave where the prophet received the theophany. The minaret represented the palm tree in a refreshing breeze where he rested exhausted after the vision in the heat of the day. The name Muslim or Islam means submission. When a Muslim enters a mosque, he is coming before his holy God (called Allah) in submission. He must therefore be symbolically clean. Just as a Jew performed the symbolic act of cleansing by the washing of hands, so the Muslim is symbolically cleanses himself by the washing of his feet before entering the mosque. He leaves his footwear outside the mosque. As he enters the mosque he joins hands with his brethren, and they become one and they approach Allah in submission.

There were numerous early sites to visit before we crossed the Black Sea to begin our visits around the Seven Churches. On the way we stopped at an early Muslim site to see the Turkish Baths. Meeting a group of students one of whom spoke English we were able to inquire where the ancient Turkish Baths were. One of the students decided to escort us to the baths. On arrival she indicated to George that he was not permitted to enter. It was only for ladies. I thought I was just going in to have a look. My guide had quite a conversation with the office girl then ushered us in. As the door opened it was difficult to see anything through the steam. It looked so unreal just shapes in a grey haze. I realized they were completely naked. It was like a surreal picture of Hades. There were about 20 or more naked women all shapes and sizes, sitting round the edge of the pool. As I stood and stared I was gradually being guided along to a dressing room and prepare to join them. I had great difficulty extricating myself from that situation in explaining I did not wish to enter only observe. That was not permitted. Eventually I was able thank my companion for the trouble and beat a retreat to the safety of the city street, a very much humiliated woman.

Sardis
It was here that an early elder of the Christian Church called Polycarp had lived in the first century. He had learned his knowledge of the Christian message from John Mark, who had been instructed by Peter when he was on a visit to Rome shortly before Peter died. Polycarp claimed to have a direct line of knowledge to Jesus from Peter and Mark.

In the early 2nd century A.D all peoples in the Roman Empire were expected to worship and pay homage to the Emperor on one day in the year. Death was the penalty for disobedience. The Caesar had become as a god to be worshipped. To the Early Church this became the greatest of all tests. It was the cause of much persecution. At the great age of 87 years of age, Polycarp was brought before the court and would not give obeisance to Caesar. In his defence he proclaimed: "I have been faithful to my God for 47 years and he has never let me down, I am not prepared to renounce him now".

In ancient times Sardis was a place of healing. It was near the village where Homer was born (the ancient Greek poet of the 8th century B.C.E.). I had heard that there were hot baths in this district, where for thousands of years the local people had used this hot curative water to cure all manner of complaints. After inquiring for the directions on a number of occasions a man offered to guide us to 'The Springs'. I was prepared to follow this man but George would not follow. This stranger led me to a bungalow and we went through the main room to a bathroom. He turned the bath water on and it came out steaming hot and indicated that I should get in. I got out of the bungalow as quickly as I could and found George, who by this time had found the ancient spring, with the water bubbling out of the ground 60 degrees, and the nearby open air baths where local people had bathed in stone baths, then lay on a stone slab and let the sun dry them. For thousands of years these open air baths had been used by generation after generation to cure rheumatics and other muscular pains. Some-time later we learned that the water was radio-active (Homer the poet had once lived there).

There was a Christian church in Sardis in the 1st century. Paul was the first to send letters out to the churches from about 48 C.E. The Gospels were not written until later (some as late as the end of the 1st century). Letters were sent to the churches to teach the story of Jesus' life. The first Gospel to be written was written by Mark who had visited Peter in Rome shortly before he died. While in Rome Peter, who had been with Jesus throughout his ministry, told Mark all he could remember. Matthew and Luke used much of the information Mark had learned from Peter when they wrote their gospels.

Mark visited Polycarp, the elder of the church at Sardis early in the 2nd century. By this time a number of letters were circulating throughout the churches, with slightly different information. This was the current method of teaching the new groups of people the story of the founders of the church. Mark had been a very young man at the time of the crucifixion. His mother's family entertained the early apostles. His father was a Greek. He had travelled with Paul on one of his journeys and according to tradition Mark had visited Peter in Rome shortly before he died. Peter told Mark of all he could remember concerning Jesus and this was the basis of Marks Gospel. Mark visited Polycarp, the old elder of the Sardis church when he was a very old man. Polycarp was delighted to be able to talk with this young man, who had recently visited Peter. Church history records him telling Mark that he could accept what Mark knew, because he had met Peter who had been with Jesus throughout his ministry.

When we arrived in Sardis we found an archaeologist working on remains of what had been an affluent district in 1st century C.E. He was kind enough to show us a building where he had found a shop with an interesting inscription over the doorway that read: 'Johanan, who is a Christian', suggesting that possibly Paul or one of his converts had been there and established a Christian community in Sardis. It was one of the churches mentioned in the Revelation. Our archaeologist had recently excavated the remains of a Jewish synagogue. Jews did not decorate their synagogues with human or animal pictures, lest they break the commandment of making an image. Two wealthy Jews belonging to Sardis had made a pilgrimage to Jerusalem for the Passover. On their return they had presented the synagogue with a stone decoration, which the archaeologist found. Sardis was one of the Jewish synagogues where sacrifice was made (sacrifice should only be made at the Temple in Jerusalem, but at Sardis and Elephantine in Egypt, this prohibition was broken).

Ephesus

Ephesus was a city visited by Paul. It is now quite a way inland compared to 2,000 years ago. Excavations have revealed the main street with its shops and its library, which was possibly the place where Paul met with a group of people in the heat of the day. In the library there was evidence of where the scrolls were stored. The Codex was new and just gaining popularity.

On the main street there was a brothel, with the baths attached, and of course nearby the large theatre where Demetrius accosted Paul (Acts 19:24-29). Because of Paul's teaching many people left the temple with its accumulation of little gods to Diana. The result was a near riot in the temple where the followers of Demetrius shouted: "Great is Diana of the Ephesians". Paul's teaching was robbing the idol makers of their living. Today the great theatre is empty, a magnificent empty shell, standing silent amidst the ruins of Ephesus. The message of Paul although silenced amidst the noise of the rioters, 2,000 years ago, still echoes throughout the world.

Ephesus was the second city in the Roman Empire two thousand years ago. It was a seaport but now it is about a mile inland. In Paul's day, the main street reached from the temple on a hilltop down to the coast. On either side of the street there were shops of every description. It has an outstanding library famous for well-known codeces and called the Place of the Scrolls. It is possible that this was a place where Paul preached in the heat of the day one Sabbath. At the bend in the road was the famous theatre where 3500 people could enjoy the play. It was here nearby the theatre where Demetrius accosted Paul (Acts 19:24-29) saying:-

> Sirs ye know that by this craft we have our wealth... hath persuaded and turned away much people, saying that they be no gods that are made with hands.

Because of Paul's teaching many people had left the temple and were not buying the gods of Diana when they came to the festivals. The result was a near riot. Demetrius proclaimed: Diana should not be despised, and her magnificence should not be destroyed. Demetrius with his silversmiths called out for a whole day: Great is Diana of the Ephesians. The whole city was filled with confusion. Paul's friends got Paul out of the city quickly to save his life.

Today, the silversmiths are no more, the great theatre is empty and its magnificence is defaced and it stands in silence. The Temple of Diana has been razed to the ground, but the message of Paul still echoes throughout the world.

Laodicea

We approached the ancient ruins of Laodicea along a dusty road. At first it appeared as a mountain covered with snow. This was an illusion. It was certainly hilly, but it was not snow covered. What we saw were hills covered with calcium carbonate, formed by evaporation. It was then we recalled the description of Laodicea in John's Revelation. John saw the church of Laodicea as neither hot nor cold. When John wrote that statement he was making an analogy between the conditions in the church as it was compared to Laodicea. It was not a factual statement. The city of Laodicea was built on calcium carbonate formed from warm carbonated water which bubbled up out of the ground and poured down the hill and evaporated. Everything was a creamy colour. The church was likened to a city that was neither hot nor cold. I arose very early in the morning to bathe in the tepid water and see the golden glow of the sunrise causing reflections. I placed a bottle in the water and after a few hours I took it out and it dried into what looked like a precious stone. Delighted with my new understanding of John's analogy I wanted to share the reality of John's writings with my husband, but he was sleeping. The lukewarm condition would finally lead to a separation from God. John's further council was "Buy of me gold tried in the fire" in other words: be hot and enthusiastic as you proclaim Me. In those ancient days much gold was found in the district of Laodicea. The city was so affluent, that when disaster struck the district, the people did not have to appeal to neighbouring cities for help. They had wealth within their own city. John's analogy of gold was contrasted with the wealth and the knowledge of God.

Then John counselled with the church to put on the white symbolic raiment of God's purity. We noticed on the hillside around Laodicea that there were still herds of black goats. Their silky black hair was used millenniums ago to make the make most expensive black garments available throughout the land. Only the very wealthy people could afford such garments. This was contrasted with the white purity or the free symbolical white wedding robe, which was offered by God.

John had said in his letter counselling the church: 'Buy of me gold tried in the fire'. Laodicea was built on a site where gold was easily available. If the city experienced a disaster, it did not have to apply to another city for help they had an abundance of gold. He counselled them: "Buy of me white raiment that thou mayest be clothed".

One morning we sat beside a local family by the edge of a stream. I sat next to grandma. She was bathing her eyes with the water and filling a bottle with some of the water. She told me she would take the water home and for three mornings she would bathe her eyes and they would get better. 2,000 years ago this water was noted for curing eye complaints. John counsels the church: "Buy of me eye salve that ye may see." Laodicea was self sufficient. She did not even need gold, she produced the most expensive silks, and the hospitals could cure eye ailments. John was drawing this analogy.

The Hittites
We went 200 miles beyond Ankara to the site of the Hittites. This was an important visit for me because during my school days I had defended my faith in the Bible, during a history class. As a young teenager I had the cheek to contradict my teacher when he declared that the Hittites were only a people of fable. I imagine that he answered me with sarcasm, because it has been indelibly in my memory ever since. I imagine I was made to feel very small and ignorant in front of the other pupils. The humiliating experience has remained with me ever since.

At the end of the war I was fortunate enough to see a newspaper report of an excavation at Antalya (Turkey) where a workman had turned over a stone on which there were three languages. The Aramaic language was well known. The Arcadian language was also known, but the other language (the language of the temple) was unknown. With having two languages making the same statement it was easy to translate the unknown language. This was an important find. It opened up the biggest library in the Middle East to historians. At Bogazkoy, the capital of the Hittites there were thousands of written stones. There was a vast library written on stone to be deciphered, concerning the early Hittites of the 3rd and 2nd millennia.

The Hittites had been one of the important peoples, for some time and equal with the Egyptians. They had this vast library. They wrote on many topics. They bred horses for warfare. Until their arrival, wheels had been solid or they had four spokes. They invented a six-spoke wheel for their chariots, which made all the difference to warfare. They learned to use metal. They had introduced a new civilization and changed warfare. My history teacher thought they belonged to fables.

It was exciting to stand at the massive Lion Gate, flanked by two towers 100 feet high. The wall looked impregnable, 8ft high re-enforced by a 20' high tower every 20 yards also a very impressive was the small postern gate opening onto a tunnel 100 yards long. The Temple, in the centre of the city had been an outstanding building. Within two miles was the great open air Temple, called The Procession of the Gods in a natural triangle. On the right hand flank stood 10' tall male Gods and on the left flank the female Gods. They met at the centre of the triangle.

At Karatepe there was the temple for the burial of the kings. Here, the walls were decorated in a low relief. The god was identified receiving the priest who brought an offering for the plaintiff. It had an air of mystery. The ills of the city were also similar to what was seen on the seals. They displayed the god, the priest, and the offering.

Visit to Greece

Tolon
For a number of years we made yearly visits to Greece where we shared Denis Conroy's Caravan Park at Tolon. When we visited Tolon four years previously on our way home from Israel, it had been a small seaside village consisting of one street, in which there was a café, a grocer's shop and a camp site, with only a few facilities. Tolon is now a 'growing seaside holiday town'. Everything had increased, including the prices. Tolon was a good centre for visiting a number of ancient sites on the Peloponese.

We liked Tolon. It had a good sandy beach; the water was warm for swimming. It was here I managed to swim 300-400 yards, so it became a memorable place for me. Every evening towards sunset we enjoyed a walk through the village to the end of the pier, to see the fishing boats return at the end of the day. One year we were in Tolon for Easter. Day by day during the week before Easter, we saw men carrying a lamb home on their shoulder. This was for the Easter Feast. We attended the Easter Service particularly to hear the Greek Orthodox Easter music. We were invited to a feast at the home of the Camp site owner. At the feast I was sitting next to a German. Not knowing exactly what I was eating, I showed my unusual looking piece of meat to my German friend who was sitting next to me: 'What do you think this is Oddo?' I asked. A brief examination of the meat and the answer came: 'It is part of the intestines'. Apparently at Easter, the

189

whole lamb from head to tail is barbecued and eaten.

In the evening we attended the village church. On entering the church each person was given a candle. Gradually nearly all the village filed into the church and by midnight the church was full. At the sound of a percussion instrument (an analogy for the earthquake) all the lights in the church were extinguished. Moments of darkness followed. Suddenly the trumpet sounded and down the aisle of the church came a priest with a lighted candle. He stood at the altar with his one solitary light. Gradually every person in the church approached the original lighted candle held by the priest, and lit his own candle from the light of the priest's. Eventually the church was ablaze with small lights. During the lighting of the candles, the trumpet sounded and the congregation sang out: 'He is risen! He is truly risen!' As the Easter Service ended the fishermen processed from the church to the pier to light the candle on their own individual fishing boat. The congregation, were expected to carry their lighted candle home and light a new candle at home from the light they had received from the church. This custom had been practised for centuries. The light had to be kept burning perpetually. The light was the bringer of good fortune throughout the coming year. Easter Day services are still very colourful and meaningful in Greece.

Spending time in Tolon made it possible to visit so many ancient sites, particularly in and around Corinth, the city the Apostle Paul visited. I went to Corinth with an ancient guidebook, which had been written by an Athenian. This I found very informative. I was able to authenticate the New Testament story of the special gift to the church from a Corinthian treasurer. Corinth in the 1st century C.E. was a fairly new city and monuments were frequently raised to commemorate gifts given to the city. In the first century a monument had been raised to this city treasurer who had also been generous to Paul's new community. This monument had been destroyed during one of the many earthquakes experienced by the city. Finally it was used as part of a pavement in a theatre. Then in the 20th century an archaeologist accidentally turned it over revealing his name and his occupation.

Apart from understanding the general layout of the city it was interesting to find all the butcher shops near the temples in the Agora. Paul in his letters speaks about 'meat offered to idols'. This saying soon became relevant in a Corinthian setting. It was the custom when giving a banquet, to offer the meat about to be served to the guests, and also to the god in the Temple. To observe this custom butcher shops were situated near the temple so that the blessings of the god could be bestowed on the meat about to be served.

Peloponese
Ancient Greek cities were all over the Peloponese. The architecture was similar each with its distinguishing feature. The high hill rising above Corinth had the temple from where the Vestal Virgins descended regularly, playing their 'tinkling cymbals' as the processed to their own special seats in the Corinthian theatre. In the theatre the 'sounding brass' was placed centrally to help produce the voices of the artists.

Games were held in a number of cities apart from Olympia. One was only a few miles away from Corinth. It was here the first running block was found and a list of all the cities where Games were held.

In each city something unique was found. At the entrance to Mycenae was by the Lion Gate, with massive rampant lions carved out of a single block of stone for the gateway. Here the great cache of gold belonging to Agamemnon was found in his Beehive shaped tomb. One item, now in the Museum at Athens was golden scales. On one balance of the scale lay a little red heart, representing the life of the person who had died. On the other balance was the wing of a falcon, representing the god of the air, before whom all appear at death for judgement. Above the entrance to the tomb was a triangular shape indicating the shape of the god.

In ancient times most people were illiterate. They thought in symbols and followed symbols. One of the ancient cultural symbols was the 'lion'. The 'king of kings' was symbolized by 'the king of beasts' the lion. Every small kingdom was ruled by a king who owed obeisance to the 'King of Kings' whose symbol was the lion, the king of beasts. When men had to follow their leader in to battle, they followed his symbol. It was easy to recognize.

As we travelled around Greece it was a learning experience. Standing outside the Parthenon in Athens, we remembered a symbol common to pagan religions and Judaism. It was that of surrogate sacrifice on the behalf of sin. A yearly sacrifice was performed in the Parthenon. Two animals were chosen. One animal was sacrificed because of the sins of the people. The other one was thrown over the precipice as a 'scapegoat'.

On these regular visits to Greece, we gradually visited numerous ancient sites. Just a few miles along the road from Tolon was the ancient city of Tyrins. It had been built in the 13th century B.C.E. when it was just as distinguished as Mycenae. Today it does not attract the same number of visitors as Mycenae. The ramparts of Tyrins were massive, from 4 ½ feet thick. Like Mycenae it had a massive Lion Gate. One stone on the wall weighed 14 tons. Seeing this helped us to relate to the massive stones used on the Jerusalem wall. Several miles away was Nauplion, reputed to have been built by the son of Poseidon. This had been a highly populated district in the 2nd Millennium B.C.E

The Corinth Canal

The Corinth Canal was very impressive and it is not difficult to understand the reason for its construction. A canal had been considered by Alexander the Great, Julius Caesar, Caligula and Nero. They all had the same ambition. The work of Nero's engineers was to reduce the long voyage by sea around the Peloponese was observed when the modern canal was cut in the 19th century.

For centuries ships had been dragged between the Ionian Sea and the Gulf of Aegina to avoid the dangerous sea voyage around the Archipelago. In antiquity channels were cut to guide the wheels of a 'bollas' a wooden platform across the isthmus. Several attempts were made to build a canal. Vespasian, after the destruction of Jerusalem 70 C.E. sent six thousand Jewish prisoners to dig a canal. He relinquished the work after he became emperor. It was not until 1893, that the present canal was built, and it was then that the remnants of Nero's perfectly straight trenches were found.

Nearby the canal was the temple of Hera, a fertility goddess and Isthmia was the centre of the Isthmian Games that were held every second year. This was one of the twelve places where Games were held in Greece although they were not as important as the Olympic Games. It was here that a peculiar mechanism was found for starting the runners of the race. It was rather similar to the starting block in use today. Corinth was only twelve miles away so it is not surprising that the Apostle Paul in his letter to the Corinthians found an analogy to the Games. He would be well acquainted with the excitement the Games evoked.

Corinth

From the 5th century B.C.E. Corinth was one of the three most important cities of Greece. Homer makes reference to its wealth and its cosmopolitan society, which was due to its geographical position. Cicero suggests it imported not only merchandise but also foreign morals. Defeat and earthquakes utterly destroyed Corinth in 148 B.C.E. It was rebuilt in the middle of the 2nd century B.C.E. by the Roman emperors and some wealthy benefactors who used poor workmen and slaves. Paul's language reflects the current conditions in Corinth in the 1st century in his letters to the churches. His letters indicate the social status of the church:

> Not many wise men after His flesh, not many mighty, not many noble.

He also draws an analogy between the church and the Isthmian Games. At the Games the winners received a crown of withered celery leaves as a prize and in a shop in the Agora there is a mosaic of this scene. Paul introduced his hearers:-

> To a crown (not withered) that will not pass away.

Corinth began to rise from the ashes during the reigns of Nero and Claudius and by the end of the 1st century C.E. it had become an elegant rich and flourishing. Plutarch refers to the moneylenders and the businessmen established there. Paul's visit was made at a vital time in its development and when Paul visited Corinth it had become a city of many temples. The sanctuary of Aphrodite on the Acro Corinth rock was wealthy and influential. It possessed 1,000 courtesans who had special seats of honour reserved for them at the great theatre. The colonists built temples to many gods. Philo the Jewish historian estimates that 2,000 Jews were to be found at Corinth with their synagogues. This was the largest community of Jews in the Diaspora. Whereas Athens retained its Hellenic image; Corinth with its mixed multitude of Romans, Greeks, Jews and Orientals built their temples to their many gods. Corinth was served by two harbours, one at each end of the isthmus. One harbour looked towards Asia at Isthmia and the other at Cenchre looked towards Italy. Most of the problems in the city and church were caused because of social and religious divisions. The rich were contemptible and the poor were wretched. Paul arrived at Corinth at an appropriate time with his solution to solve the problems of Corinth. His letters are replete with the language of this cosmopolitan city.

The Temple of Aphrodite was situated on the top of the rock called

Accro Corinth, and it had a 1,000 courtesans. This contributed to Corinth's reputation for immorality to which Paul alluded (1 Cor. 6:9-20. 2 Cor.12:20-21). According to Pausanias, the image represented the goddess as armed and bearing a bow. She had images both of the Sun and of Love. As the courtesans regularly processed down the hillside to the theatre, they played on their brass instruments and tinkling cymbals (1 Cor. 13:1). An Archaeologist found a large brass drum like object. It had been placed in the theatre to control the acoustics.

Paul arrived in Corinth after an overland walk from Athens, along the Sacred Way of Eleusis. This would have been a difficult 10 or 11 miles walk, taking three to four hours. He would have passed through the cypress groves of Craneum with its gymnasiums and sanctuaries. His arrival in Corinth almost coincided with the arrival of Jewish Christians, Priscilla and Aquila who had escaped from Rome, because of the persecution of the Jews by Nero. This expulsion has been recorded by Seutonius in his 'Life of Claudius'. He related the cause of this Jewish persecution to be because of the confusion and trouble the Jews caused. At the instigation of 'Chrestos', the Jews were evermore tumultuous. Nero blamed the Jewish teaching of 'Chrestos' as being responsible for the trouble in Rome at the time of the fire; but it was thought he started the fire himself and it gave Nero the opportunity he wanted to expel all Jews from Rome.

Paul being a Jew attended the Jewish synagogue in Corinth (Acts 18:3. 6) where he addressed both Jews and Greeks. It was a courtesy in Synagogues when a stranger attended a synagogue, to offer them an opportunity to speak. Paul used this opportunity on the Sabbath when he visited synagogues in the Diaspora. When he was at the Corinth synagogue, Silas and Timotheus arrived from Macedonia. This prompted Paul to testify to both Jews and Greeks that Jesus was the Christ. This was possibly one of the most significant interruptions in Paul's ministry and as a result he was inspired to write his first letter to the Thessalonians 48 or 49 C.E.

In the 20th century archaeologists found, at the foot of a gateway leading to the Lechion Road, a lintel stone inscribed with seven letters that translates 'Synagogue of the Jews'. It may, or it may not have been the synagogue Paul attended. There has also been found on the floor of the theatre a marble impost on which was carved a design including three menorahs (the seven branched candlesticks) with palm leaves. Unfortunately they do not identify the place of the synagogue. We learn that when Paul was opposed and blasphemed in the synagogue (Acts 18:6) he declared:

I am clean henceforth I will go unto the Gentiles.

He had given the Jews in Corinth the opportunity to accept the Messiah, now he was going to offer his good news to the gentiles. After his expulsion from the synagogue he went to live in the house of Titus Justus, a worshipper of God, who lived in a house next door to the synagogue. In the first century many people were impressed with the morality of Jewish people and they became known as 'God Lovers.' They accepted Judaism but not circumcision.

The other follower whose name has come down to us from the Corinthian synagogue is name of the ruler of the synagogue. He was called Crispus an elder. He believed in God, along with his household. It was the current custom for the extended family and their slaves to worship the god of the head of the household. These accounts for the New Testament reference to: the household. Other households mentioned were Stephanus and Giaus with whom Paul found a home on his next visit to Corinth (1 Cor. 1:124). In a night vision Paul was given confidence that he would do a good work in Corinth. Confirming the time of Paul's stay in Corinth a stone found at Delphi that identified the time when Gallio the brother of Seneca was the proconsul in Achia. This was during the time Paul was in Corinth (Acts 18:12). Although most of Paul's converts were lowly people Erastus was an exception. A stone was found in a secondary use on the floor in the theatre. It had been a commemoration stone, with letters set in bronze. It read "Erastus, in return for his leadership, a Roman man of influence and wealth laid this pavement at his own expense". Paul gave Erastus mention (Rom. 16:23). The stone must have been in existence at the time of Paul.

Mycene
We were near Mycene, which had been inhabited since Neolithic times. Its period of greatest power was between 1600 –1000 B.C.E. To those who have read Greek history it is better known than some on the cities of ancient Greece. Myths and legends have originated from this period of internal strife and dissension made famous by Agamemnon, who fought in the Trojan War. Schielmann who discovered the Grave Circle was astounded at the amount of gold in the graves. Little is known about the details of religion but burial and eternity were connected. Gold had a special significance to the

195

ancients. Its colour was reminiscent of the sun and the symbol of the divine. The sun played an important part in worship. The Egyptians believed that the wearing of gold could achieve immortality for them. Kings and leaders wore gold so that they would acquire greater divinity.

The dead face of Agamemnon, was covered in a gold mask (now in the museum in Athens). It was also used to make votive objects, which were thought to assume special powers. Much of the gold that has been found was in graves because it was believed that gold given to the dead found its way to the wielders of divine power.
Visitors today are astounded as they approach the big Lion Gate and see the cyclopean walls bearing witness to a people of great wealth and ability. Above the gate is the massive triangular symbolic window (the Egyptians believed the triangle to be the shape of the god). Below were the sculpted lions, each one reaching upwards towards divinity, with their feet planted on an altar. Upward through the gate, past the granary to the great Grave Circle, which until recently had the appearance of a mound. It was the resting place of six kings surrounded by golden jewellery, bronze swords with ivory hilts, and daggers with inlay decorations. Agamemnon's face was covered with a golden mask (all these are now on display in the Athens Museum).

Epidaurus

Not far from our Greek home was Epidaurus a place of healing. The most important temple was the Temple of Hygeia, where the god Asclepeia was honoured. Myth has it that he was the son of Apollo. The sanctuary was built in the 5th century B.C.E. It continued to function until the 5th century C.E. Visitors entered by the east gate and progressed through the sanctuary first of all by performing ablutions, then entering a temple for prayer. This was not entirely a religious experience; they were expected to visit the Odeon where they were to be soothed by music. They then went to the gymnasium and then to the theatre.

The theatre is one of the best preserved ancient theatres. The acoustics are nearly perfect. George dropped a coin on the stage and I could hear the sound on the top row. He also did his 'Friend Romans and Countrymen speech' from William Shakespeare's, Julius Caesar. The theatre has 34 rows of seats, divided into 12 sections, and it can accommodate 12,000 people. The lowest row was reserved for important visitors. Concerts are still given there today. The healing was performed by the use of hallucinatory herbs, encouraging the patient to sleep and dream in the temple. The dreams during the night helped to release the tension causing the illness. There is a museum full of tales of cures.

Visit to Israel

We visited Israel at least three times. On each occasion we stayed at the Scottish Hostel, a building facing the old walls of Jerusalem. On our first morning to Jerusalem I was up before dawn and from my bedroom window I gazed on 'Jerusalem the Golden', as the morning sun illuminated the ancient sandstone walls with a golden hue. It was a picture to behold.

The Scottish Hostel commanded a spectacular position from which to get the first glimpse of that ancient city and three times we returned to wander like ancient pilgrims and absorb its history. On our first visit we learned of an excavation a few yards from our dwelling. Although close inspection was not permitted, we learned from an archaeologist who was working on the site, that the oldest piece of stone inscribed in ancient Hebrew with the name of Yahweh had been found in the tomb that was dated 8th century B.C.E.

During the same visit, I asked the Hostel housekeeper if anyone inquired about the tomb found on the site, before the hostel had been built. She was rather horrified at what I knew and hoped I would not inform any of the guests, lest they wish to leave.
 During our visits we found many interesting details pertaining to the old city. There was the pavement, underneath the level of the road going back to the 1st century. We were able to visit underneath the temple where there are numerous indications of an earlier structure. There was the odd corner on the S.E wall caused by an attempt to straighten an earlier wall. On the South West corner there was a cornice still protruding where the trumpeter had stood to proclaim the arrival of the Sabbath and Feast Days. One Sabbath afternoon we visited, probably the most nostalgic place in Jerusalem. We sat on the ceremonial steps of the temple, where the woman taken in adultery was accosted by their accusers, and the place where Jesus had said to her "Go and sin no more". In front of this wide ceremonial stairway to the temple were the relics of what had been mikveh baths where the pilgrims could ceremonially cleanse themselves before going into the temple.

The Walls of Jerusalem

The walls are of historical interest and the gates belong to various periods, but not the first century. The gateways look and are ancient, but are are not 2,000 years old. They have been places of defence. One of the gates on the south side, near the Temple would have been 'the Gate of the Essenes. It was built because of the theological differences between Orthodox Jews and the Essenes. The gate provided a way whereby the Essenes could enter the temple without becoming contaminated by orthodox Jews. Josephus records one of the many customs of the Essenes, which made them distinctive. Josephus had spent some time at Qumram as a young man and has recorded this peculiarity. On the Sabbath the Essenes did not believe in contaminating the ground by urinating or defecating. At the close of the Sabbath all the people of Essenes persuasion in the temple, rushed towards their own private gate to make a quick exit to relieve themselves away from the temple area.

Mount of Olives
Most pilgrims arrange a visit to the Mount of Olives so reminiscent of the time of Christ. The Temple was built on Mount Zion and is separated from the Mount of Olives by a valley. At the north end of the valley is the Garden of Gethsemane and on the hillside at either side of the valley are the tombs of orthodox Jews. On the night of the Last Supper, Jesus and his disciples resorted to one of their favourite places on the Mount of Olives. It was while resting there Jesus was arrested. It was also here he made his last appearance shortly before his Ascension.

It is probable that it was here Jesus was crucified. According to the Roman law, a person was crucified, in the place where he was arrested. At the place and time of Jesus' crucifixion, the people who were standing at the foot of the cross, could see the veil of the Temple being rent in twain. This could have happened at the time of the earthquake. The place of the crucifixion had to be within site of the temple.

The Eastern Gate
This gate has been identified, by archaeologists recently and is under the Eastern wall of the temple, overlooking the Mount of Olives. According to the Oral Tradition the sacrifice of the Red Heifer took place on the Mount of Olives opposite the Golden Gate. The place of the sacrifice was reached by crossing a double arched bridge crossing from the temple to the Mount of Olives. This was necessitated by the fact that the priest performing his duty in the temple must not be contaminated by the unclean graves on the Mount of Olives. By using

198

the arched bridge he retained his purity as he approached the altar for the sacrifice of the Red Heifer. This symbolized the utter destruction of sin. The sacrifice of Jesus was the sacrifice for the utter destruction of sin. The altar on the Mount of Olives was therefore a symbolic place for Jesus' sacrifice to be made.

The House of the Potter
One ancient site we found fascinating was to visit the house of a potter who was also a priest.   This excavation caused more interest than any other had done within recent years.   The house had been destroyed during the destruction of 70 C.E. Very little in Jerusalem could be clearly identified as belonging to that time. The news of the find relating to 70 C.E. was kept as a secret for as long as possible. When the news did eventually break, there was a rush of Jews to the site to gather a little earth from 70 C.E. The house owner had been a priest. According to law every priest had a trade (Paul was a tent maker). The house of the potter priests was near the temple. In his house was his pottery wheel with a half made pot. A servant who had not managed to escape was lying on the floor protecting his sword. Historically this priest could be identified. His name was known. First century literature referred to him as a cheat. Although a priest he was not honest in his dealings with other people and 2,000 years later his bad reputation has followed him.

Nazareth
Nazareth is not the little country village it once was, but it is now to a sizeable town. Although Muslims dominate, Nazareth there is a large Christian Church, built on top of a deep cave. It is said that is where an angel appeared to Mary. There is still a village well. Near the village is a hill where it is said Jesus disappeared out of the sight of his critics. What is not mentioned in the Gospels is that only four miles distance away from Nazareth there was a large affluent Roman city named Sephorisis. No doubt artisans from Nazareth found employment when Sephorisis as it was being built. Sephorisis is well known in history as the city where the Zealots destroyed the Treasury. Resulting from that incident the Romans withheld many privileges that the Jews had once enjoyed. During the life of Jesus the authorities feared His influence would again bring down the wrath of the Romans upon them.

Tiberius (Sea of Galilee)
Tiberius was a large influential Roman city where hot healing springs attracted the wealthy for healing in the 1st century. It was situated near the south end of 'The Sea' of Galilee called locally 'Sea of Tiberius'. It

199

was the sea for Jewish fishermen. What is not always realized when reading the New Testament is that 2,000 years ago Jewish enclaves were small and few and far between. At the north end of the Sea of Galilee was Capernium, a Jewish town under Roman supervision. At Capernium, a generous Roman soldier had built a synagogue for the local Jewish people and it was here Jesus healed his servant. On the lakeside there had been the miraculous feeding of the five thousand and possibly the Sermon on the Mount. Looking across this Sea of Galilee the distance are the Golan Heights.

Galilee and Synagogues

I had been attending Birmingham University and my tutor had requested me to try to identify the places where synagogue had stood years ago (synagogues could also be a house). The presence of synagogue buildings had become a point of controversy by some minimalist theologians. This was a wonderful project that I really enjoyed. The Church of Scotland minister at Capernium recommended me to visit an archaeologist, who had worked at the site of the miraculous distribution of bread and fishes to 5,000 people. He was a busy man who was happy to give me some guidance. At his suggestion that we should cross the lake, go up over the hill, then turned north, and go nearly as far as the Jewish border. Then we should descend the hill to an excavation of the ancient town of Gabeta which had been destroyed 65 C.E. There, after much searching I found what appeared to be the ruins of a synagogue. It faced Jerusalem. It was an oblong building. Just outside the building there was what had obviously been a mikveh bath with six pillars, to hold up the roof of the building, which was customary in ancient synagogues. At the far end of the building was an apse where the scrolls were kept. It had all the identifying marks of an ancient synagogue. It had not been destroyed until 65 C.E so it must have been in existence at the time of Jesus. That was a triumph. During the remaining weeks of our time in Israel, I saw a foundation stone in the Rockfeller Museum and the foundation of other synagogues in Herodium and Massada.

Galilee was known as 'Galilee of the Gentiles'. Two thousand years ago the land was occupied by the Romans, but scattered abroad in Galilee were conclaves of Jews. In their villages were synagogues, sometimes in purpose made buildings, sometimes in the Jewish homes. At Capernium there was a synagogue. Synagogues were usually oblong buildings, supported on six pillars. It was in the synagogue that the scripture was read. In the synagogue excavated at Sardis there was written on the wall "Here the scripture may be read". On the Sabbath the deacon would stand before the ark and pray and then he would take the appointed scrolls for the day out of the ark, and give them to the seven chosen readers, who would then read the portion of scripture for that Sabbath. Those who lived more than a Sabbath day's journey from the synagogue could hear the readings on the Tuesday or Thursday when they would be again read. In one year Jewish people would hear the whole of the scripture.

From the beginning of his ministry Jesus visited the synagogue on the Sabbath. He proclaimed His message in the synagogue (Lk.4:21). His message involved Him occasionally breaking the current rules of the synagogue. He brought a woman who had been unclean for eighteen years, out of her place. The place of women in the synagogue was either in a balcony or behind a curtain. Jesus brought her out of her place into the centre of the synagogue where only men were permitted (Luke 13:11-13) and healed her on the Sabbath day. He ate with the unclean tax collectors, fishermen and shepherds. He touched and raised the dead. His whole life was spent in breaking the traditions of the Jews. This we learned as we walked around Galilee. The leaders of religion sought him for years, but until they could find two witnesses to testify against him, they could not harm him. He was popular with the people and so they could not touch him. He was condemned to death by an unruly mob and the leaders of the day.

Jerusalem

We made three visits to Israel. The first visit was for two weeks, the next was a month and the third time was for a six-week period. At this time we visited Sinai. Each time we had accommodation at the Scottish Hostel where I could view the walls of Jerusalem and ponder on the tombs which for at least 8 centuries had been excavated into the rock. The one that especially interested me was the oldest recorded name of Yahweh was found on an 8th century blessing.

Jerusalem has been in continual occupation since the Calcolithic period 4,000 – 3,000 B.C.E. From that period four tombs and two houses were found and pottery which had come from Crete. Jerusalem was mentioned in the Egyptian Excretion Texts of Curses, 2,300 B.C.E. Also in Saquarra, where on the back of a bull, was written the names of Canaanite cities that were to be obliterated.

Jerusalem was built on four small hills, Moriah, Zion, Acra and Bezeitha, between the valleys of Kidron and Hinon and was only 15 acres in size. This is where Abram went to sacrifice Isaac, (he was directed to Mount Moriah). There is no mention of Jerusalem between 1,400 - 1,200 BC.E. (the late Bronze Age). As a city of the Amorites it was called Jebus. The name is interesting Jer means 'to form' and salim means 'god is life'. It was named after a Bedouin tribe. In 1,400 B.C.E., it was mentioned in the El Amarna papers when the king of Jerusalem was Asonijah-Zedec and when Joshua took Ai. When David conquered it, it was already 3,000 years old (2 Sam. 24:19-25). Araunah sold the city to David for 50 shekels. The Jebusites were still in Jerusalem when David was crowned at Hebron. He reigned in Hebron for 7 ½ years, when he challenged his military leader to take the fort by stealth (2 Sam.24: 25). It then became the political and religious centre of Judaism.

Dome of the Rock
Recent excavations have found that The Dome of the rock is built over a tomb to venerate ancestors, going back to 2,300 B.C.E. This custom of veneration for dead ancestors goes back beyond the time of Abram, who bought land from the Hittites, to prove his faith in Yahweh's promise of land. The Hittite land was the symbol of what he would possess according to the promise. The symbol of bondage was to own no land. When David took the city, his general who made the capture possible was a Hittite general named Aron. David entered Jerusalem with the Ark of the Covenant and all his people. (1 Chron 15:3). He placed the Ark in Jerusalem and according to (2 Sam. 24:25) he provided the materials for the building of the temple, which had been supplied by the King of Tyre (2 Chron 5:4, 14). Recently cypress and cedar wood was found under the mosque at the Dome of the Rock (this wood was over 3,000 years old). Solomon took the Ark of Covenant to the Temple he built over the Dome of the Rock. This had been prepared by David as a place in which to serve God. Solomon did not take his Egyptian wife to the temple. She was housed outside the city because of her Egyptian ancestry.

The Temple
The temple was rebuilt 536 B.C.E and restored 446 B.C.E., at the same time as that Nehemiah built the wall and expelled the gentiles (John 4:9). A letter to Aristeas in 167 C.E. shows that Jerusalem was reclaimed from the Selucids and rededicated. Since then Hanukkah has been named to be a perpetual feast until the end of time. Jesus attended this feast just before his crucifixion (the Feast of Dedication) (John 10:22). At the time of Jesus, Herod had rebuilt the temple which included the Council House, from where everything in the Temple area

could be observed. The gymnasium was just outside the temple, where athletes appeared naked. There were five gates, the North Gate with two large triangular stones, the West Gate, called the Nicanor gate, the East Gate or Golden Gate opening onto Mount of Olives, with its arched bridge over to the Mount of Olives (used by the priests to take the Red Heifer over for final destruction (Heb.13: 8-10) and the South Gate or Huldahs's Gate approached by a wide stairway. This was where several incidents in the New Testament are recorded.

Recently a fascinating find was made where a glass factory had once been 2,000 years ago. Amidst the broken glass was found the bowl of a glass used at the time of Passover Feast on which was engraved 'Drink ye all of it', confirming that the Last Supper was observed at the time of the Passover, when Jesus used the Passover liturgy.

In Galilee we also stayed at the Scottish Hostel, facing the Sea of Galilee (Tiberius). It was not difficult to recall the sites visited by Jesus. The contours of the countryside have not changed much. The lakeside at which the fish and bread was multiplied to feed 5,000 has not changed a great deal. It is still surrounded by villages and backed by small hills. It was here that the most successful part of Jesus' ministry took place among fishermen, tax collectors, shepherds and people with leprosy. They were all unclean people in the estimation of the religious leaders and all who were prohibited from receiving the mercies and love of God. Jesus' preaching to them was like a breath of fresh air, or like a cup of cold water to the thirsty. He revealed to them what God was really like. He gave them a hope for eternity and his message was the word of a prophet.

Capernaum
We found evidences of 1st century synagogues. The remains of the synagogue at Capernaum, is 3rd century C.E. An earthquake destroyed the 1st century C.E. synagogue. It was the tradition to rebuild on top of a holy place that had been destroyed. It is very possible that the remains of this 3rd C.E. century synagogue had been built on the foundations of an earlier synagogue. I did find 1st century C.E. foundation stones. Then at Gamla, situated on the east side if the Sea of Galilee we found the remains of six pillars, a place for the ark, and just outside the remains of a mikveh bath. In the Rockfeller Museum was the foundation stone, naming the family responsible for the building of this synagogue which was located near the Temple where Jews from the Diaspora could be ceremonially cleansed in preparation to enter the Temple. There were also foundations of one

at Herodotus, near Bethlehem and another at Massada.

Visit to Sinai

We had made an attempt to visit Sinai on our second visit to Israel, but this had not been possible as the mountain was closed to all but Greek Orthodox for a festival. To ensure that this did not happen again I spent some time investigating the possibilities. A travel group in London offered us a chance of a visit. They insisted we call at their office and become acquainted with the arrangements. This we did. The office was on the attic floor of a four-story building, with no lifts. By the time I had climbed all the steps I was somewhat breathless but Dad was not too bad. The girl in the office at the top of the stairs took one look at us and decided the tour they offered was not for us. It was for teenagers. Dad was over eighty years. I insisted that I had an appointment with the manager and must see him. He was surprised to see we were not teenagers. His tour involved sleeping in the open and on the sand. He attempted to discourage us and would not take a booking. "Go home and discuss it with your family" said he. I do not recall discussing it with the family but sent the deposit. The following correspondence offered to try and supply us with a tent. It never materialized. We joined a group of 10 teenagers at Elat and transportation was by minibus.

We soon left the road and were on the desert sand. Our driver must have travelled by compass or landmarks. The minibus pulled up at a sheltered area for the night. We had already stopped to gather firewood on which to cook supper. This first night was the most memorable. The two guides cooked the meal, which was very adequate. We then had our instructions. "When you go to the toilet, take toilet paper and a box of matches and burn the paper. We must not defile the desert. If you see your urine is becoming white, come to me immediately and I will give you a jab". I was not used to examining my urine! For a bedroom we all found our own crevice in the rocks. The party was scattered around. I had taken blow up beds and night attire. There was no privacy for undressing, but with a struggle I got into a nightdress and we settled for our first night in the desert. I began to understand how the Israelites would find suitable protected stopping places. In the early morning I heard what I thought may be a mountain lion and nudged George. He may have had his deaf ear towards me however he was not interested in identifying the roar. After some time it did eventually stop. I discovered in the morning, it was our Egyptian driver snoring, not a wild beast

The desert night sky was spectacular. I had never before seen red or blue stars or so many stars in the heaven. When I would woke up in the night, I found going to sleep again difficult. The starry heaven was such a new experience. I was completely captivated. By day we saw foliage we had never before seen, and birds, quite new to us. Our minibus occasionally got stuck in the sand, and everybody had to get out and push, except me. Daily we had to collect scrub for the evening fire but the driver would not permit a lady of my age to collect scrub or to push the coach. I had never before been treated to such reverence. It was lunchtime and very hot, the driver found a large area where we could shelter from the burning sun. I could not help but recall, the hymn that I had heard as a child, with the line: "the shelter of a mighty rock within a desert land". It was so applicable

After four days of travel, each night sleeping on the sand, we were told, "tonight we sleep at the Hilton". It sounded wonderful. But on arrival we were confronted with an enclosed area of about 30-40' long. It was surrounded by wall made with stones and erected on the wall was a canvas top. It had the appearance of a circus tent. It was the Hilton. Nearby were toilets and shower. They were a welcome addition. Dad and I went to bed fairly early. The group had to be up at 3 am. to climb the Mount Sinai. I planned to spend my time at the monastery. Dad and I arranged our place for sleeping at one end of the 7' stone bench that went the length of the wall. We went to bed at the far end. Next morning I awoke, to find a strange man, sleep right beside me. I whispered to Dad saying "Look!" and pointed to the man beside me. Since we have been married I have never had a strange man sleeping by my side. He thought it was very funny. Dad joined the group going to the top of Mount Sinai. I had a wonderful time at the monastery, seeing the ancient windows and mosaics, also visiting the library where the Codex Siniaticus had been found. I went to see, what was called the burning bush. About lunchtime, I saw one of the guides coming down the mountain, so I quickly went over to him to see how Dad had fared. He was over 80 years at the time. I was greeted with: "He is a lion of a man". Having enjoyed the hills for many years he was used to pacing himself on difficult gradients. Although he was climbing with young people he did not hold them back. They all got to the top where there were two small churches, one Orthodox and the other Catholic. On the descent they met the guide called Moses (he was German). He had prepared breakfast for the group. Dad was delighted to tell me he had breakfast on Mount Sinai prepared by Moses.

On the return journey we were able to visit some ancient beehive tombs. It was the custom with wandering tribes, that if they had a death in the family they were to prepare the cadaver, and keep it with them until they came to a sacred place for burial. It could have been weeks before they committed the corpse to a final resting place. Beehive tombs have a very ancient history. Articles to accompany the dead have been found in some of these beehive tombs. Those we saw were empty. I managed to get inside one to inspect it, but had great difficulty getting out of it and I had to come out backwards with a gentle pull from Dad, much to the amusement of some of the young people.

As we were coming near civilization, I was speaking to Moses one of the guides and told him how much Dad had enjoyed the trip. In fact he said it was the best holiday he had ever had. Moses assured me that the young people were amazed at the pair of us. We had not been a cause of holding up the trip. We had fitted into all the arrangements as though we belonged to their age group!

People
We met a lot of Israelites and also Arabs. When we were in Jerusalem Arab cleaners came up from Bethlehem every morning. They were delightful to know. We met an Adventist who was an Arab shopkeeper who had a shop in the precincts of the church at Bethlehem. The most interesting Arab story we heard concerned the eldest son of a village elder. When he was a child the Zionists came to his village telling his father that wicked men were about to raid his village. They suggested the patriarch should take all his people to the hills for safety. While the villagers were on the hills, the Zionists came to the village and stole everything of any value. They even cut down the tree his old father had planted at the time of his marriage, for the benefit of his children and grandchildren. His father a Christian Arab, was devastated at the destruction of all he owned. The local bishop arranged for his eldest son to get his education in Germany, away from the dangers of the Zionists. This young man was the first Arab to be accepted at the Hebrew University, where he was working to make it possible for Arab children to receive similar education to that of Jewish children. While we were in Israel, education for Arabs was not included in the responsibility of the State. It had to be paid for independently.

Birmingham University
It is now nearly 40 years since retirement and life has had numerous avenues of interest that I had never even considered possible. I was able to attend Birmingham University for two years doing some

research in Judaism and New Testament History. These were two very influential years in as much as the value of my study opened up the background and understanding of scripture in a way I had never approached. My tutor was **Michael Goulder**, was a professor of world-wide reputation. He had open lectures many of which I was fortunate enough to hear and meet some of the foremost men in biblical studies. For instance W. H. Anderson and his family a well known theologian, also in the States also James Charlesworth and his family, an eminent Bible scholar known world-wide for his work on Inter Testament Literature, Judaism, and The Dead Sea Scrolls etc. I also met Richard Elliot Friedman, known as one of the most eminent Jewish scholars, who was well into his 80's and was still publishing books and papers each year. It was unusual because he was Jewish scholar of the New Testament. His work covers a wide area. I also met Ceza Vermes, born a Jew who became a Christian and then reverted to Judaism. He was a fascinating speaker. I also met Alan Millard from Liverpool University who was well known internationally. Tom Richard Elliot Freidman, an American Jew one of the most famous Hebrew scholars from Houston and a popular writer, who serves on the committee for the translation of the Bible. Lein Ritmyer the Dutch architect, who spent months under the foundations of the temple in Jerusalem identifying early foundations. Hershel Shanks the editor of Biblical Archaeology Review (BAR). I also attended lectures by W.D. Davies, James Dunn, and John Polkingthorne who held the chair of Physics at Cambridge but resigned to become an Anglican priest. There were many many others.

Chapter 10

Memories of my marriage to George Bell

During our last few years of my married life we made visits by air to several islands, such as Madeira etc. By this time long car journeys across continents had lost some of their glamour. Now some of local districts captivated our interest. One very interesting journey was made to Scotland with Fiona. We gradually went up as far as John O'Groats. There we learned that there was a boat trip to Orkney the next morning. This we arranged to take at 12 hours notice. It was well worth the decision. When I was still a schoolgirl I had been fascinated with the discovery of an ancient village being exposed after a terrible storm had blown an enormous sand dune away exposing the ancient village. This was on the itinerary. The village was dated 8th century B.C.E. It revealed a village of eight houses, with sanitation and running water. Under one house they found skeletons. The guide emphasised this mystery. He had never been able to understand why the skeletons were there or find out how they came to be there. To him it was a mystery. I ran after him as he went to open up his shop and advised him about a similar custom in the Middle East. There are records of ships leaving the Mediterranean and sailing up the west coast of Britain going as far as Scandinavia. He assured me he would add this information to his little discourse. It was an interesting visit and we were shown 2nd millennium tombs and stone circles. An engineer in the 1930s had visited every stone circle in Britain, and found them all oriented to the same direction, at the same time of the year in the sky. He implied they were used to determine the length of the year and to advise the people on when to plant crops.

Our last trip before George died was down to Dartmoor and district. I did most but not all of the driving. We had been out for nearly a fortnight and were about to come home but George felt he would like to go to church at Torquay so we waited for the Sabbath. That particular Sabbath **Sydney Beardsall**, an old college friend of Dad's was speaking at church. He was so glad to see him again. Immediately after church we drove straight home. That was our final journey. The end was near.
 Before I bring this story to a close, I must highlight one of Dad's great abilities to communicate with children. Although he was not good with foreign languages he had a wonderful ability with sign language and was marvellous with children. He did tricks with his hands and with

play and sounds would keep children amused and entertained. Language was not needed. Even if the children did not know a word he was saying they were entertained. I have watched him at the door of a Bedouin encampment hold the attention of four or five Arab children. I have seen him in Turkey communicate with street children who knew nothing of what he was saying.   At No 9 Bedford Road, Sutton Coldfield (1965-'91), it was quite a regular thing for us to have the local children coming home from school to visit him in the hope of some entertainment or to play with him. He would also mend their bikes. Just before he went into hospital for the last time, I remember two children knocked at the door to ask if he could come in to play with Mr. Bell (they called regularly on their way home from school came for their few minutes of fun). He was very poorly but he would not let me send them away. "They must not be turned away" he said. He tried so hard. As I watched I saw it was just too much for him and distracted them with some ice cream. They were the last two he entertained.

I remember when we started life at Parkstone I wrote an account of our honeymoon journey. That first year was the dedication of our life to God's service. The following was our dedication prayer:

Lord Give us strength to go through with our task,
This is our prayer.

Not to be spared from the strain or stress,
But to be able to work with some success,
The job that we are given, and not to fail,
Nor grumble, nor flag, nor even to wail.

Not to be given an easier part
But to be given the will and the heart
To tackle our problems with courage and zest,
In spite of all hindrance, just doing our best.

Not to be led along pathways that please,
Taking our pleasure and walking with ease,
But to be shod for the storm and the flood,
The hills and the stones, the ruts and the mud.

Thus may we welcome the jolts and the jars,
Keeping our eyes on the light of the stars,
Conquering self, in our deeds and our speech,
Learning the lessons that life has to teach.

209

Just after a holiday:-

This is Happiness.
To wake up slowly on a bright Spring morning,
To enjoy the song of the birds as they make music to the sun,

To leisurely stroll on a country lane,
To have time to stop, and talk to village worthies,
To walk along the margin of a bay,
To pick driftwood and treasure from the sea,
To watch the sun make pattenrs like tinsel on the water
This is happiness.

To gather shells and pebbles on the beach,
To lie on hot sand, to drink in the sheer beauty of the day.
To meander home when day is done,
And hear again the evening song of birds on treetops.
This is happiness.

This joy and happiness may only happen one or two days in the year.
But the elation and the beauty of the earth is mine,
It takes me through the dark days of the year,
This happiness of seeing the perfection of this beautiful earth is mine,
Its brilliance, its colours light up the dark days of the year with beauty.

On our 25th Anniversary I wrote:

Today I look back and remember the times long since past
And we can truly say with the Psalmist,
Our lives have been laid in pleasant places.

Today I look back and remember,
The joy that came with the smile of the child so small
It was the joy only a mother can know,
It was an intense happiness, beyond all understanding,

Then one by one I saw the children grow up,
Become confident, and even independent,
It was a great joy

210

Today I look back and remember.
Friends scattered across the world,
The joy they have given me, as we have communed together.
From time to time to receive their messages of love.
This makes my heart leap up with joy.

Another Poem:

Today I look back and remember, places of great beauty we
visited
The sheer ecstasy of seeing the autumnal glory of the Blue
mountains,
The elation of standing on a high mountain.
Seeing the patchwork meadows below
The staggering beauty of sunrise on Galilee
It was great joy

Today my heart is full of joy,
The joy I have had in just living with an understanding
companion
We share each other's thoughts and memories,
The joy of his faithfulness to me and mine to him
It has been a knot of love that has bound us together
Thank God for that joy.

At Christmas time

Throughout the years at Christmas, with my gift of love I always
enclosed a special verse. I found them all in an envelope in his desk
after he died. I instantly destroyed them. This I have regretted, they
were what he treasured.
While George was in hospital and we both knew the end was near I
brought this little verse to him. During the eight weeks he frequently
asked me to read it to him.

Pastor George Bell requested this poem in the last few weeks of his
life,

Through all the years we've travelled together dear,
Along life's highway,
Through all the years we've loved and laughed together dear
Along life's highway.

211

Today I cannot do much to help you dear, but sit and stare,
But love has been unending joy, though all the years.

Pastor George Bell asked that this be read at his funeral:

Weep not for me now,
My life is o'er
My rest has come at last.

My life was full of love,
And service for the Lord
Weep not for me now, my life is o'er.

Weep not for me now,
My work is done,
Dwell on the joy, the happiness
Our friendship brought

Weep not for me now,
Remember how we served the Lord,
From youth to old age, I faltered not.
Weep not for me now my life is o'er.

Towards the End

During our retirement, requests came to me to give talks to groups. It really began at a W.I. meeting, of which I was a member. The speaker had not arrived, and I had the temerity to ask if the group would like me to give the talk. As it was near Christmas I spoke on the origins of Christmas traditions. It must have been interesting because within a month I had a request to give the same talk at the local parish church. This was the beginning of a new venture in my life. George was delighted to be able to transport me, not only in the Birmingham area, but occasionally many miles away. On one occasion I went to Abingdon, and on another occasion to Leicestershire. I was frequently invited to church midweek Women's meetings. I counted up once and realised I had spoken in over fifteen non-Adventist churches. Before George died I was giving between 50 – 60 talks in a year, occasionally two in one day and sometimes two to three in a week. I only spoke from September to March so this did not interfere with our love of travel. There was no stopping me I really enjoyed being able to entertain groups and convey to them unusual and interesting knowledge. I was delighted when hard of hearing people would say to me: I heard every word you said. On a few occasions I spoke to blind people. That was very rewarding.

Since George's death I have had to curtail my speaking appointments. I used to use a projector on some occasions. The first appointment I had with the projector after Dad's death, June came with me to help get me established. We were in a large hall with a fairly low ceiling and nearly 100 people there. June had to hang the screen from the ceiling. I instantly knew I could not cope with such a problem and speak as well. I had to work without a projector and just talk. This demanded some readjustment in the topics I offered. As a speaker I was rather unusual in the number of topics I offered. The programme secretaries were always delighted to have my list. They could invite me four or five times. I reduced my list to eight talks. As long as I was able to drive I was really kept busy. Last year I gave my car to Fiona. Now if people wish me to give a talk, they have to come and collect me from the house and bring me home again. During 2001 I gave sixteen talks. This is quite a come down, but I am delighted to still be able to give them.

Recently I was asked to speak at a Probus Club, in front of 50 men. My subject was 'The Dead Sea Scrolls'. When one of them got up to give me a vote of thanks he said: We pride ourselves in the quality of the speakers we have, but Alice Bell has excelled herself. George would have been delighted. Within a month I had a call from a Methodist Church to give the same talk. I advised them that I had to be collected and brought home. "No problem!" they said. Just recently I have had another invitation for the same topic. This is November 2001 and I have four appointments already for 2002. My present list of topics:-

      Let's Look at Christmas
      Let's Look at Superstition
      Let's Look at Tradition
      Let's Look at Words
      Let's Look at Cookery through the Ages
      Let's Look at the Dead Sea Scrolls
      Let's look at Amulets
      Let's Look at Egypt

Let's Look at Christmas I must have done 40-50 times. I have been doing it for at least fifteen years and some years I have given it five times. My topic of Words has been just as popular. I have about 20 words or phrases, beginning with 'Madam' and ending with: 'The weak go to the wall'. I give the historical background to their origin. 'The weak go to the wall' is a phrase with a cathedral origin. In days gone by the church was not equipped with seats. The congregation had to stand. In the time of our Wars of Religion, sermons became very long. A good sermon was an hour. A very good sermon could be two hours or more. This was a very long time for people to stand, particularly if they had rheumatism. The solution was quite simple. On the north and south wall of the cathedral they built a stone bench, so that the weak could go to the wall. With that I announce that "I also am beginning to feel a bit weak, and I will 'go the wall'.

Epitaph

(This was written by Alistair Euan Bell with the co-operation of his mother at the same time as she wrote her autobiography).

A girl called Alice was born in Leith, the first child of George and Alison McDonald Anderson. At her birth she was greeted by her maternal grandmother, Elspeth Thomson saying: 'She's a bonnie we lass. Her early years were spent between Leith and Sunderland, during the First World War. Alice was left fatherless at the age of six when her father, who was in the Merchant Navy, was torpedoed in 1917 off the coast of St Nazaire, France.   His last moments were on the bridge of his ship as she made her last courtesy into the depths of the sea.

Alice, a child of the First World War became rather fearful and her paternal grandmother taught her to say this prayer:-

> Four angels round my bed.
> One to watch around my head,
> One to watch and one to pray,
> Two to bear my soul away.

Although she was left without a father at the tender age of six, her father's belief in the importance of education was inculcated into her young mind.   Her mother constantly reminded her of her father's ambition to have the best education he could afford for his children. As she grew up her mother constantly inculcated his wishes to his daughter. There was never a time in her long life when she stopped learning. In her later years every day she sought out new knowledge.

Alice was greatly influenced by four other people in her formative years. At Leith Academy, it was from her history teacher that she gained an enduring love of history. He was a man, who strutted around the classroom making history the most exciting thing to be discovered. From, him she developed her enduring and great love of history, which dominated her many years. At church, it was her Sabbath-school teacher, the wife of a doctor from Barbados who was studying medicine at Edinburgh, who influenced her. This lady loved Alice as her own child and implanted in her mind a love of the Bible. Alice loved her with an enduring love, and when Mrs Cave had to leave Edinburgh with her husband to open a health centre in Barbados, she extracted a promise from her protégé that she would attend Stanborough College and would become a 'worker for God'. As a

215

teenager she began the fulfilment of that promise. She went to Stanborough College. She became a Bible worker in Scotland and Wales. She co-operated as a Bible worker with my father, Pastor George Bell throughout their years in the Ministry and even in her years of retirement she still fulfilled her early promise.

Another mentor was Miss Jane Archibald, a remarkable woman. In retrospect she was a minister, but was called a Bible worker. She possibly did more for the work of the church in Scotland than any other worker of her generation. As she prepared Alice at the age of fifteen years to go to Stanborough College and impressed upon her mind the idea of the equality of the sexes. More than once she said, you can do as well as any boy. Jane Archibald was an unusual lady, very much in advance of her age and undoubtedly it was her influence that was behind my mother's teaching on 'The Place of Women in the Bible'. In numerous churches in the 1970's through out the Midlands and beyond, she was able to speak in churches, from as far north as Dundee in Scotland down to Cornwall on this topic.

Alice's other mentor was George Baird, the history teacher at Stanborough College. She recalled the many times she was transfixed as she listened to this Irishman's approach to history. His influence led her into a life-long interest in archaeology. These four mentors were all good communicators, they infected their listeners with their enthusiasm; those who listened to them remembered for years what they had heard. The magnetism of communication of each of these mentors rubbed off on my mother. Her one pride and joy, which her family tried to keep in check, were the numerous times people said to her: I remember the sermon you gave 'x' years ago. This happened with regularity throughout the years and gave her great joy.

As many church members will recall, my Mother like her four mentors before her, had the capacity to convey the interest and the enthusiasm of her topic to others. She became a well known and revealing preacher not only in Adventist churches. She also had the privilege of being invited to fifteen non-Adventist churches, including Catholic and Brethren. Her sermons were noted for revealing the historical background and original meaning of the original language. To a large extent she acquired some of this knowledge after she was sixty years of age. She frequented University Theology lectures and as was the custom at the end of a lecture she occasionally asked a question or made a comment. On one occasion **Dr. Goulder** said to her as she left the classroom: I do not think what you were correct in what you stated. Her reply was: I will send you a copy of the quotation. On a later occasion when the Chair of New |Testament had given the lecture, she again made a statement at the end of the lecture. The lady questioned what she had said. Dr Goulder who was in the Chair, said publicly: "If you question a statement made by Mrs Bell you will have a copy of the original by the middle of the week." With Dr Goulder's encouragement she was able to have two post graduate years at Birmingham University at the age of seventy (this was unusual at this time to start serious study) and she studied with a well known New Testament lecturer and a Jewish Rabbi. This was for Alice a most exciting and a very rewarding intellectual experience. It laid the foundation for over thirty years of her research into the understanding of the colloquial language, the background history and the culture and customs of the Bible. She constantly described this experience as if she had had a magnifying glass over the sacred word. She began to understand the implicit message of the Bible, as it was originally written, and not as it had become cluttered with the presuppositions and misinterpretations of modern times. This knowledge she felt impelled to share with hundreds of people through her books: 'Magnify They Word', 'Jesus Judaism and Miracles', 'Jesus Judaism and Parables', 'Genesis - Primeval Age', 'Genesis - Patriarchal Age', and her preaching.* (p 176) She preached not only in Adventist churches, but wherever she had the privilege to speak. Her great pleasure was to hear one of her congregation say: "I am going home to re-read my Bible". For many years she gave 50 to 60 talks between September and March. When she became slightly handicapped, she gave an average of 16 talks a year at churches and clubs throughout Birmingham and the surrounding area. During her later years, when people wished her to speak they had to collect her, and return her home after the talk. In her ninetieth year, she spoke at a Probus Club to over fifty men, on the topic of the 'The Dead Sea Scrolls'. The member who gave the vote of thanks after her talk said "We pride ourselves in the quality of our speakers, but Alice Bell has excelled them". Her response was 'Oh if only George could have heard that what a joy it would have been to him. He was the one with whom she wished to share all her joys. Within a few weeks of that event a call came to speak to the Methodists. Her usual response was "You know I am slightly handicapped you would have to collect me and bring me home again. "No problem", came the reply. Within the next three to four months she had to speak on the same topic at five churches and clubs. Very often at the end of her talk, people rendering personal thanks would call her 'a remarkable woman'. She would add:

217

"Oh no, I'm not! I'm just doing what God has empowered me to do". Frequently she was thanked for making the Bible more understandable.

Alice throughout her life always followed an individual line. Her length of days, were spent in learning. Leading where truth led her. She spent her life in a long search for truth and whenever she found it, she led where it followed and sought to lead others where truth led her. Towards the end of her life she was frequently heard to say: I have had a good life. I have been able to accomplish much more than I ever anticipated as a teenager. I have had a good husband and family, I have travelled far beyond my early dreams or hopes. I have worked hard, I have been greatly blessed, I have lived long enough. I am ready to meet my Maker. Today the Great Scorer has come to write against her name. May she rest in peace.

*June has put all her mothers work into three books

Alice Bell's research into Genesis and the names for God

The New Testament,
The beatitudes
The Sabbath miracles
The Parables
 Jesus attitude to women
 Wine in the New Testament
 The life of Paul (Saul)

 Autobiography a girl called Alice

They can be purchased as a printed book, or as an E-book from Amazon

Appendix

The Bell story

The grave in South America

George Richard Bell (1897-1914) was buried in Punta Arenas and his grave was in the main cemetery for the first 10 years because the company had made a payment for the maintenance of the grave for the first 10 years. Then when no further payments were made he was moved to a communal grave. This is normal procedure in South America. A friend of June's visited the cemetery in 2005 and was able to get photocopies of all the details.

Richard 'George' Bell with his wife Hannah and children - Dorothy Irene and George

Richard George Bell 1879-1914
The Great Grandfather (George Richard Bell) died in 1895 leaving his children orphaned. The children were George Richard, Joseph, Susan and Lizzie. George Richard went to work for his Uncle William who was a foreman fell monger in Carnforth, Lancashire, and the others who were younger were taken into Dr Barnardo's Home at Birkenhead; because the relatives had large families and were unable to help. Eventually Joseph was sent to Canada to work on a farm and the sisters worked as maids in the Manchester area.

Unknown to us the Grandfather George Richard Bell had sent money to his brother Joseph who was in Canada and this money helped him buy a bicycle. These details were on a Post Card sent from Punta Arenas to Joseph and discovered by his Grandson Keith. This helped to re-unite the family in the 1990's.

219

George Richard courted Hannah Bland on the banks of the river Lune, she had a beautiful head of very long hair and the Grandfather was completely smitten. Hannah spent much of her teenage years with an old aunt who taught her to crochet and sew. She would not marry George Richard until he had saved £100. They married and moved to Merthyr Tydfil, South Wales where he managed a fell monger business. They had a flat above a row of shops and in the 1970's the then owner of the shop could remember where the factory had been and told us it was demolished in the 1920's. During this time they attended the Methodist church and sang in the choir. They were well known in the area and took an active part in the community. Their first child Dorothy (1902-2003) was born here. Just after this time they moved to a new work contract in Southern Ireland (Wexford Eire) where George (1905-'91) was born. They then returned to Merthyr where Irene (1907-'51) was born.

They saw an advertisement for a Manager's job in Punta Arenas, South America and they left for what they thought it would be a better life for the children. They did not realize how isolated and rural this factory would be. They were 5 miles away from the town. The supply ship arrived twice a year. They had to take care of their yeast and save some of it for the next bake in order to make their daily bread. The children were given a chop instead of sweets. They were dependent on a lot of meat for nourishment and for this they killed one sheep every week. The area was wild and windy. They found plenty of wild mushrooms which they picked and cooked and this was their only fresh vegetable. They fenced in a garden to try and grow a few vegetables.

The Family
The children rode to school on horseback. One day when they were leaving school Dorothy's or Irene's horse tore the skirt off the teacher as she was helping her onto her horse. Edward (1911-2000) was born out there. Their closest friends were the Buchanan's and they were 10 miles away. One Christmas Eve the children hung up their stockings for Father Christmas and when they woke up they had many more presents than usual; so the following year they thought they would help Father Christmas by hanging up pillowcases. In the morning when they woke up the pillowcases were full of wood for the fire. Their dad knew he had to teach his children a lesson and this one was remembered for the rest of their lives. Children should not to be greedy.

George and the Police

One memorable day George took some friends back to the town in the horse and cart, he was chosen to go because he was smaller than an adult, he could squeeze in to the seating space and he was also a very good driver. When he was returning home he was chased by the police, but they could not catch him. The road was badly rutted and he was very knowledgeable about the ruts and tracks. George was in one track and the police were in the other track. When the tracks split into two, George was in the one that led home and the police were in the other track and could not catch him. George went racing along in his cart track got home safely. The police did not normally leave the town but there had been a murder and they thought George could help them. When the police found they had lost George they returned to the safety of the town. Outside the town there was no law and order and it was every man for himself. Each family had to look after their own security.

George and the Crayon Stuck in his Ear

Another time George stuck a crayon in his ear and Hannah (his mother) had to return with him to Liverpool for surgery which was unsuccessful. It was not until they were on their way back to South America and on the high seas that the crayon eventually came out; unfortunately he suffered from ear ache and ear infection for the rest of his life.

The Shackleton Expedition and George Richard Bell

After an unsuccessful expedition Shackleton (the Antarctic explorer) was frozen into the sea ice for the winter. When the sea ice melted his ship the Endurance sank leaving Shackleton and his men with two life boats. They got as far as Elephant Island and then Shackleton made one good boat from the two and sailed 800 miles to South Georgia, but due to the wind and tides he landed on the wrong side of the island. They then had to climb the 10,000 foot glaciated mountains to get to a whaling station on the other side of the island. This was the only human habitation on the island. They arrived in an utter state of exhaustion. The Whalers took them to Punta Arenas to get help. Shackleton had great difficulty in finding help. But eventually the traders of Punta Arenas grouped together and collected enough money to hire a boat in which Shackleton returned to rescue his men. It was a dangerous under taking, the boat was not very seaworthy, but the men were rescued. They were fortunate in that there was a very short break in the weather and ice and the men were snatched from the island just in the nick of time and they all returned safely. On arrival at Punta Arenas the traders lined the harbour to welcome the rescued men raising their hats in salute their bravery and endeavour. George Richard Bell was one of the traders giving the welcome.

George and Rifle Practice
Every weekend George was taken out by his Father for target practice with a rifle and he became a good marksman. It was essential for the protection of the family. They slept with a riffle under the bed in case of intrusion. He would ride to town with cash that needed to be banked. He seemed to have responsibilities of an adult but when he returned to the UK he was only 10 years old.

The Factory
The factory employed many men, some were from the UK. They had good and bad times out there. George Richard Bell was well liked for his happy cheerful relationship with everyone. Unfortunately there was tragic accident in 1914 caused by one of the machines. His protective coat was pulled into the machine (he may have been pushed into the machine). Hannah returned home with the children. She visited the relations in Birkenhead and they remember the girls, Dorothy and Irene wearing beautiful dresses. But the relatives could not help, so they went to Merthyr and eventually settled in Newport, South Wales where they ran a Health Food Store and general shop. In turn all the children helped in the shop.

How the Bells joined the Adventist Church
In Merthyr Hannah rented a house and a lady came to the door asking if she could have a room. This lady was an Adventist and she gave Bible studies with the family and persuaded the family to join the church. The family moved to Newport, Monmouthshire, and mother Bell bought a shop (this was probably paid for from the compensation money given by the company). The children went to school but had to help in the shop when they came home. The family was active in the Newport Adventist church.

Dorothy became a nurse in the hydro at Stanborough Park, she married William Hyde and became a missionary in West Africa for 20 years. Most missionaries died after a few years but I think Dorothy's early years in South America had taught her how to live in a harsh environment. After being in Africa Will worked in Australia as a college lecturer and eventually went to the church university in California, Pacific Union College, where he was a professor. This is where they spent they rest of their lives.

Will Hyde and his wife Dorothy with their 2 children Anne and Heather

Irene Pullinger née Bell

Irene was the cleverest member of the family and went to the grammar school. When she finished school she became a teacher. She got a job as a private tutor to children of an ambassador's family. She went with the family to Egypt and Mexico. In 1937 she married her childhood sweetheart Sydney Leonard Pullinger (born 20th October 1905 died 28th July 1943) who she had known from the grammar school. At the time of their marriage Sydney was an architect. Sadly Irene died in 1951 of a nervous breakdown and pleurisy. The nervous breakdown was made worse by the death of her husband in 1943. Lieutenant Sydney Leonard Pullinger was travelling home to see his wife when his plane crashed into a mountain near Shannon in Southern Ireland where he received fatal injuries. Sydney was a Lieutenant Colonel and during the war was in the army and was Chief Engineer who was responsible for the Suez to Aden pipeline.

Sydney Pullinger

Sydney Pullinger 1905-1943

Sydney's received the following WW11 medals:-
1939-45   Star
Battle of Britain
1942-43   Africa Star
1st or 8th Army North Africa
1939-45   Defence Medal

1939-45   War Medal

On July 28th 1943 Sydney died in a plane crashed in poor visibility. He was returning home on compassionate leave to see his wife who was very unwell. The plane was travelling between Lisbon and Foynes when it crashed into high ground on the Dingle Penninsula (above Slieveglass and Brandon villages). All the 7 crew and 11 passengers were lost. Foynes flying boat museum have an engine, wing-tip float and other parts. Some wreckage still existed at the site in 2008.

Edward Bell (known as Eddie) married Violet Haining (this family is on p78). He went to work in California in order to meet up with his childhood sweet heart. He returned to the UK with her and eventually became a very successful farmer just North of Watford. To start with he had a lorry and did deliveries as well as farming. He hand milked in the open air and was able to build up a good herd of cows. He was very hard working. To start with he rented land but was eventually able to buy his own farm. At one time his milk went on the Queen's Royal Yacht Britannia

George and friend out for a summer selling books

George, the second eldest child had missed out on his basic education when the family were in South America and his education would have been in Spanish. When he came back to Wales he spelt his name in the Spanish way (Jorge). He attended Newbold College on two separate occasions. After the first session at college he became in charge of the book sales for North and South England. Then he went back to college to finish his education and in 1935 he became a pastor in the Adventist church. In 1937 he married Alice Anderson. And the rest is history.

Grandfather Richard George Bell 1879-1914

Written for ANNE HYDE Eldest daughter of Will and Dorothy Hyde (Dorothy is George's elder sister)

Your grandfather George Richard Bell had managed a fell mongers factory for treating animal skins in Lancaster. Hannah and George met in the Lancaster area; he fell in love with her being attracted by her beautiful hair. She was a talented needlewoman, but she would not marry until he had saved £100. She determined on this to secure her future. A local business man had started with ten pounds and he became the wealthiest man in the area. So she felt she would be secure with £100!

Your Great grandfather had four children two boys and two girls and both parents died within a short space of time leaving the four children homeless. Your grandfather was the eldest of the four (Richard George, Joseph, Susan and Lizzie). When the mother died the eldest

226

George being 12 years old and old enough to work was taken into the business by an uncle. The other three children were taken in by Doctor Barnardo's Children's Homes.

The next eldest boy Joseph was sent by Barnardo's to Canada to work on a farm. When he left Barnardo's would have been supplied him with a new suit of clothes and a small leather case for his processions He later served during the Great War and it was his grandson Keith found a post card and diary from Richard George. From the information kept by Dr Barnardo's it was discovered that Richard George had sent money to him when he was at Barnardo's and then money was sent to Canada for a bicycle. You and your mother (Dorothy) visited the family and Dorothy met her cousin and his son Keith in California. Keith is probably in Texas now. The remaining two girls (Susan and Lizzie) went into service as maids and we met up with Auntie Lizzie in the I960's in Birkenhead.

The eldest (Richard George) went to Liverpool and then went onto Merthyr Tydfil to open a factory for himself. This is where Dorothy was born. In the late 1960's or early1970's we found the flat where they lived above a fruit shop and this where Dorothy was born. We found the man who owned the shop, and he remembered the Father's factory, and said that it was demolished in the I920's.

While there, they attended the Methodist Church and both parents sang in the choir and were friendly with other traders who had businesses in the town. At that time it was thriving church with hundreds attending but by the 1970's only 4 or 5 attended the Sunday night service. It was at this time they saw an advertisement for a Manager's job as a Fell monger in Punta Arenas, Chile, South America. They soon left for South America probably at the beginning of the 1905. It must have been a fairly large factory with other UK residents and local people working for him. The hides were preserved in the factory and shipped to Liverpool Docks. They entered the country tax-free. The family found they were very isolated and their nearest neighbours were 10 miles away and Punta Arenas was five miles away. The area was very primitive; and no vegetables would grow there except mushrooms which grew wild. They fenced in an area to try and grow their own vegetables. Everything was very basic and they had to keep their yeast going from week to week. Goods only came in by boat twice a year. They killed a sheep every week and hung it up in the kitchen and this was their staple diet. Instead of sweets the children were given a meat chop to chew.

227

Comments on the factory
The estate where the factory was situated is still there.
The people are still producing sheep.
Cowboys on horse-back still shepherd with the help of dogs.
Anne Hyde knows someone who visited estate in the 1990's.

27109457R00130

Printed in Poland
by Amazon Fulfillment
Poland Sp. z o.o., Wrocław